2616

8 Connable Dr.
Toronto M8R 1Z8

416 924-4554

Knowing Practice

Studies in the Ethnographic Imagination

John Comaroff, Pierre Bourdieu, and Maurice Bloch, *Series Editors*

州中医学院第五届留学生进修结业留念 84.3

Souvenir photograph commissioned by the Guangzhou College of Traditional Chinese Medicine at the close of the author's first period of research there. In the back row are Foreign Affairs Office staff (left to right) Huang Huixia, Chairman Lu Shang, Chen Tang, and Li Daosheng. Front row: Vice President Ou Ming, Vice President Li Renxian, Judith Farquhar, and Professor of Medical History and Natural Dialectics Huang Jitang.

Knowing Practice

The Clinical Encounter
of Chinese Medicine

Judith Farquhar

WESTVIEW PRESS

Boulder • San Francisco • Oxford

For my parents
and my sister Ann

Studies in the Ethnographic Imagination

All photographs are by the author unless otherwise attributed.

Published in 1994 in the United States of America by Westview Press, Inc., 5500 Central Avenue, Boulder, Colorado 80301-2877, and in the United Kingdom by Westview Press, 36 Lonsdale Road, Summertown, Oxford OX2 7EW

Library of Congress Cataloging-in-Publication Data
Farquhar, Judith.
  Knowing practice : the clinical encounter of Chinese medicine /
Judith Farquhar.
     p.   cm.—(Studies in the ethnographic imagination)
  Includes bibliographical references and index.
  ISBN 0-8133-8533-4
  1. Medicine, Chinese.   I. Title.   II. Series.
  [DNLM: 1. Medicine, Chinese Traditional.   2. Diagnosis.
3. Therapeutics.   WB 50 JC6 F16k 1994]
R601.F34   1994
615.5'3'0951—dc20
DNLM/DLC
for Library of Congress   93-25947
                                                                            CIP

Printed and bound in the United States of America

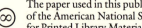

10   9   8   7   6   5   4   3   2   1

Contents

Tables and Illustrations

Photographs

Acknowledgments

MY DEBTS ARE MANY, and it is particularly important in a book that emphasizes continuities of knowing practice over individual creation to acknowledge them. I have had wonderful teachers in and out of classrooms: Carleton Gajdusek, Arthur Hummel, Sr., Stephen Toulmin, Jean Comaroff, Huang Jitang, Ernesto Laclau, and Nathan Sivin (in roughly chronological order) stand out among them. At various stages in the long progress of this study I benefited from the insights, criticisms, and cheerful assistance of Michael Alpers, Roger Ames, Joyce Canaan, Barney Cohn, John Comaroff, Michael Dalby, Gail Henderson, Dorothy Holland, Jia Huanguang, Eric Karchmer, Andrew Kipnis, William Lachicotte, Gail Langley, Andrew Lass, Donald Lopez, Susan Maingay, Tomoko Masuzawa, Nancy Munn, Ralph Nicholas, Della Pollock, Rafael Sanchez, Jim Sanford, Barry Saunders, J. P. Seaton, Penny Taylor, Cynthia Visness, Raul Zaritsky, and Angela Zito, among many others. A number of graduate students at the University of North Carolina helped me refine my views on medical anthropology, and undergraduates in my course on Chinese philosophy and science forced me to see the forest as well as the trees. I am in Nathan Sivin's debt for his extensive critical notes on my dissertation, which are chiefly responsible for this book's substantial difference from that much less accurate work. Jim Hevia critically read the whole manuscript several times; my responses to his demands for clarity of thought, rectitude of language, and honesty to the Chinese sources were among the best revisions made.

A great many dedicated and energetic doctors, students, and administrators at the Guangzhou College of Traditional Chinese Medicine contributed directly and indirectly to the successful completion of my first long period of field research. I want especially to thank Foreign Affairs Office chairman Lu Shang, Vice President Ou Ming, and Professor Lai Shilong. The group of faculty members selected from various departments of the college in 1982 and 1983 to study oral English with me enriched my life and my understanding in ways that went far beyond medicine. Other foreign students in Guangzhou, particularly Chiaka Diakite, Jebali Ezzedine, Ikai Yoshio, and Jani, generously shared with me the results of their study of Chinese medicine as well as much else. For a few months in 1991 I enjoyed the kind hospitality of the Institute of Medical History and Literature of the Academy of Chinese Medicine in Beijing.

Field research was supported by three generous grants from the Committee on Scholarly Communication with the People's Republic of China of the U.S. National Academy of Sciences. The speed and efficiency with which I was able to write my first version of this book were much enhanced by a grant from the American Association of University Women and two William Rainey Harper fellowships from the University of Chicago. Additional archival research was funded by grants-in-aid from the American Council of Learned Societies and the American Philosophical Society. And the Department of Anthropology at the University of North Carolina has been extraordinarily generous with research leaves and research assistance. I am most grateful to these agencies for displaying such palpable faith in an unusual topic and an untried investigator.

Naturally I take full responsibility for the excesses and deficiencies of this study. I am well aware that it contributes little to the advancement of Chinese medicine as a healing art and clinical discipline. But I still dare to hope that parts of it have risen to the challenges presented to me by my teachers in Guangzhou, especially Professor Huang Jitang, who more than anyone demonstrated to me that "the subtleties of discerning these transformations dwell nowhere but within the doctor."

Judith Farquhar

Introduction: "We Take Practice to Be Our Guide"

IN THE FALL OF 1982 I began an eighteen-month period of study and participant observation at the Guangzhou (Canton) College of Traditional Chinese Medicine. Among many other services provided to me by the college were regular "guidance" sessions, which I could use to question teachers in various specialties about the contents of the readings and lectures in my classes. In the course of these wide-ranging conversations, I sometimes pointed out apparent contradictions between textbooks or clinical scenarios in which conflicting explanations might be equally plausible. My question often was "How do doctors know which statement or explanation is correct?" Invariably the answer was "We take experience [*jingyan*] to be our guide," or, rebuking me for my literal-mindedness, "We take practice [*shijian*] to be the main thing." Later, in interviews with a few senior Chinese doctors (formal affairs in which the wisdom I collected was almost indistinguishable from their published writings), these statements came up again and again: Questions about disagreements between doctors, the work of textbook committees, the design of medical college curricula, and the involved technical disputes between schools of thought were all met with the same insistence on experience and practice.

The long process in which I came to accept these responses as "the answers" for an ethnographic study of Chinese medicine has led to the structure and argument of this book. I began to realize as I gained more familiarity with Chinese medical textbooks, clinical practices, and technical literature that my questions about logical contradictions and hypothetical situations had been forged in an intellectual environment quite different from that occupied (and generated) by my teachers in Guangzhou. Their answers were not so much evasive as they were effective in casting doubt on the value of my questions. By following their advice and altering the abstract epistemological bent of my original interests, I was able to perceive these notions of practice and experience, not as residual categories full of idiosyncratic, repetitive, or imponderable miscellany, but as complex generative formations in their own right. These formations of social activity provided most of the coherence for the written sources in which I had previously assumed I would find systematic knowledge.

The Chinese terms for practice and experience evoke no simple divide between theory and practice or between booklearning and worldly activity. *Shijian,* a word that connotes concrete realization of a potential, is much more intentional and intrinsically formal than the rather gritty practice, which is "theory's" passive partner in English. And *jingyan* is a good deal more historical, collective, and discursive than the individualistic life narratives that the word experience connotes. To accommodate these important differences, what began for me as a study of "culture-specific (Chinese) ways of knowing" had to become much more attentive to clinical priorities in medical work. Statements in discourse remained important, but in a new way. They had to be seen as weapons against illness, resources for action, rather than as claims about nature or representations of truth. The emphasis of this book, then, remains epistemological in the broadest sense but organizes itself around a practical form: the phases of the clinical encounter.

This mundane practice, in which patient and doctor "look at illness" (*kanbing*) together, has proven in the more than ten years in which I have been attending to it to be a remarkably sturdy form. The medical work that continues to go on in clinics and hospitals of traditional medicine all over China retains this logical and temporal sequence. And many kinds of new knowledge, including facts and techniques derived from "Western medical" sources, have been appropriated to its structure.

By allowing practice, the form of the clinical encounter, to be the occasion and the organizing principle of this reading of the contemporary discourse of "traditional" Chinese medicine, I have tried to show how the daily work of healing continues in relation to an ancient, vast, and still growing literature of healing experience. The clinical encounter as it is described here both draws on and generates medical knowledge, disciplining doctors to the rational use of proven methods while allowing, even demanding, that they intervene creatively in the ever-new challenges of illness. In close relation to this everyday practical form, the collective accumulation of expertise through scholarship, teaching, and healing generates doctors as embodiments of virtuosity, a form of experience that links practice to history and practitioners to knowledge.

I will argue (in Chapter 1) that my teachers' insistence on practice and experience was, and to a certain extent still is, an epistemological formation with a specific historical importance. There is no doubt that in a modernizing medical system these terms became prominent partly for strategic reasons, helping to ensure a continuing place for traditional medicine in China's official health care system. But their ubiquity in the life of the contemporary profession was far from being a cynical manipulation of public opinion and official resource allocations. A large part of the appeal of these terms was the way in which they accorded with, and continued to reproduce, Chinese doctors' deeply held understandings of how truly effective healing had to be organized. Their emphasis on the linked themes of practice and experience was far more than (or other than) an instrumental deployment of terms made fashionable by Mao Zedong's essays (e.g., "On Practice") and a modernizing romance with "Western" empiricism (*jingyanzhuyi*).[1] For many of the leaders of institutional Chinese medicine in the 1980s, the ground on which diverse techniques and texts made sense was practical, and the actor who made medicine fitting and effective was experienced. In many different ways, Chinese medical writers and teachers sought to demonstrate that practice and experience had long been core strengths of their field, and many staked their future and that of their students on the enduring value of these two terms.

Anthropological readers will realize that the practical emphasis of this book is as much a convergence of themes as it is a "field" discovery. Although *jingyan* is quite different from an Anglophone notion of experience (not, for example, a good candidate for founding a Chinese version of phenomenological anthropology), the *shijian* of modern Chinese usage (derived from Mao) and the practice that has become important in anthropological theory (thanks most notably to Pierre Bourdieu) have much history in common.[2] Both can claim Karl Marx as an ancestor, and both have been advanced to resolve complex social and intellectual divides between ideas and action, thinkers and doers. Though Bourdieu has developed the scholarly implications of a theory of practice perhaps more lavishly than Maoist theorists have, contemporary Chinese people can be said to have lived, sometimes bitterly, a "practice of practice," the social and personal consequences of which we in the non-Maoist world perceive only dimly.

Both Mao's and Bourdieu's writings on practice can also be interpreted as reductionist. Although Mao argues that "man's social practice" takes many forms,[3] the dominant reading of his early philosophical essays in the People's Republic of China (PRC) usually includes the insistence that "man's activity in production [is] the most fundamental practical activity, the determinant of all his other activities."[4] As for Bourdieu, anthropol-

---

1. Mao Zedong, "On Practice," in *Selected Readings from the Works of Mao Tsetung* (Beijing: Foreign Languages Press, 1971), pp. 65–84.

2. Pierre Bourdieu, *Outline of a Theory of Practice* (Cambridge: Cambridge University Press, 1977).

3. Mao, "On Practice," p. 66.

4. Ibid., p. 65.

ogists often express discomfort with his apparent unconcern (in *Outline of a Theory of Practice*) with thought, knowledge, and intention except as epiphenomena or mystifications of unverbalized bodily, spatial, and temporal practices.[5]

Any study of practice must limit itself somehow. "The entire activity of human beings acting to transform nature and society" is not a subject for study,[6] even if (for my purposes) a subuniverse called medicine were to be unequivocally discernible within it and rigidly focused on. Rather, an emphasis on practice is a denial that certain narrower topics that are classically studied (e.g., ideas, texts, behavior, verbal or economic exchanges) are quite adequate to the complexity of social life. "Activity" is a key word in the Maoist definition, permitting much and excluding little and incidentally rendering pointless any attempt to claim that a practice approach can yield final or comprehensive knowledge. What a practice approach can provide, I think, is more satisfying ways of understanding action in all its historicity and specificity, exploring concrete settings in which the inseparability of intention and event, word and deed can be taken for granted, while the specific constraints on and resources for a contingent human agency can be articulated. An anthropological or Chinese medical centering of practice invites us to locate unconventional (but still rather everyday) subjects for our research, delimitable social forms through which "ideas" and "behaviors" merge into many strands of signifying and world-altering activity. The clinical encounter in the contemporary practice of Chinese medicine is such a form.

*   *   *

The research on which this book is based was begun when I first read Manfred Porkert's *The Theoretical Foundations of Chinese Medicine*.[7] That research took its first major turn as a result of my opportunity to study at the Guangzhou College of Traditional Chinese Medicine, and it has continued at a distance through several years of reading the recent Chinese literature of traditional medicine. Subsequent research visits to Guangzhou, Beijing, and Shandong have allowed me to supplement the original fieldwork with observations of clinical work outside the College setting and further interview-

---

5. See, for example, Jean Comaroff, *Body of Power, Spirit of Resistance* (Chicago: University of Chicago Press, 1985), pp. 4–5.

6. Cihai Editing and Compiling Committee, ed., *Cihai,* compressed character edition (Shanghai: Shanghai Dictionaries Press, 1980), s.v. *Shijian* (Practice).

7. Manfred Porkert, *The Theoretical Foundations of Chinese Medicine* (Cambridge, Mass.: MIT Press, 1974). See also my "Problems of Knowledge in Contemporary Chinese Medical Discourse," *Social Science and Medicine* 24, no. 12 (1987):1013–1021, in which I critique Porkert's tendency to idealize Chinese medical knowledge along lines similar to those I develop here.

ing. And I have been able to pursue historical questions at the library of the Academy of Traditional Chinese Medicine in Beijing.

My methods and interests are primarily ethnographic, but in this book I have tried to expand the practice of ethnography beyond its traditional emphasis on social relations, social structures, and cultural hermeneutics. At the same time I have made no attempt to be holistic about Chinese society or to discover cultural systems underlying and unifying many domains of Chinese social practice. In general I find Chinese culture to be far too large and vague an object to address with the interpretive and field methods open to cultural anthropologists. This book remains ethnographic mainly because fieldwork has been essential in its development of a focus on knowledge as a practice and on the deployment of historical resources in medical work; study of traditional medicine in the social context where it is both formed and formative has been the source of most of my interpretive hunches. Nevertheless, the published (and some unpublished) literature of Chinese medicine provides most of the material for this book. As I have just argued, the structure of this book derives from practice, specifically from the phases of the clinical encounter, but practice is often best explained in the words of those who have devoted much of their lives to teaching it. The pedagogical and professional voices of Chinese scholar-doctors have proven useful here because their explanations result from considerable reflection and writerly work, much of it collective and cumulative over at least the last few decades. I urge close attention to their considered explanations.

In Chapter 1 I place the contemporary practice of traditional Chinese medicine in its historical moment and briefly describe features of its institutional existence in the PRC. One of the aims of this chapter is to identify the knowledge reported in the rest of the book as the possession and product of a particular group of people and set of institutions that came into existence at roughly the same time as the People's Republic itself. Chapter 2 introduces a few of the cosmological assumptions with which any reading of Chinese medical writing should be informed. These constructs are clarified through a discussion of certain early Chinese philosophical fragments, texts that are used in teaching traditional medicine's "theoretical foundations" in recent textbooks and classroom materials. Ancient philosophical formulations need not be thought of as historical foundations that have remained in place in China for more than two millennia, but they do help uninitiated readers see the sense of the technical medical material that follows. Chapter 3 provides a preliminary description of how work is done in clinics of Chinese medicine and focuses on the readily observable activities of doctors and patients in a hospital affiliated with the Guangzhou College of Traditional Chinese Medicine. This chapter also presents and partly reproduces three published case histories, the "strangeness" and technicalities of which are slowly unraveled in the course of the analysis to follow. Some problems of terminology are also discussed in Chapter 3, and the general form of the clinical encounter is abstracted and summarized in Figure 3.2.

Chapters 4, 5, and 6 compose the core of the book, analytically leading in and out of the recurring practical form that I have called the clinical encounter and that Chinese doctors think of as looking at illness (*kanbing*) or "syndrome differentiation and therapy determination" (*bianzheng lunzhi*). Some general conclusions on an overview of the clinical encounter are taken up in Chapter 7.

The technical terminology of Chinese medicine has presented special problems of translation. Certain terms that already enjoy considerable currency in North American English, such as qi (romanized in the Wade-Giles system as ch'i) and yinyang, are treated herein as English words and supplemented with commentary. A few terms that simply lose too much in translation remain in romanized Chinese; see Chapter 3 for a discussion of some of these. I have translated most technical and conventional terms following excellent precedents set by Nathan Sivin and Shiu-ying Hu. Where these terms refer to notions that are radically different from those attaching to the English words, I have capitalized them as a sign of their difference and as a reference back to earlier passages that explain Chinese medical terms and their uses. Examples of the terminology for which this capitalization technique has been used are the visceral systems of function (Heart, Liver, etc.), the illness factors (Heat, Cold, Damp, etc.), and the conventional names of drug formulae (e.g., Opening Bones Powder). Unless otherwise noted, all translations from the Chinese are my own.

* * *

Certain sources have proven valuable so often that they deserve special mention here. Nathan Sivin's *Traditional Medicine in Contemporary China* is a very useful introduction to the history and teachings of Chinese medicine.[8] It is cited often herein as a historical and conceptual macrocosm to my own more microscopic investigation. Its latter half, a translation of a 1972 foundations of Chinese medicine text, has provided the authority for most of the translations of medical terms I have used. We do, however, use different systems for romanizing Chinese words: Sivin, along with most others writing on Chinese medicine in English, uses Wade-Giles romanization, whereas I use hanyu pinyin. A conversion table is provided as Appendix A to aid comparison of Chinese terms.

I have also extensively consulted two recent works by senior scholars at the Guangzhou College of Traditional Chinese Medicine, Huang Jitang's

---

8. Nathan Sivin, *Traditional Medicine in Contemporary China* (Ann Arbor: Center for Chinese Studies, University of Michigan, 1987).

Zhongyixue Daolun (Introduction to Chinese Medicine) and Deng Tietao's *Shiyong Zhongyi Zhenduanxue* (Practical Diagnosis in Chinese Medicine).[9] Beyond these, I have relied most heavily on textbooks, especially those designed for courses in the foundations of Chinese medicine: Those by Deng Tietao, Liu Yanchi, and Zhao Fen have been very useful on theoretical matters,[10] and those produced by the Beijing College of Traditional Chinese Medicine, the Office of the 1977 Physicians of Western Medicine Class in Chinese Medicine of the Guangdong College of Traditional Chinese Medicine, and the Jiangsu Province Department of Health have been authoritative sources in that they are backed by the work of large committees.[11] Textbooks, of course, have a special charm for anthropologists since they can be taken to have a stronger relationship to the needs and intentions of large groups of people than do some of the individually authored works also cited herein. In this respect I make no apology for not always preferring works that have resulted from "superior scholarship," and even where the study of canonical works is concerned, I have tended to cite widely used contemporary texts.

9. Huang Jitang et al., ed., *Zhongyixue Daolun* (Guangzhou: Guangdong Higher Education Press, 1988); and Deng Tietao, *Shiyong Zhongyi Zhenduanxue* (Shanghai: Shanghai Science and Technology Press, 1988).

10. Deng Tietao, ed., *Zhongyi Jichu Lilun* (Guangzhou: Guangdong Science and Technology Press, 1982); Liu Yanchi, Song Tianbin, Zhang Ruifu, and Dong Liantong, eds., *Zhongyi Jichu Lilun Wenda* (Shanghai: Shanghai Science and Technology Press, 1982); and Zhao Fen, ed., *Zhongyi Jichu Lilun Xiangjie* (Fuzhou: Fujian Science and Technology Press, 1981).

11. Beijing College of Traditional Chinese Medicine, ed., *Zhongyixue Jichu* (Shanghai: Shanghai Science and Technology Press, 1979); Jiangsu Province Department of Health, ed., *Zhongyi Jichu* (Suzhou: Jiangsu Science and Technology Press, 1977); and Office of the 1977 Physicians of Western Medicine Class in Chinese Medicine, ed., *Zhongyi Jichuxue* (Guangzhou: Guangdong College of Traditional Chinese Medicine, 1977). The structure and conventional content of this genre of textbooks is preserved in Liu Yanchi's English-language work *The Essential Book of Traditional Chinese Medicine,* 2 vols. (New York: Columbia University Press, 1988).

1

Chinese Medicine as Institutional Object and Historical Moment

THE PEOPLE I KNEW at the Guangzhou College of Traditional Chinese Medicine in the early 1980s were initiating a new era in their field. The antiexpert policies and practices of the Great Proletarian Cultural Revolution (1966–1976) had recently been replaced by an emphasis on "the four modernizations" (industry, agriculture, science and technology, and the military), a national policy shift that benefited the institutions of traditional medicine as it did other academic and scientific units. Doctors, cadres, herbal pharmacists, nurses, and research scientists were beginning to aggressively exploit and contribute to the new resources and new ideas becoming available during this dynamic period.

On the campus new buildings had been recently completed, more were being planned, and a badly needed water tower was under construction. Some of the land appropriated from the college by a neighboring agricultural commune during the Cultural Revolution had been returned; by the end of the decade a laboratory research building had been built on it. The curriculum was quickly revamped in the late 1970s to include a training period of five years, after a decade of being limited to three years; thus, the "class of 1977,"[1] the first for almost a generation to be admitted to the college through a competitive examination, had graduated shortly before I arrived. Many members of this newly professional generation had been assigned to jobs in the college; others had tested into a recently instituted

---

1. College classes in the PRC are referred to by their year of matriculation rather than their year of graduation. Thus, the members of the class of 1977 entered Guangzhou College in that year and worked through their courses as a stable cohort.

graduate program. A nationally distributed journal of Chinese medicine, *Xin Zhongyi* (New Chinese Medicine), had resumed publication on campus after the long hiatus of the Cultural Revolution;[2] it provided a forum for lively debates on science, theory, history, laboratory research, and clinical work. A number of coordinated textbooks, edited by national committees, supported a demanding sequence of courses in traditional medicine, basic bioscience, and "Western medicine."[3] By the early 1980s these authoritative works were already being supplemented by more specialized and idiosyncratic works, also published by state presses, which were enthusiastically collected by faculty and graduate students.

This upsurge of professional activity was also in progress at the other provincial colleges of traditional Chinese medicine (there were twenty-three of them in 1983). Although the Guangzhou College was one of the largest such institutions, with about fifteen thousand students, faculty, and staff living on campus, it was only one of numerous intellectual centers. Each had its own reputation: The Beijing College served as home to a larger number of famous scholar-doctors and published the bulk of the early technical textbooks; the Shanghai counterpart of these institutions was known for an emphasis on scientific research; and many smaller schools had reputations for particular projects and groups of scholars. Each of these academic institutions was formally affiliated to numerous clinical units—hospitals and outpatient clinics—in which students were placed for internships and favored graduates were given permanent work assignments. Other graduates of such schools received assignments to practice in hospitals more remote from their alma maters or to teach traditional medicine in lower-level schools (e.g., three-year health academies). Many of the faculty and advanced students in colleges of traditional medicine belonged to one or several state-supported professional organizations and attended national and regional meetings at their work unit's expense. The journal published in Guangzhou was one of eighteen such periodicals (appearing monthly, semimonthly, or quarterly) in 1983, a number that has grown since then. *New Chinese Medicine* remains one of four periodicals that is widely read in national Chinese medicine circles, the other three being published in Beijing and Shanghai. By the

---

2. No professional journals of TCM were published during the Cultural Revolution. The very few medical journals that appeared during the period concentrated on the work of barefoot doctors and (as far as I can tell from the incomplete collections I have seen) contained no substantive Chinese medical information.

3. Comparisons between "Chinese medicine" (*zhongyi*) and "Western medicine" (*xiyi*) were constantly made in conversations at the college. The pervasive use of these terms for very complex and, in the twentieth century, interwoven bodies of knowledge and clinical practice reflected a sense of struggle in which two oversimplified combatants were discursively reproduced. I will mostly refer to Western medicine as "biomedicine" herein.

time I arrived in Guangzhou, six years after the death of Mao and the close of the Cultural Revolution, it was hard to see the future of Chinese medicine as anything but bright. The sheer size and visibility of its institutions and activities argued against an early demise, despite what some interpretations of modernization might predict.

It was tempting when I was first there to see the social relations and institutional arrangements visible at the college as natural to "Chinese medicine." The particular proportions of time faculty members spent in the classroom, office, and clinic; the lectures I received on the "holism" (*zhengtiguan*) and "preventive emphasis" (*yufangxing*) of Chinese medicine; the intellectual leadership of senior doctors and the deference younger doctors seemed to accord them; and the elegant order of knowledge laid out in clearly written textbooks—all these had a certain logic and correctness. They appeared to be continuous with the cultural and epistemological differences that spoke to me from the pages of ancient books, and they seemed to offer a refreshing alternative to the "impersonal" and "objectified" world of practices I was coming to call, along with my friends at the college, "Western medicine" (*xiyi*).

It was only later, and in connection with certain interpersonal divides and intellectual contradictions, that cultural features of Chinese medicine began to appear quite newly minted, as young as the institutional arrangements that allowed them to flourish.[4] The field of traditional Chinese medicine (TCM), which caused such a stir in Western public health circles in the 1960s and 1970s and on which a few European and American anthropologists and historians have commented since then, came into existence in its modern institutional form only after the 1949 founding of the People's Republic of China (a date referred to in China as Liberation). Contemporary TCM organizations locate their inception as fully legitimate entities

---

4. The brief historical discussion that follows is largely based on lore I picked up in interviews with senior doctors, in prefaces to many different kinds of books, and in the autobiographies of senior Chinese doctors (see my "Rewriting Traditional Medicine in Post-Maoist China" [Paper presented at the Conference on Epistemology and the Scholarly Medical Traditions, McGill University, Toronto, May 1992]). Ralph Croizier, *Traditional Medicine in Modern China* (Cambridge, Mass.: Harvard University Press, 1964); and David M. Lampton, *The Politics of Medicine in China* (Boulder: Westview Press, 1977), both cover the recent history of Chinese medicine, and this discussion is written as a supplement to their (now somewhat outdated) work. I have perhaps made more of an effort to incorporate into my account the indigenous (i.e. Chinese medical) reading of this recent history than they do. In this I have benefited from the important work of Zhao Hongjun, *Jindai Zhongxiyi Lunzhengshi* (Anhui: Anhui Science and Technology Press, 1989); and I have also drawn on Fu Weikang, *Zhongyixue Shi* (Shanghai: Shanghai Science and Technology Press, 1990). In addition, the research assistance of Jia Huanguang has been invaluable in tracking down Chinese historical sources; his thoughtful analysis of twentieth-century medical history has importantly influenced my own thinking.

with Mao Zedong's 1955 proclamation that "our motherland's medicine is a great treasurehouse."[5] The first few colleges of TCM were founded in the mid to late 1950s, pre-Liberation professional associations were revived and enlarged with public support, and the Chinese Medicine Bureau was moved from the Ministry of Commerce to the Ministry of Health.[6] The diverse and scattered practitioners of traditional medicine, with their small academies and family clinics, were organized into a rapidly growing national hierarchy of clinical and academic institutions. TCM suddenly acquired a clear-cut professional identity.[7]

The Institutionalization of Chinese Medicine

As far as I know, no detailed social history of TCM since 1949 has been attempted either in English or Chinese. But the development of the field as a profession since Liberation, as well as an earlier-twentieth-century context of elite pressure to abandon or Westernize "traditional" knowledge, significantly influenced perceptions of TCM's character and mission in the early 1980s. Before 1949 most practitioners of Chinese medicine worked as individuals in private clinics, cooperating with apprentices (often their sons or nephews) and developing idiosyncratic specialties and local reputations for particular types of efficacy. Some gained large numbers of students and followers, set up academies and hospitals, and participated actively in professional organizations and publishing projects. Even so, these shifting groupings remained largely regional. Although many in the mid-twentieth century argued that a united national front against the challenge of Western medical modernization was required, the national organizations

---

5. This constantly quoted phrase apparently first appeared in Mao Zedong's Instruction to the Leading Party Groups of the Ministry of Health in 1958.

6. Lampton, *The Politics of Medicine,* suggests that public support of TCM was motivated in part by the need for the new government to deliver universal health care in the absence of an effective national biomedical service structure. More important, however, he provides a history of early health policy in which TCM became a focus in a long-standing struggle between the Chinese Communist Party (CCP) and health bureaucrats, who were mainly scientifically oriented biomedical doctors. Like many in the world of TCM today, Lampton credits an "idiosyncratic" interest in Chinese medicine on Mao Zedong's part with much of the responsibility for its institutional expansion in recent decades.

7. See Nathan Sivin, *Traditional Medicine in Contemporary China* (Ann Arbor: Center for Chinese Studies, University of Michigan, 1987), pp. 21–23, on the wide variety of social forms healing practices took in premodern China. He makes clear that it is inappropriate to see classical medicine as a "profession" prior to the twentieth century and the encounter with "Western medicine." See also Paul Unschuld, *Medical Ethics in Imperial China* (Berkeley and Los Angeles: University of California Press, 1979), for a study of social issues in the history of Chinese medicine that somewhat oversimplifies the identity of the profession.

that emerged prior to the triumph of the revolution were weak and embattled.

When a coordinated national structure did emerge, it benefited from many years of concerted effort. Contemporary Chinese doctors recall the pre-Liberation years as years of struggle against powerful agencies that wished to see traditional medicine eliminated and replaced with "modern" biomedical institutions.[8] Ralph Croizier, in his intellectual history of the fortunes of medicine in modern China, documents a wide variety of elite initiatives to abolish or radically reform Chinese medicine.[9] These polemical and, increasingly throughout the 1920s and 1930s, administrative efforts were received with understandable anxiety by practitioners of herbal medicine and acupuncture. As early as 1929 defenders of the practice of traditional medicine organized a national association, Guoyi Guan (Institute for National Medicine), to combat these legal and ideological challenges. Perhaps a more significant achievement, however, considering that this institute and later similar organizations actually did little to alter opposition to TCM at high levels of government,[10] was the success of Chinese medicine's proponents in identifying "national medicine" as a patriotic issue. The writings of medical and nonmedical people from the turn of the century forward apparently produced a relatively new coherence for indigenous medical practices by labeling them national medicine and conflating them with a precious "national essence." As debate on medical modernization and the requirements of building a modern state on the wreckage of the old imperium moved forward, a wide variety of defenders and reformers of Chinese medicine managed to present their cause as inseparable from that of preserving the national essence.

In conflating traditional medicine and national essence, practitioners of Chinese medicine joined their voices to those of nonmedical intellectuals who are now thought of as conservatives and traditionalists. At the same time that "Mr. Science" and "Mr. Democracy" were becoming irresistible forces in the world of Chinese letters, numerous new characterizations of the essence of Chinese culture and critiques of Western scientific "mecha-

---

8. The general histories of medicine presently available in the PRC tend to lay the blame for this "devastating pressure" against TCM at the door of the National People's Party, or Guomindang (GMD). This is an oversimplification in that it ignores the influential voices of many CCP intellectuals who argued vigorously against traditional medicine during the 1920s and 1930s. But contemporary professionals credit the CCP with according the field its current state of legitimacy and state support, and the pressures of maintaining a coherent historiography of the party have influenced the mainstream narrative of medical history.

9. Croizier, *Traditional Medicine*.

10. Lampton argues that opposition in the Ministry of Health to official support for TCM continued throughout the 1950s in spite of party directives to integrate Chinese and Western medicine. See *The Politics of Medicine,* Chaps. 2, 3.

nism" and "imperialism" emerged.[11] Parallel developments in Chinese medical discourse that sought unimpeachably Chinese foundations for a reformed TCM now look rather quaint to contemporaries who are accustomed to arguing for the dialectical materialist virtues of TCM. The reformist positions of writers such as Zhu Peiwen and Yun Tieqiao, with their complicated theoretical rationales for the virtues of ancient medicine, were overwhelmed in the more radical language of the 1949 revolution.

But nationalist and anti-imperialist themes have continued to inform the rhetoric of the field. Advocates of continuing or expanding support for Chinese medical institutions have had to cobble together nationalist, socialist, scientific, and modernizing values and link them to central characteristics of the profession and its knowledge. In other words, discourses on knowledge and practice in the PRC have been intensely political.

Senior Doctors

It should be borne in mind that even for contemporary educated people in China, "modernization" is not an unambiguously positive value. In the twentieth century it has been difficult to untangle an imperative to modernize (whether to combat economic and military incursions or to provide a better standard of living for the masses) from the particular cultural and political projects of the powerful states (the United States, the Soviet Union, Japan) on which success in such an undertaking must partly depend. Despite the obviously high stakes of health for the people, the task of medical modernization is a highly problematic project that is significantly colored with a history of Western and Japanese imperialism and considerable popular anxiety about "China's backwardness."

Because early-to-mid-twentieth-century medicine must presently be viewed through the memories of those whose professional identities have been forged within socialist bureaucracy and in relation to a medical system that is thought of as a discrete unit, little can be said with certainty about the popular social existence of the Chinese medicine that immediately preceded the highly organized structures of the present. As has been noted, the important work of building a national hierarchy of intellectual and therapeutic institutions in the late 1950s did much to define, delimit, name, and "purify" a certain strain of nonbiomedical healing practice. Fields such as traditional Chinese medicine that are constituted in this kind of collective endeavor tend to be quickly naturalized. They are subject thereafter to representation within triumphalist histories, accounts that eject in advance all

---

11. See D.W.Y. Kwok's excellent study of important writers of this period, *Scientism in Chinese Thought, 1900–1950* (New Haven: Yale University Press, 1965), Part 1.

elements inconsistent with the historian's sense of the essence of his or her object of study. In the case of pre-Liberation Chinese medicine, it is unlikely that many practitioners of herbal therapies had a clear commitment to practicing only the "medicine of systematic correspondences" (as Unschuld calls TCM), with its naturalistic biases and reference to a large but restricted body of classic texts. Given how herbal medicine is incorporated within shamanic healing and temple-based divination practices elsewhere in the Chinese world,[12] it is unlikely that before 1949 TCM was a particularly discrete unit for the majority of practitioners.

The production of such a unit, in which knowledge and social structure could be mapped over each other and reproduced through large-scale educational institutions, was a major historical project authorized in the early years of the PRC. Most of the work was done by leading urban doctors under the watchful eye of Communist Party cadres; many doctors at this time became party members and cooperated enthusiastically with the party in building their field. The new institutions, especially that of the provincial-level college, produced unique intellectual and practical challenges. Within this new form of collegiality, doctors suddenly knew much more about each other's particular teachings and clinical habits; they were placed in horizontal relations with many others of their same rank, egalitarian modes of social practice that were unfamiliar for many of them. (Before the introduction of large Western-style medical institutions, teacher-student and elder-younger relations effectively organized local medical groupings. A partial exception is the schoolmate relationship, the *tongxue* bond that has been so important in twentieth-century Chinese culture. But few doctors of traditional medicine attended the modern academic institutions that fostered these horizontal relationships.) In the work of setting up clinics and hospitals, in textbook committees and curriculum planning groups, previously autonomous scholar-doctors were newly subject to criticism or even ridicule; at the same

---

12. See Arthur Kleinman, *Patients and Healers in the Context of Culture* (Berkeley and Los Angeles: University of California Press, 1980), esp. pp. 1–9, for a view of how diverse healing services might have been on the Chinese mainland prior to socialist reorganization. For similar indications of pluralism in Chinese societies, see Marjorie Topley, "Chinese Traditional Etiology and Methods of Cure in Hong Kong," in Charles Leslie, ed., *Asian Medical Systems* (Berkeley and Los Angeles: University of California Press, 1976), pp. 243–265; Katherine Gould-Martin, "Ong-ia-kong: The Plague God as Modern Physician," in Arthur Kleinman, ed., *Culture and Healing in Asian Societies* (Cambridge, Mass.: Schenkman, 1978), pp. 41–68; Emily M. Ahern, "Chinese-Style and Western-Style Doctors in Northern Taiwan," in Kleinman, *Culture and Healing,* pp. 101–110; and Jack M. Potter, "Cantonese Shamanism," in Arthur P. Wolf, ed., *Religion and Ritual in Chinese Society* (Stanford: Stanford University Press, 1974), pp. 207–232. These studies of contemporary Chinese situations that have not developed within socialist administration present a complex problem of historical comparison; but they are instructive in their descriptions of the many combinations of healing traditions that can be kept in play in a setting where there has been less pressure to define and delimit professions than there has been in the PRC.

time many discovered that they could be newly powerful in realizing their favored accounts of Chinese medicine's essence.

This group of seminal figures, almost all men who were at the height of their powers in the 1950s and 1960s, came to be thought of as a generation of "senior Chinese doctors" (*laozhongyi*). By the early 1980s many of them were very old or deceased, and a slightly younger generation of leaders was being honored with the *laozhongyi* appellation.[13] I was impressed at the time with the respect that was accorded both groups of seniors and the many ways in which their personal intellectual habits seemed to be reflected in the official writing of the field.[14] These men were visible as authoritative leaders in firm control of their profession; somewhat less visible were the administrative roles of a nonmedical cadre group and the resistant activity of groups of younger professionals who sought to "scientize" (*kexuehua*) Chinese medicine.

The *laozhongyi* seized their moment starting in 1980. Prior to that time, during the early years of collective institution building (during which period individuals received little credit or renown for heroic efforts) and throughout the Cultural Revolution, the intellectual and clinical leaders of the field of TCM had foregone many of the benefits that (they must have felt) should accrue to teachers and supervisors. But in mid-1980 the quarterly *Shandong Zhongyixueyuan Xuebao* (Bulletin of the Shandong College of Traditional Chinese Medicine) began publishing a series of autobiographical essays under the title "Ming Laozhongyi zhi Lu" (Paths of Renowned Senior Chinese Doctors). The journal's editors planned to include two or three of these personal histories each quarter, seeking to "unearth the expert professional heritage [of Chinese medicine], introduce scholarly and therapeutic experience, . . . salvage precious research materials, and enrich research on medical history." The editors also noted that "the significance [of this project] lies in inspiring future scholarship; we can learn from [the ways in which] a generation of famous doctors has matured."[15] In keeping with these goals, the essays focused on recalling the formative experiences of study, clinical work, and (sometimes) political involvement of their authors, the paths by which the senior doctors who had for several decades led the field of TCM had reached their present eminence. In this publishing ven-

---

13. The terms *laozhongyi* and *ming laozhongyi* (renowned senior Chinese doctor) are quite recent. One highly placed doctor in his late fifties told me in 1991 that until the late 1970s there were regulations governing the usage of the honorific form of address *lao* (old or senior) for leading doctors. He could think of only two doctors in Beijing who could properly be addressed with the word *lao* before about 1980. Now, although he is a bit young for the appellation, he and many many other senior doctors are honored with the usage.

14. This impression resulted from comparing textbooks and journal articles with interviews, lectures, and clinic observations in which I could witness local *laozhongyi* at work.

15. *Shandong Zhongyixueyuan Xuebao*, 1980, no. 2 (cover essay).

ture, which was welcomed enthusiastically by mature doctors all over China,[16] the *laozhongyi* openly seized the leadership of the field and inscribed themselves and their lives as national mentors for the young, exemplars for the future of Chinese medicine.

Over the next few years the essays published in the *Bulletin* and others solicited by and volunteered to its editors appeared in a three-volume book.[17] Chinese medical readers I spoke with agreed that these stories of their elders' lives were inspiring and instructive, especially for students of medicine. But many pointed out that the direct lessons of these narrative were few; the conditions and tasks of clinical and academic work had changed so much in the last decade or so that the lives of senior doctors (as opposed to their clinical insights, which were felt to be important) were becoming less and less relevant to contemporary situations.

Scientizing

It appears now that the moment seized by the *laozhongyi*, the years in which they inscribed their authorship and their authority in biographies, was fairly short-lived. It became more difficult in the late 1980s, amid a general conservative trend, for Chinese medical people to publish in genres associated with history and social pedagogy. And continuing efforts by young, vigorous, and increasingly well-educated scientizers to recast the central problems of the field as biological and clinical issues were producing a division between scholarly historical work (which was less and less often done by clinicians) and laboratory and statistical research designed to serve clinical work.

The aspirations of this younger cohort of scientifically oriented professionals will not be easy to fulfill, but they will not, I think, be abandoned either. Everyone acknowledges that the problem of rendering Chinese medicine more "scientific" is a knotty one. The work has been going on for a long time, however. Continuing initiatives begun early in the twentieth century, pharmacists have been working for decades to chemically analyze the Chinese materia medica, and their findings are readily available in standard reference works.[18] Clinical trials have been conducted for a huge variety of

---

16. Numerous letters in response to the "*Ming Laozhongyi zhi Lu*" series were published in the *Shandong Zhongyixueyuan Xuebao* 1980, nos. 3, 4.

17. Zhou Fengwu et al., eds., *Ming Laozhongyi zhi Lu,* 3 vols. (Jinan: Shandong Science and Technology Press, 1981–1985).

18. Jiangsu New Medical College, ed., *Zhongyao Dacidian,* 3 vols. (Shanghai: Shanghai People's Press, 1977). Volume 3 organizes chemical analyses according to drug name for reference. Although I often refer to the traditional materia medica herein by speaking of "herbal medicines," not all the drugs in question originate from plants. There are also drugs derived from animal and mineral substances.

techniques and medicaments, publication of which research takes up many pages of TCM professional journals. But it was only in the late 1970s that ethical objections to the use of control groups in clinical research were lifted by the Ministry of Health, so scientists of the 1980s who wished their clinical research with human patients to meet international standards had to consider doing a great many projects again, this time with "normal controls."

My young scientific acquaintances at the Guangzhou College in the early years of the decade planned ambitious research to address major theoretical issues in the evaluation of TCM (many of these involved immune system theory and systems theory), although they had great difficulty obtaining funding. And graduate students studying English and Japanese dreamed of going abroad to study advanced medical and bioscience techniques that they could use in research on TCM. If these are the leaders of tomorrow's traditional medicine, the field will quickly move far from the vision of the senior Chinese doctors.

One of the points to be made in my own discussion of Chinese medicine is that its practical logic and its ways of seeking efficacy are thoroughly inconsistent with the epistemological strictures of the Western natural sciences. I have said as much to many clinicians and researchers in the contemporary institutions of Chinese medicine and have been met with substantial agreement. Even leaving aside the classic texts of an ancient tradition, anyone who has studied the post–Cultural Revolution literature of TCM can see that its epistemological habits are not at all like those of bioscience. This difference, about which much more will be said, was partly signaled in the early 1980s in the widespread insistence on TCM holism. Experimental design being what it is, any scientific evaluation of Chinese medical knowledge ends up fragmenting and controlling the variables of its historical and practical reality right out of existence.[19]

But science cannot be so easily dismissed in today's China or today's world. The anxious comparisons that are constantly made between Chinese medicine and biomedicine on both sides of the Pacific are not idle epistemic exercises. In China, state funding for education, hospitals, and research is required if the structures within which practitioners of TCM now live and work are to continue to reproduce and legitimate the field. The policy concerns that nurtured TCM in its early post-Liberation years, such as national-

---

19. This is arguably true of any medical practice. Rigorous clinical research distorts everyday clinical practice in the interest of isolating the minimal active factors necessary to achieve narrowly defined therapeutic goals. Laboratory research in the basic biosciences is of course even more remote from the world of the clinic and the decisions of the practicing doctor or nurse. The arguments that link bioscientific facts to Western medical clinical values are complex indeed, although they are often forgotten once the connection has been consensually legitimated.

ism and self-sufficiency, have lost prominence since the Cultural Revolution, being overshadowed by the four modernizations and a commitment to global competitiveness. Government resources aimed at rapidly developing science and technology are being poured into research in the cosmopolitan physical and biological sciences. Even in the decades before new economic policies under Deng Xiaoping were instituted and stabilized, a strong discursive emphasis on "scientific socialism" influenced Chinese medicine toward a certain empiricist apologetics in the interest of earning a share of research funding.[20]

In short, for some time now there has been no material advantage to be gained from insisting on the "unscientific" character of TCM's particular forms of knowledge. If the legacy of several thousand years (*jiqiannian de yichuan*) of clinical experience has to be broken up into researchable fragments and subjected to a discourse and technology of epistemological legitimation to survive, then there are those who are prepared to undertake this arduous task. Among those members of Chinese medicine's next generation of leaders who have glimpsed the world of cosmopolitan science (many have by now studied abroad, and all are tired of competing with better-trained bioscientists for research support), there seems to be little nostalgia for a "pure" Chinese medicine of practical clinical work. Science is the weapon of their generation in a struggle to ensure a future for themselves and their students.

Chinese Medicine Beyond the Institutions

There are others who have a stake in the future of Chinese medicine, but their interests are in many respects distinct from those of the professionals. Patients I have spoken with, for example, do not seem to care much whether the Chinese medical care they are seeking is scientifically legitimated.[21] As is true of pluralistic medical fields elsewhere in the world, many of those who use traditional medical care suffer from long-term chronic illnesses. Having discovered that many of their most stubborn complaints can neither be

---

20. See Kwok, *Scientism,* esp. pp. 18–20, for a discussion of Chinese communist and Marxist commitment to scientific socialism, advocacy of technological modernization to combat military and economic imperialism, and opposition to "feudal elements." Before the Long March and the Yan'an period, traditional medicine was one of these feudal elements for leading communist thinkers.

21. Apart from conversations with acquaintances from outside the world of Chinese medicine, I have not systematically interviewed patients who prefer to use biomedical services in China. This discussion is based on encounters with people who for one reason or another chose to use the services of a TCM clinical unit.

cured nor even directly addressed within the framework of biomedicine, they are desperate and willing to try anything that might work. These patients and their families often spend large amounts of money traveling to clinics and purchasing exotic herbal medicines. They shop around for doctors, try out new clinics and new practitioners as they hear of them, and often seek recommendations to renowned specialists from friends and family.[22] And they sometimes form strong loyalties to particular doctors, to whose clinic they will return every week, sometimes for years, for continuing management of their symptoms.

Not all patients of Chinese medicine are seriously ill, but they rely on the ready availability of TCM services anyway. Many prefer to use TCM remedies for minor illnesses and as part of continuing programs of preventive home care. People of this sort argue that Chinese medicines are safer than those of biomedicine, having, for example, no side effects; although such therapies work slowly, they are said to "treat the root" of the ailment. In my experience these are the same people who maintain careful health regimens for themselves and their family members; they can talk at length about the medicinal properties of various foods, the dangers of dressing too lightly in the winter, and the most wholesome times of day to bathe or sleep.

A large Chinese pharmaceutical industry produces, and vigorously advertises, a vast array of "made-up Chinese medicines" (*zhongchengyao*). In contrast to the decoctions of herbal medicine prescribed by most doctors of TCM (see Chapter 6), which require time-consuming boiling and reboiling, these are patent medicines: pills, powders, and infusions that can be readily bought in neighborhood pharmacies and then quickly prepared and consumed at home. These products are used in the treatment of common complaints such as colds and flu, indigestion, arthritis, constipation and diarrhea, high blood pressure, nervousness, and the aches and pains of old age. Their composition is usually based on classic formulae from the literature or formulae developed by famous doctors. In addition to use in self-care, these medicines are often given as gifts, forming part of the regular prestations that sustain family life and social relations; tonics for old men are a particularly popular offering.

The new economic policies that have encouraged sideline businesses and valorized getting rich have stimulated business for herbal drug factories,

---

22. A complaint I heard frequently from patients and their families in the late 1980s and early 1990s was that the only way to ensure careful medical care was through "connections" (*guanxi*). Whenever possible, experienced patients approached doctors with an introduction from a mutual friend; gifts and bribes were also sometimes in evidence in clinics. Whether it was true that health care improved when there was a personal relationship (and many doctors I knew went far out of their way to allay this impression), patients thought this was the case. Some said that the *guanxi* problem was much worse for biomedical institutions than for those of Chinese medicine.

which now provide many nonclinical jobs and consulting contracts for graduates of TCM colleges. The new policies have also allowed some TCM practitioners to go into private practice. Although this is especially the case for those with established specialties and reputations, who can carry loyal patient populations with them, doctors of many types (young or old, male or female, renowned or just starting out, formally or informally trained) can now be found running small clinics of their own. The large hospitals and academies that in the past had their pick of graduates of the TCM colleges are increasingly on the defensive, trying to keep their senior staff and attract skilled junior doctors away from growing industrial and commercial sectors.

These complex developments in response to a continuing demand for Chinese medical treatment may be as crucial to the direction of knowledge in the field as the scientizing tendencies that thrive within its large institutions. While official traditional medicine may be narrowing, growing more and more rigorously scientific, popular medicine may be rediversifying to meet patients' demands, respond to competitive activity by drug companies, and guarantee doctors' livelihoods. And as elsewhere, the divide between professional and lay knowledge is permeable and fluid.

The knowing practice that this book describes takes its place in a particular historical moment framed by the events and constructions just outlined. Once it seemed natural and necessary to me that Chinese medicine should function in clinics with little or no reliance on laboratory tests or penetrative imaging devices; that it should reveal the specificities of particular illnesses, rather than place each illness in an abstract nosology of diseases; and that it should embody a relation between doctors and the past, between clinical experience and the ever-new demands of practice. A few years having passed, I now realize that many of the particular epistemological and therapeutic formations I observed in the early 1980s and describe herein are under contest. This clinical encounter, it must be admitted, is a possession and creation of the senior Chinese doctors who still dominated the field when I was first at the Guangzhou College of Traditional Chinese Medicine. Although the practical logic that I outline here is still the dominant form in which clinical work is done, and as such can appropriate numerous kinds of knowledge and put them in play in clinical work,[23] it is impossible to say how long this particular form of clinical encounter will survive in mainstream institutions.

Much of what follows, however, will argue for the historical toughness of this non-Western healing practice. People know that the herbal medicines

---

23. For example, the results of many biomedical tests (hematology and urinalysis, X-rays and sonograms) are sometimes consulted in the process of analyzing the illness and classifying the symptoms. See Chapter 4.

and acupuncture therapies they administer and accept are often effective, and they have a very involved language in which to speak of, understand, and manipulate this effectiveness. The language of science, which even in Chinese incorporates a borrowed metaphysic, is inadequate to the experience of Chinese medicine and the illnesses articulated within it. But regardless of whether the very great differences investigated herein have a future apart from that of global science and medicine, it is worth attending to them as they presented themselves in the discourses of traditional medicine in the 1980s. It is to those differences, and their implications for understanding knowing practice, that I now turn.

2

Preliminary Orientations: Sources and Manifestations, Unity and Multiplicity

People of old, by way of a long period of observation of natural phenomena, came to the realization that the universe was permeated by two kinds of material force that were both opposed to each other and united with each other, these being yin qi and yang qi; and qi is the material foundation of the genesis of the myriad things. The two qi of yin and yang are from beginning to end ceaselessly moving and transforming. The gathering and dispersing of qi are the mutual push and pull of yin and yang; the rising and falling of qi are yin and yang summoning responses from each other; when qi is a dense fog, this is yin and yang softening relative to each other. Mutually opposed, interdependent, and controlling each other, moving and changing, yin and yang embody the basic principles of change and development of all the things in the universe.[1]

The preceding passage appears on the first page of the first chapter of a textbook about the theoretical foundations of Chinese medicine; it was published in Fujian Province in 1981, edited by Zhao Fen and other faculty at the Fujian College of Traditional Chinese Medicine. The book's vocabulary, style, and content resemble both Han period (206 B.C.–A.D. 220) philosophical works in which qi and the yinyang relationship were extensively elaborated and certain much more recent works in Chinese Marxist dialectics.[2] This use of ancient and uniquely Chinese concepts to open the

---

1. Zhao Fen, ed., *Zhongyi Jichu Lilun Xiangjie* (Fuzhou: Fujian Science and Technology Press, 1981), p. 1.

2. The relationship between yin and yang aspects of phenomena is referred to in modern Chinese as yinyang. The compound term thus refers to the complex dynamic discussed in this chapter. I use it frequently to avoid implying that yin or yang qualities can be characterized independently of their relative value.

topic of theoretical foundations in a contemporary textbook suggests a long and continual history of systematic knowledge. Combining Han dynasty and Maoist language, it admits of no contradictions deforming or rupturing the history of Chinese medicine. Even (or especially) the revolution of 1949, it is implied, has continued the fulfillment of Chinese medicine's ancient promise. In placing such abstractions at the beginning of the book, Zhao requires that readers first come to terms with a certain philosophical idiom and outlook before embarking on the more technical and clinical material that follows. He locates yinyang and qi, and the literature in which these notions were first systematically inscribed, in a foundational position, suggesting that ancient philosophy together with a Marxist dialectic style of thought should function both to frame the more specific science that follows and render it more comprehensible for the novice.

Although Zhao Fen is more artful than most, this approach to opening introductory works was utterly conventional in the discourse of Chinese medicine in the 1980s. Invoking, even insisting on, qi as a substance or force and yinyang as an explanatory method is both risky and (many feel) necessary in the global culture of the late twentieth century. In both China and North America, readers schooled in textbook science and empiricist common sense take these words, and the conceptual structures of traditional medicine in which they function, to be superstitious or mystical. The physiology and pathology that make sense of the language and techniques of traditional Chinese medicine violate the canons of causality and anatomy that Western readers have come to see as basic to any true science of disease or the body. This epistemological dis-ease presents a special challenge for this book. Although my readers and those to whom Zhao Fen addresses his book are quite different, I wish to adopt part of his strategy here, invoking eloquent and powerful writing from early in the history of Chinese scholarship to encourage a more coherent and respectful reading of medical writings in the present. Thus, in both Zhao Fen's project and my own, classic Chinese philosophy is recruited to serve as a first step toward Chinese medical understanding.

Chinese Medicine's Challenge to Comparison

Chinese medicine heals in a world of unceasing transformation. This condition of constant change, this fluidity of material forms, stands in sharp contrast to a (modern Western) commonsense world of discrete entities characterized by fixed essences, which seem to be exhaustively describable in structural terms.[3] Theories of relativity and indeterminacy notwithstanding, in our everyday life we still assume a Newtonian world of inertial masses, a world in which motion and change result from causes external to entities. Events must be accounted for in a logic of cause and effect, an ultimately mechanical relationship that requires the radical reduction of the plenum of phenomena to its most effective or significant elements. In this process a single reality, both universal and originary, is (never quite completely) constructed as it is "described." Basic changes in object status and life and death per se remain final mysteries that seem to escape the reductionist and causal logics of "science." In other words, phenomena that are not easily reduced to quantifiable relations between discrete objects or analyzed as a system of "structures" and "functions" are a problem for explanatory methods grounded in Western materialist metaphysics.

In the early Chinese sciences, by contrast, where generation and transformation are intrinsic to existence, fixity and stasis occur only as a result of concerted action and therefore demand explanation; motion and change are a given and seldom need be explained with reference to their causes. One consequence of this dynamic bias in Chinese medicine is that the body and its organs (i.e., anatomical structure) appear as merely contingent effects or by-products of physiological processes.[4] Basing a pathology on anatomical

---

3. The essentialism of our commonsense understandings of the world is everywhere evident but (like all commonsense) difficult to define. The inherited philosophical use of the concept of "essence" is well summarized by Alasdair MacIntyre in the *Encyclopedia of Philosophy* (New York: Macmillan and Free Press, 1967), pp. 59–61. A strain that runs through the epistemological arguments he reports is the notion that essences are possibilities of form that, when existence is conferred on them, make it possible for humans to identify things as what they are. This is a classically idealist structure in which the differences and characteristics of things, their structures, derive from their instantiation of timeless essences.

Much recent social theory and scientific practice has attacked essentialist formations. Richard Rorty's revision of pragmatism has been particularly effective in widening philosophical understanding of this problem (*Contingency, Irony, Solidarity* [Cambridge: Cambridge University Press, 1989]). See also Donna Haraway, "The Biopolitics of Postmodern Bodies," in *Simians, Cyborgs, and Women* (New York: Routledge, 1991), pp. 203–230, for insights into contemporary immunology that are in many ways parallel to those of this book; Ronald Inden, *Imagining India* (Oxford: Blackwell, 1990), esp. the introduction, for a critique of essentialism in history and anthropology; Tony Skillen, *Ruling Illusions* (Sussex: Harvester, 1977), pp. 12–15, for a discussion of essentialism in regard to the Western idealist tradition; and Steve Woolgar, *Science* (New York: Tavistock and Ellis Horwood, 1988), p. 30*ff*, for a look at essentialism in relation to assumptions about representation. A very thoughtful antiessentialist study of early Chinese philosophy is David L. Hall and Roger T. Ames, *Thinking Through Confucius* (Albany: State University of New York Press, 1987).

4. Judith Farquhar, "Body Contingency and Healing Power in Traditional Chinese Medicine," *Discours Social/Social Discourse* 3, nos.3–4 (1990–1991):53–70; and Judith Farquhar "Objects, Processes, and Female Infertility in Chinese Medicine," *Medical Anthropology Quarterly* (NS) 5, no.4 (December 1991):370–399.

structures and structural abnormalities would be like closing the barn door after the horse has fled. For the scholar-doctor, as for the classic philosopher, attention to the patterns of the "myriad phenomena" (*wanwu*) as they emerge into the manifest world is a way of discerning "the changes." The seasoned adept notes the qualities and forms of manifestations and the changing time and space relationships among them, looking for effective combinations that can influence developments in a desired direction.

This difference between a world of fixed objects and a world of transforming effects accounts for many of the difficulties encountered by moderns who attempt to understand Chinese medicine. Assumptions about the nature of being cannot be "proved"; no evidence can support or refute them. Like the solid inertial world of modern natural science traditions, the processual and transformative world of Chinese medicine seems to exist prior to all argument, observation, and intervention. Perhaps with a certain discomfort, Western readers must acknowledge that "their" abstractions about such things make as much sense as "ours."

Classically in the Western philosophical tradition, the problems presented by differences at this apparently fundamental level have been considered under the heading of "metaphysics."[5] The troubled relationship between truth (taken up in epistemology, with its array of arguments, claims, and formal correspondences) and existence (the domain of ontology, with its idiom of insight and "natural" common sense) has kept questions of first principles and their evaluation central to Western philosophical discourse. The commonplace assertion that all sciences, all systems of knowledge, are founded on "a metaphysic" or "system of first principles" that is beyond proof or argument has not, however, prevented numerous attempts to apply epistemological standards to ontological principles.

This historical commitment to a separation and an interdependence between "metaphysics" and knowledge presents special problems to comparative historians of science.[6] Together with sociologists, they have made it difficult to ignore the way in which all systems of knowledge, or better, languages of science, seem to rely on some body of metaphysical assumptions,

---

5. For a conventional definition of metaphysics see P. B. Gove, ed., *Webster's Third New International Dictionary of the English Language, Unabridged* (Springfield, Mass.: G. and C. Merriam, 1969), where the term is glossed as "the system of first principles or philosophy underlying a particular study or subject of inquiry." See R. G. Collingwood's extensive discussion and critique of the history of Western metaphysics (*An Essay on Metaphysics* [Lanham, Md.: University Press of America, 1972]). Collingwood seeks to radically historicize metaphysics, but he continues to accord it a foundational position in a stratigraphic metaphor of levels of knowledge.

6. The massive work of Joseph Needham on the history of Chinese science is thoroughly comparative and remarkable for its sensitive attention to "metaphysical matters," especially in vol. 2 (*Science and Civilization in China* [Cambridge: Cambridge University Press, 1956]). More recent Anglophone scholarship in the history of science, which conventionally traces its origins to Thomas Kuhn *The Structure of Scientific Revolutions*, 2d ed. (Chicago: University of Chicago Press, 1970), has contributed substantially to what many philosophers have seen as a relativistic

regardless of whether these are explicit; in a parallel set of debates, what has interested anthropologists is that cosmologies, ontologies, whole worlds of practice and discourse, have varied so much.[7] If metaphysics cannot be found true in a strict sense, then the systems of knowledge that rely on universal acceptance of certain metaphysical foundations for their coherence can make no strong truth claims either. As anthropology and history relativize metaphysics, they uncover logical contradictions that shake the universal pretensions of the natural sciences that emerged within Western modernism. This situation is, of course, widely acknowledged by scientists and by those who write about science within other disciplines.[8]

For an anthropological study of knowledge, it seems unwise to rely too heavily on standard divisions provided by the history of Western philosophy. In particular I want to guard against the almost unconscious way in which ultimate questions of being (ontology) and universal form (cosmology) are expressed as foundational to knowing (epistemology). This and other forms of foundationalism in epistemology have been challenged by recent philosophers in widely influential arguments;[9] they have, among other things,

crisis. Also see Barry Barnes *Interests and the Growth of Knowledge* (London: Routledge and Kegan Paul, 1977); and Barry Barnes, *T. S. Kuhn and Social Science* (New York: Columbia University Press, 1982). Concerning the genealogy of these developments, Kuhn himself acknowledges important influence from a rich and long-standing Continental tradition of critical histories of science via the work of Ludwik Fleck, *The Structure,* pp. vi–vii.

7. This interest has been most explicitly developed in the now nearly defunct "rationality" debate. See Bryan R. Wilson, ed., *Rationality* (Oxford: Basil Blackwell, 1977), for a collection of essays that draw on the seminal ethnographic and speculative work of Lucien Levy-Bruhl and E. E. Evans-Pritchard. For a critique of the debate, see Paul Hirst and Penny Woolley, *Social Relations and Human Attributes* (London: Tavistock, 1982), pp. 211–273.

8. See R. C. Lewontin, Steven Rose, and Leon J. Kamin, *Not in Our Genes* (New York: Pantheon, 1984), p. 32n, for a pragmatic characterization of "true statements" for scientific purposes. For a critique of transposing the methods of a positive science into the social sciences, see Donald McCloskey, *The Rhetoric of Economics* (Madison: University of Wisconsin Press, 1985), pp. 3–19. See also Bruno Latour and Steve Woolgar, *Laboratory Life* (Princeton: Princeton University Press, 1986); Woolgar, *Science;* and Allan A. Young, "Mode of Production of Medical Knowledge," *Medical Anthropology* 2, no. 2 (1978):97–122. More philosophical treatments of truth as a social problem can be found in Paul Feyerabend, *Against Method* (London: New Left Books, 1975); and Paul Feyerabend, *Realism, Rationalism and Scientific Method,* vol. 1 (Cambridge: Cambridge University Press, 1981); and Jean-Francois Lyotard, *The Post-Modern Condition* (Minneapolis: University of Minnesota Press, 1984). For a reference to these problems in anthropology, see James Clifford and George E. Marcus, *Writing Culture* (Berkeley and Los Angeles: University of California Press, 1986), pp. 10–11.

9. See Richard Rorty, *Philosophy and the Mirror of Nature* (Oxford: Basil Blackwell, 1980); Paul Feyerabend, *Against Method;* Jean-Francois Lyotard and Jean-Loup Thebaud *Just Gaming,* (Minneapolis: University of Minnesota Press, 1985), pp. 73–92; Jacques Derrida, *Of Grammatology* (Baltimore: Johns Hopkins University Press, 1976); Michel Foucault, *The Archaeology of Knowledge* (New York: Harper and Row, 1972), esp. the introduction; Michel Foucault, "Nietzsche, Genealogy, History," in *Language, Counter-memory, Practice* (Ithaca, N.Y.: Cornell University Press, 1977), pp. 140–164; and Barbara Herrnstein Smith, *Contingencies of Value* (Cambridge, Mass.: Harvard University Press, 1988).

encouraged studies that investigate historically and culturally specific knowledge practices, looking for modes of organizing thought, experience, and action in ways that were previously undreamed of in our philosophies.

Cosmogony and Transformation

The brief excerpts from early Chinese philosophical and medical texts that follow continue to be cited in the present; courses are taught in medical colleges on the central classic of Chinese medicine, the *Huangdi Neijing* (The Yellow Emperor's Inner Canon), and on the Daoism of Laozi as well as on several other works from China's classical philosophical corpus. These texts are poetic and (by virtue of being constantly referred to by scholars) powerful statements on the nature of being. Perhaps in the contemporary world of Chinese medicine they function more as allegorical resources for clinical thinking than as first principles, but the fact remains that moderns still read them. Within a medicine that insists on its specificity and historicity in a global scientific culture, this is neither an accident nor a mere cultural survival.

Because this book is primarily concerned with medical knowledge and practice in the present, I have in my translations followed the lead of modern Chinese paraphrases of and annotations to classic texts. The paraphrases, which are more verbose versions of ancient writings, use some of the same vocabulary and usually retain the same overall structure and sequence as the original, but they also incorporate a distinctly modern understanding of their message as well as a rendering of ancient terms that sometimes ignores historical variation. More important, modern Chinese "translations" of classical Chinese texts reduce the polysemy of ancient language, rendering them in a more specific and limiting modern syntax in the interest of intelligibility to more readers. (This problem is even more severe, of course, for translations of classical Chinese into English, in which a greater syntactical rigidity is compounded by an almost entirely separate language history.)

Under these circumstances it is surprising and significant that early medical and philosophical texts preserve so much of their suggestive density in their modern Chinese versions. The practice of publishing the "original text" (*yuan wen*) along with historical and linguistic notes and modern Chinese translations maintains an important contrast in the medical literature. It also encourages an active comparative reading, in which the reader's "text" is compiled from several levels of commentary. Paraphrases continue to use some ancient technical terms even (or especially) when there is considerable controversy over the meaning of such words; but the use of a more restrictive modern language of paraphrase reduces the likelihood that the inexperienced will read the texts in ways entirely inconsistent with medical practice.

The following excerpts, with the exception of the one from Laozi, are from the medical classic *Su Wen* (Basic Questions). This work is the first of two books composing the *Inner Canon*. The work has been dated from the Han period.[10] Like other philosophical and scientific works of China's classical period, *Basic Questions* (in part) speculates about cosmology and cosmogony, tracing phenomena back to their roots in time prior to time periods, matter prior to form, action prior to agents, and life prior to birth and death. The imagery and phrasing of many other contemporaneous philosophical works are embodied in *Basic Questions* (in its fully compiled versions) without attribution. And the medical insights recorded in *Basic Questions* have much in common with those of more renowned Han dynasty philosophical texts. The book figures particularly prominently in contemporary teaching of the theoretical foundations of Chinese medicine, serving as a fund of ultimate explanations on which many modern writers draw.

All the following excerpts consider the nature of transformation and existence in a cosmogonic framework. The first is a particularly complex example:

> The emperor said, "I want to hear how the five cyclic components [*wuyun*] divide to rule the four seasons."
>
> Gui Yuqu said, "Each of the five components can rule one year; it is not that [each] solely or independently rules [one of] the four seasons."
>
> The emperor said, "Can you explain the reasons to me?"
>
> Gui Yuqu said, "Your servant has studied the *Notebooks on the Ultimate Beginnings of the Heavenly Origins* at great length. In this work it says, 'The vast and limitless heavenly void is the foundation of the root and origin of the generation and transformation of matter, and it is the beginning of the production of the myriad things. The five components move through the Dao of Heaven, ending only to begin anew, distributing the steady original [*zhenyuan*] qi of heaven and earth, epitomizing and comprehending the root and origin of generation and transformation upon the great earth, among the nine stars twinkling in the sky, and among the seven planets that revolve according to the degrees of heaven. Consequently, ceaseless change results from the myriad things having yin and yang aspects, having different characters of hard and soft, while opaque darkness and clear brightness emerge according to a certain positional order, and cold and heat come and go according to certain seasons. These mechanisms of ceaseless generation, this Dao of inexhaustible transformation, and the differing forms and manifestations of the world's myriad things all [in this way] come out and are manifested where they can be seen.'"[11]

---

10. Cf. Nathan Sivin, *Traditional Medicine in Contemporary China* (Ann Arbor: Center for Chinese Studies, University of Michigan, 1987), p. 5 n. 3.

11. This is a modern Chinese paraphrase from Shandong College of Traditional Chinese Medicine and the Hebei College of Medicine, eds., *Huangdi Neijing Suwen Jiaoshi* (Beijing: People's Health Press, 1982), *juan* 19, sec. 66, pp. 847–848.

This description posits three main moments in a cosmogonic sequence: "steady original qi" pouring forth from the void, a "distribution" of this qi into differentiated forces (i.e., processes of differing character), and a manifest world whose forms (the "myriad things") change ceaselessly as a result of this differentiation. An original generative unity is divided into the opposing and interplaying aspects of yin and yang, hard and soft, dark and bright, and cold and hot, and these differences in turn enable the bewildering variety of the world's manifest (and inexhaustibly transforming) forms.

A simpler and more cryptic passage in *Basic Questions* argues against any overly literal classificatory application of these cosmogonic relationships:

> The emperor said, "I have heard that sky is yang and earth is yin, that the sun is yang and the moon is yin, that the long and short months form a year of 360 days, and that man corresponds to this. But now I hear that bodily threefold yin and threefold yang do not correspond to the enumeration of heaven and earth, yin and yang. Why is this?"
>
> Qi Bo responded, "Yin and yang enumerated can be ten and extended can be one hundred, further enumerated they can be one thousand, further extended they are myriad, and the myriads can be multiplied beyond counting— still their essence is unity."[12]

In other words, the dualities that emerge as the "Dao of inexhaustible transformation" turns unity into multiplicity are neither mutually exclusive categories nor opposed forces nor kinds of stuff. Rather, this frequently quoted text asserts that yin and yang are the principle of worldly differentiation and intertransformation itself, a simultaneously logical and material polarity that characterizes activity at any level this side of the most ultimate beginnings. Yin and yang need not, however, be used to account for the process of generation itself; generation is rooted in that unity of steady original qi that is prior to all form and differentiation. This numerically framed explanation also suggests that ultimate causes are beyond all knowing since knowledge can only be of that which is already differentiated.

A similar cosmogony which appears to place the notion of Dao in a more originary logical and cosmogonic position than *Basic Questions* does can be found in Laozi: "The Dao generates one, one generates two, two generates three, and three generates ten thousand things. These myriad things carry yin on their back and yang in their arms; pervaded with qi they can achieve harmony."[13] Here the Dao seems to replace the Void as ultimate origin, but

---

12. Cheng Shide et al., eds., *Suwen Zhushi Huicui, juan* 2, sec. 6, (Beijing: People's Health Press, 1982), p. 110.

13. Chen Guying, ed., *Laozi Zhuyi ji Pingjie, juan* 42 (Beijing: Chinese Book Company, 1984); cited, by way of explaining Laozi's use of the concept of Dao, in Xiao Shafu and Li Mianquan, eds., *Zhongguo Zhexueshi*, vol. 1 (Beijing: People's Press, 1983), pp. 111–112. This latter text was used in teaching the history of Chinese medicine to graduate students at the Guangzhou College of Traditional Chinese Medicine when I was there in 1983 and 1984.

the same one-two-three sequence already evident holds: Two presumably refers to yinyang and all allied dualities, whereas three usually means the three moments of yin, yang, and the unity formed by their interdependent relationship. Endless multiplicity flows from the intimate interplay of yin and yang and other such differences. Therefore, the myriad things are never really separate from interactive difference (yinyang) or from the fundamental generative process of which qi is the common name. In other words, cosmogony is not confined to the unimaginable past—the temporal pattern described in these texts is the way in which the manifest world continues to come into being.

Partly because of this, manifestations also multiply and change according to the relations that hold among them; it is possible to analyze worldly time in terms of sequences of production and destruction operating in regular and repetitive patterns:

> The eastern quarter generates Wind, Wind generates Wood, Wood generates sour, sour generates Liver, Liver generates muscle, muscle generates Heart, Liver rules the eyes. This [process] in Heaven is dark generative potential [*xuan*], in man is the Dao, on earth is transformation [*hua*]. Transformation generates the five flavors, the Dao generates wisdom, dark potential generates vitality. Vitality in heaven is Wind, on earth is Wood, in the human frame is muscle, among the viscera is the Liver, among the colors is blue-green, among the musical notes is *jue*, among the inflected tones is *hu*, in movement is grasping, among the orifices is the eyes, among the flavors is sour, and among the intentions is anger. Anger injures Liver and sorrow overcomes anger, Wind injures muscle and Dry overcomes Wind, sour injures muscle and pungent overcomes sour.[14]

This passage could be analyzed as a technical problem in the correspondence relationships of medical entities and qualities, but its interest here is more general. The "generation" and "injury" relationships listed should not be seen as mechanically causal ones. They are better thought of as relations of commonality, enabling, or constraining among phenomena that are naturally caused by a much deeper process, that of unceasing spontaneous (*ziran*, or self-so) world generation. Free of any obligation to explain why things happen at all (they happen of themselves), Chinese scientists could focus on the usual sequences in which they happened, the conditions that influenced the forms of happening, and the interventions that could nudge happening in desired directions.

Finally, here is a passage from *Basic Questions* that shows cosmology and medicine to be inseparable and that functions in contemporary discourses as a central charter of Chinese medicine's unique features:

---

14. Cheng et al., *Suwen Zhushi Huicui, juan* 2, sec. 5, pp. 82–83.

Yin and yang are the Dao of heaven and earth. They are the network of the myriad things, the father and mother of alteration and transformation, the root and beginning of life-giving and death-bringing, the abode of vitality and intelligence. The treatment of illness must trace this root. Thus it is that collected yang is heaven and collected yin is earth. Yang ends life; yin begins [life in] latency. Yang transforms qi; yin brings forms to maturity. When cold reaches an extreme, it gives rise to heat; when heat reaches an extreme, it gives rise to cold. Cold qi generates turbid [yin]; hot qi generates clear [yang]. When clear qi is in the lower [parts of the body, which are relatively yin], it gives rise to "rice-gruel" diarrhea; when turbid qi is in the upper [parts of the body, which are relatively yang], it produces swelling and distention. This is the opposed action of yin and yang, the countermovement and following movement of illness.[15]

One of the many fascinating features of this passage is the relationship between classification of phenomena as relatively yin or yang and the dynamic polarity of phenomena so classified. Effects such as heaven and earth, life and death are named as yin or yang and in the same moment placed in a polar relationship to each other. The polarity of yin and yang thus allows numerous positions on the continuum of possibilities between its extreme points; just as hot shades into cold and clear can become turbid by degrees, the difference between life and death is discernible as infinite particularities of the yinyang relationship. Because all manifest phenomena can be placed on such a continuum, the yinyang of the bodily person and of the medical techniques through which she or he can be read is little different from that of the cosmos as a whole. Medicine focuses a powerful analytic technique on the particular problems of maintaining health and treating diseases. In its practice there is both a partnership and tension between classificatory and dynamic aspects of the yinyang dyad the significance of which will be illustrated at length in the later analysis of diagnostic practices (see especially Chapter 4).

Sources and Manifestations

Figure 2.1 generalizes two sequences of cosmogony, or world production, from the texts just quoted; this figure cannot claim to be appropriate for all of ancient Chinese philosophy and medicine, but a general movement from a unitary source through duality to the myriad manifestations is discernible in many early cosmogonies. This formation has been evident in most of the preceding brief texts: Steady original qi (for example) flows forth from the

---

15. Ibid., pp. 68–69.

A.

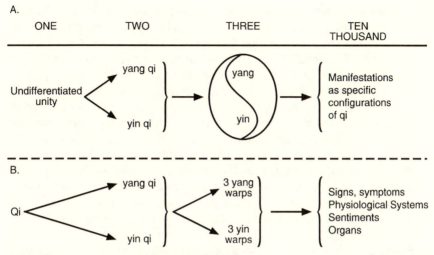

FIGURE 2.1   Two sequences of world production

vast and limitless heavenly void, emerging after a process of yinyang differ-entiation as the myriad things. This cosmogonic terminology is only one example of the things that can stand in a source-manifestation relationship; but if the general relationship between sources and manifestations is borne in mind through the more technical material to follow, the intellectual co-herence of Chinese medical practices will be more apparent.

The first sequence (A) in Figure 2.1 is general and cosmic; the second (B) is medical. Four moments can be identified, corresponding to the four columns in the figure. For the one, two, and ten thousand (myriad) mo-ments of the process, the correspondence between cosmic and medical phe-nomena is clear, but the things counted by three are quite different in the two sequences. The "six warps" (*liu jing,* see Chapter 4) are a specific orga-nization of the intimate relationship between physiological yin and yang, whereas the threeness of yin, yang, and their polar unity is a philosophical abstraction that seems logically entailed in the process of getting from one to many.

Although only sequence B deals specifically with illness and physiology, both sequences relate to medicine. The former cosmic order includes ex-ternal illness factors and herbal drugs in its cosmogenesis, and the latter body order clarifies physiology and pathology. The cosmic order encom-passes and accounts for the body order, which is then an important speci-fication of cosmogenesis. Herbals that (like everything else) belong to the world of the myriad things can be brought to bear on that subset of the myriad things that is the body and its illness effects.

Modern textbooks commonly define qi as the minimal essential substance that flows in the body *and* as the functions of organs and tissues.[16] In ways that can be differentiated only contextually, qi is spoken of both as a concrete fluid and an abstract notion that is often glossed as the "characteristic activity" of a functional system. Sections in texts are devoted to explaining the functions and transformations of the substances "qi, Blood, *jing* [transitional qi], and dispersed body fluids"; hence it is reasonable to say that the qi (i.e., characteristic activity) of the Spleen system is to transmit and assimilate substances (of which qi is one). Although there have been modern efforts to definitionally reduce qi to only a "substance" (*wuzhi*),[17] it is difficult to account for the full range of the word's semantic functions when such a definition is promulgated. There are many types of physiological qi (e.g., defensive qi, primordial qi) that are distinguished from one another entirely in functional terms. In these usages qi is both structural and functional, a unification of material and temporal forms that loses all coherence when reduced to one or the other "aspect." In other words, qi may be a substance, but it is at present too elusive and multiple to define using a substantive language of essential characteristics or structures.[18]

English translations of qi vary, but most rely on the concept of energy to make its simultaneously active and material nature clear. All these approaches to qi are oversimplified, however. Readers of the many classic and other premodern texts that remain important in the world of contemporary Chinese medicine can hardly fail to note the variable functions and the connotative richness of earlier notions of qi.[19] Modern concern with defining, scientifically characterizing, and translating both the word and "the thing" qi distorts these premodern discourses. Perhaps some definitional imperative has arisen in contemporary China from the convergence of dialectical materialism, economic and technical modernization, and scientific Marxism. One suspects that qi is being posited as a discrete and unitary substance simply

---

16. Editing Committee of the Dictionary of Chinese Medicine, *Jianming Zhongyi Cidian* (Beijing: People's Health Press, 1979), p. 149.

17. Hong Menghu, "*Ping 'Qi' ji Biao Wuzhi you Biao Jinengde Liangyishuo,*" *Zhongyi Zazhi* 24, no. 3 (March 1983):4–7.

18. Some authors have posited a relationship between substantive and functional senses of the term, arguing that substantial qi is the material basis of qi function, which is in turn the functional expression of substantial qi. See Beijing College of Traditional Chinese Medicine, ed., *Zhongyixue Jichu* (Shanghai: Shanghai Science and Technology Press, 1978), p. 22. See also Deng Tietao, ed., *Zhongyi Jichu Lilun* (Guangzhou: Guangdong Science and Technology Press, 1982), p. 37. The formal analogy of this type of argument to Marxist-Leninist concerns with theorizing the relationship between base and superstructure is, of course, no accident.

19. Manfred Porkert, *The Theoretical Foundations of Chinese Medicine* (Cambridge, Mass.: MIT Press, 1974); and Sivin, *Traditional Medicine,* have developed the most helpful scholarly discussions of qi in Chinese medicine. Their discussions of classical and premodern meanings of the term are important supplements to this book not least because so many of the texts on which they draw remain prominent in contemporary teaching and scholarship in the PRC.

because the word exists and is central to Chinese medical writing and clinical practices. A pressure to define terms and demonstrate the "objective" (*keguan*) reality of their referents (as if a word without a concrete measurable referent could never be admitted to the language of science) is undoubtedly felt by the compilers of textbooks and dictionaries.[20] Thus, although a "systematically" defined unitary qi has become important as Chinese medical theorists respond to subtle scientizing pressures, it need not be confused with the steady original qi of the classic cosmogonies. And regardless of what the dictionaries say, the many ways in which "configurative force" (Porkert's translation of qi) is both unitary and multiple in physiology and pathology continue to be embodied in the knowledge and practice of Chinese doctors.

All generation involves the specification of qi into the myriad things. Yin and yang—the opposed aspects of phenomena that are rooted in each other, "struggle" with each other, and can transform into each other—are the general form of a universal dynamic that is at once unitary ("seen as single, it is simply a waxing and waning"),[21] dual, and triple (in that the aspects are both two and one at once). Relations of struggle and interdependence among phenomena naturally take yinyang form. Thus, yinyang is the name of the dynamic process in which the ever-various manifest world continues to self-generate.

There are many medical specifications of this process, and, as commentators have argued, apart from early cosmogonic speculation it is not appropriate to think of yin and yang as forces that are (even logically) separable from the concrete phenomena that display these polar aspects.[22] Insofar as the bodily effects with which Chinese doctors are daily confronted are consistent with the logic of sources and manifestations diagramed in Figure 2.1, the clinical discussions to follow will in a sense be a long exploration of the subtleties and technicalities of yinyang reasoning.

Clearly, the world-generative process diagramed here need not be solely

---

20. Recent critiques of the concept of representation have denaturalized the word-referent relationship indicated here. See Timothy Reiss *The Discourse of Modernism* (Ithaca, N.Y.: Cornell University Press, 1982); Michel Foucault, *The Order of Things* (New York: Vintage, 1973), pp. 63–67; Louis Marin, *Portrait of the King* (Minneapolis: University of Minnesota Press, 1988), pp. 3–15; Dalia Judovitz, *Subjectivity and Representation in Descartes* (Cambridge: Cambridge University Press, 1988), pp. 149–159; Woolgar, *Science;* and, a particularly important book for the point made here, Timothy Mitchell, *Colonising Egypt* (Cambridge: Cambridge University Press, 1988).

21. Song Dynasty philosopher Zhu Xi, cited in Sivin, *Traditional Medicine,* p. 64.

22. Clarifying discussions of yinyang can be found in Marcel Granet, *The Religion of the Chinese People* (New York: Harper and Row, 1975), pp. 48–52; Joseph Needham, *Science and Civilization,* vol. 2, p. 273*ff.*; Porkert, *Theoretical Foundations,* pp. 9–43; and Sivin, *Traditional Medicine,* pp. 59–70.

about past origins of present entities. As was pointed out, it works as well to summarize continuing processes of transformation that operate in the present. Consequently, as medicine in treating the illness traces the root, it must come to terms with the continuing transformation of the manifest. Doctors must join the benign influences that they can organize by way of drugs and practices such as acupuncture and massage to the continuing activity of "the ensemble of processes" that is a living person in the hope of altering a pathological development.[23]

Yin can be brought to bear on yang, and Pungent can overcome Sour. Since qi pervades things, manifestations resonate among themselves, and juxtaposition of like or unlike can strengthen or undermine effects. The idea of resonance, that "things of the same genus energize each other," has been brilliantly discussed by Joseph Needham and has become classic in both Euro-American and Chinese studies of the traditional Chinese sciences.[24] Resonance has, however, been understood in subtly different ways by different writers, and the convenience of the concept in substituting for mechanical causation may have led at times to insufficiently historical treatments. I do not propose to advance a new or wholly adequate theory of resonance here but rather to invite attention to the forms of effectiveness that are envisaged within contemporary Chinese medical practices. An awareness of the continuing emergence of manifestations through the interaction of yin and yang aspects is important, I think, to any complete grasp of the concept of resonance. The cosmos is active and generative of itself; it is caused, but by forces and in ways that only speculative philosophers need care about. Doctors focus instead on the forms and sequences of emergence of effects, attending to resonances and interactions among manifestations that, as Needham suggests, "could be considered a kind of cue from one declining process indicating that it was time for the proper rising process to come on the stage."[25] Armed with this focus on time, difference, and form, we can now take up in detail the nature of Chinese medical intervention in the world.

Understanding Clinical Action

The clinical encounter in contemporary Chinese medical practice is a process through which illness is formed into an actionable pattern and is acted on.

---

23. Sivin, *Traditional Medicine,* p. 91.

24. See Needham, *Science and Civilization,* vol. 2, p. 285*ff.,* for the classic discussion of resonance. See also Charles LeBlanc, *Huai Nan Tzu* (Hong Kong: Hong Kong University Press, 1985), pp. 123–131; Tjan Tjoe Som, trans. *Po Hu T'ung,* 2 vols. (Leiden: Brill, 1949, 1952). For a consideration of the related principle of nonaction in Confucian theories of rulership, see Roger T. Ames, *The Art of Rulership* (Honolulu: University of Hawaii Press, 1983), pp. 28–64.

25. Needham, *Science and Civilization,* vol. 2, p. 283.

Classificatory logics play an important role in this formative process. Effects (e.g., symptoms, not "diseases") are classified at successive levels of generality to develop a detailed picture of the current state of dynamic relations in the pathological process. Classificatory analysis then resolves into a therapeutic intervention that is completely specific to the illness thus formed. This process incorporates both a mode of explanation and mode of treatment and hinges on the reinvention of a relation to the past—prior medical experience—that subsumes explanation and action in a field perceived to have specific features that can guide the understanding and management of the whole illness episode.

An investigation of Chinese medical modes of explanation, understood as relying on classifications of dynamic forms, rather than on a reductive analysis of causes, is an important first step beyond a mere mechanical transposition of Chinese medical drugs and techniques into Western discourses. Some studies of Chinese medicine in Western languages, in their haste to appropriate holistic and alternative therapeutic systems, have introduced major "contradictions" in Chinese medical "theory" through simplistic translating. The two most usual responses to these contradictions have been to generalize to a point that transcends the difficulty but leaves medicine looking a lot like mysticism or superstition[26] or to resolve the perceived contradictions with reference to a few carefully selected loci of authority in the classical texts, thereby creating new theory in an attempt to rectify or purify an essential Chinese medicine.[27] In the determination to make Chinese medicine conform to one or another causal and systematic style of logic, both procedures illegitimately idealize it, failing to perceive the positive value that the improvisational play of classification holds in the process of diagnosis and treatment.

Problems of translation are rooted in differences characteristic of whole cultural fields. In the case of Chinese medicine, the "peephole metaphysics" of modern science,[28] premised as it is on a subject-object distinction seeking to achieve pure observation, is a recent uncomfortable import. Certain characteristics of modern Chinese language and idiom make it difficult to sustain a clear subject-object divide even in technical texts, and some of the best writing in the field tends to adopt premodern syntax to resolve confusions introduced by attempts to scientize Chinese medical knowledge. The net-

26. This is characteristic of most "popular" accounts and also afflicts the only English translation of the *Inner Canon:* Ilza Veith, *Huang Ti Nei Ching Su Wen* (Berkeley and Los Angeles: University of California Press, 1966).

27. I make this argument at length in my article, "Problems of Knowledge in Contemporary Chinese Medical Discourse," *Social Science and Medicine* 24, no. 12 (1987):1013–1021. In addition to Porkert's complex technical purification of Chinese medicine, see Paul Unschuld, *Nan Ching* (Berkeley and Los Angeles: University of California Press, 1986), pp. 11–16.

28. Theodor Adorno, *Negative Dialectics* (New York: Seabury Press, 1973), p. 139; cited in Paul Smith, *Discerning the Subject* (Minneapolis: University of Minnesota Press, 1988), p. 58.

work of dualisms that has developed within our own intellectual tradition has introduced misleading distinctions—for example, between theory and practice, scientific knowledge and its technological applications, even doctor and patient.[29]

One aim of this book is to replace these ill-fitting dual categories, which have long seemed universally applicable to medical work, with a more specific language for speaking of knowledge and healing. In this attempt to avoid imposed frameworks, I have tried to emphasize the temporal and processual character not only of Chinese medical physiology and pathology but also of Chinese medical work. The source-manifestation logic previously described entails a great attentiveness to temporality, an understanding of illness developments and healing techniques as process.[30] This stands in contrast to a medicine of anatomical structures and fixed lesions, reductive causality, and mechanical influence—or any healing system that encourages a romanticization of the wonder drug and the brilliant surgical correction. Such Western therapeutic models cannot, of course, be removed from time; drugs take time to work, and surgery is a craft in which timing can be very important. But the intellectual appeal of such ideologically valorized elements of biomedicine has little to do either with their temporal characteristics or with the practical exigencies (the very word is revealing) of their application.

A focus on the clinical work of Chinese medicine that privileges the practical and the temporal reveals Chinese medical classification as a method of deploying material from the medical archive within specific projects of healing, a continuing subordination of formalized knowledge to the concrete demands of the moment. Such an orientation can restore practice to a

---

29. Filling "Western" categories with "Chinese" content has accorded a certain intellectual and scientific dignity to Chinese medicine, but it has done so only by imposing a theory-practice division on a mode of practice that is not "naturally" ordered in that way. Note that Porkert has followed his ground-breaking work on Chinese medical theory (*The Theoretical Foundations*) with a "practical" work on diagnosis, *The Essentials of Chinese Diagnostics* (Zurich: Chinese Medicine Publications, 1983). A recent two-volume work on contemporary Chinese medicine, Liu Yanchi, *The Essential Book of Traditional Chinese Medicine,* 2 vols. (New York: Columbia University Press, 1988), devotes one volume to "theory" and the other to "clinical practice." Unschuld's companion volumes entitled *Medicine in China* are subtitled *A History of Ideas* and *A History of Pharmaceutics* (Berkeley and Los Angeles: University of California Press, 1985, 1986). Contemporary texts of Chinese medicine in the People's Republic of China are similarly divided as part of the recent institutionalization of training and publishing. But an active clinical life is still considered to be the real arena of learning traditional medicine, and the textbook divide between "theory" and "clinical practice" is maintained rather more briefly in China than it is in the discourses of the Western natural sciences.

30. See Judith Farquhar, "Time and Text," in *Paths to Asian Medical Knowledge* Charles Leslie and Allan Young, eds., (Berkeley and Los Angeles: University of California Press, 1992), pp. 62–73.

certain intellectual dignity but makes it difficult to reconstruct an overarching system of disembodied and self-consistent traditional knowledge. Once the forms of intellectual and clinical practice within which Chinese medical people live and work are taken seriously on their own terms, abstract, comprehensive, or ahistorical knowledge systems no longer clarify very much. This is arguably as true for the Chinese medicine of the past as it is for that of the present.

A great many problems of the Western scientific causal model, such as mutual exclusivity or economy of causes, are therefore not at issue in this study of Chinese medicine. The standards of argument by which we judge our own most rigorous explanations cannot be applied to Chinese medicine without fundamentally altering its nature prior to any understanding of what that nature is. In what follows, then, I propose to examine the ways in which and the purposes for which principles and rules are deployed, texts and common knowledge are drawn on, and symbols and metaphors are reflexively put into play in the process of dealing with illness.[31] The way in which these principles, texts, and metaphors are generated out of and formed within ongoing processes of medical practice should become clearer as well. In this examination of the clinical encounter, I will try to show why flexibility and responsiveness of knowledge constructs are more valued in Chinese medical practice than are explanatory "rigor" or generalized predictive power. At the same time I will consider the complex relation between (1) the particular situation presented by each illness, including the methods and experience brought to bear by the doctor, and (2) the roles played by formal classificatory systems within the temporal structure and the specific teleology of the clinical encounter. In other words, a mode of movement from the specific to the general, from significance outside medicine to significance as part of it, and back again, will be described in the following discussion of the clinical encounter.

---

31. Many historians and commentators of Chinese medicine in the PRC emphasize the preventive character of Chinese medicine, pointing out that "the superior practitioner treats the not-yet-ill" (*shang gong zhi wei bing*). This saying quotes the second-century work *Huangdi Bashiyi Nan Jing, juan* 77. For a modern reprint of a fourteenth-century edition, see Hua Shou, *Nan Jing Benyi*, vol. 18 of *Gujin Yitong Zheng-mai Quanshu* (Taipei: Yiwen Yinshuguan, 1967), p. 513. Western histories of Chinese medicine have not yet found a way to link the histories of therapeutics with a full consideration of techniques for cultivating life (*yang sheng*) or refining the self (*xiu shen*) in premodern China. The focus of this book is the treatment of illness; this aspect of the broader medical field in China is the only one that enjoys marked institutional support in the contemporary PRC and so presents itself as an object of study that is (perhaps only recently) drawn apart from older cultures of self-cultivation.

3

The Clinical
Encounter Observed

THE DOCTOR SITS AT A TABLE, on which there is a small cloth pad (where patients rest their wrists for pulse taking), a glue pot, and some blank prescription forms. If he is a senior doctor, he is usually assisted by a younger colleague or medical student, who may conduct the preliminary stages of an examination (when the patient load is heavy, freeing the older doctor to deal with each patient only at a later stage of examination) or copy out a prescription according to the older doctor's instructions.[1] A patient, often accompanied by family members or friends, enters carrying a small slip of paper with a clinic registration number for that day and a case record booklet. Blanks of such booklets can be purchased at the registration desk if this is the patient's first visit to the clinic or if the patient has lost a case record used previously. (For the outpatient clinic no permanent case histories are kept at the hospital. Patients keep their own case record booklets. But some work units maintain files for the health records of their members in which these booklets are stored.)

The patient sits down at the side of the table (i.e., facing the doctor with a corner of the table between them) and gives the registration slip to the doctor or assistant, who glues it to the top of a prescription form. If the patient does not immediately begin reporting illness signs, the doctor may ask, "What are your discomforts?" (*You shemma bushufu?*) or "What (where)

---

1. The vast majority of doctors of Chinese medicine are men; Chinese medical gynecology is now heavily populated by women, although its oldest practitioners are almost all men; and the overall predominance of men in the field may be changing somewhat with the youngest generation of school-trained doctors. Nevertheless, it is not a misrepresentation to use the masculine pronouns *he* and *his* to refer to the doctor. Patients, of course, are more evenly distributed by gender, and I refer to them by an alternation of male and female pronouns.

is your illness?" (*You shemma bing? Nali you bing?*). The patient describes the history and characteristics of the illness, prompted by questions from the doctor regarding, most commonly, presence of fevers or sensitivity to cold; sweating; aches and pains; sleep (somnolence or insomnia); appetite, dryness or bitter flavors in the mouth; quantity, quality, and timing of urination and defecation; and, the case of women, menstrual irregularities. Care is taken to note the timing of the appearance of such signs both relative to each other and to the time of the examination.

In contemporary urban hospital practice this interview is seldom private. Clinic rooms are usually shared by two or more doctors with their retinues, and patients and members of their families often crowd into the room while waiting their turn. Doctors and patients may lower their heads and their voices to prevent bystanders from hearing, and doctors occasionally ask the most casual onlookers to go back into the hallway.

The doctor jots down significant signs of illness in a dated entry in the case record booklet. In a few important categories, most notably those of urination, defecation, and appetite, he notes the condition even if it is normal. During this questioning the doctor observes the appearance of the patient's face and examines affected parts of the body as appropriate (e.g., skin eruptions or swellings. In most of the examining rooms there are curtained examination tables at the back of the room where patient and doctor can go to look at parts of the body that require disrobing; but in all cases only the clothes immediately covering the affected part are removed or moved to one side, even for gynecological examinations). The doctor looks at the color and quality of the patient's tongue and its coating. He takes the pulse at each wrist in turn, using the middle three fingers of his hand placed on the palm side of the wrist, his middle finger placed just in front of the distal radial epiphysis (Figure 3.1). The results of these examinations are noted in the case record booklet. If time permits, the doctor points out and discusses salient features of the patient's condition with the colleague or student (or anthropologist) at his side.

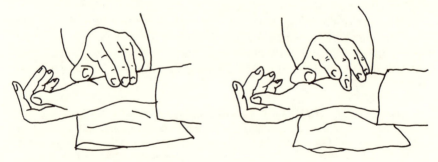

FIGURE 3.1   Technique of palpating pulse

The doctor then writes (or dictates to an assistant) an herbal prescription, sometimes using a piece of carbon paper to record it simultaneously in the case record booklet; otherwise, the assisting doctor later copies the prescription into the booklet. The prescription usually consists of the names of four to sixteen herbal medicines written in two or three columns with the desired quantity (in grams) written as subscripts to the names. The number of days this medication will be required (seldom more than three) is noted at the bottom of the form. The patient's name and the date are filled in at the top of the form, and the doctor signs the form at the bottom. His signature is either transferred into or directly written into the booklet, too, but not necessarily by him; the assisting doctor may do it.

The patient's case record book thus contains the symptoms and signs, both those reported by the patient and those observed and elicited by the doctor, and the complete herbal prescription or acupuncture protocol to be used. Illness factors, mechanisms, and locations; diagnosis; treatment principle; and other categories of information discussed in teaching texts often do not appear in the case record booklets of outpatient clinics, although case histories maintained on hospital wards usually include a fuller discussion of the case written by the medical personnel involved.

Occasionally a modern Chinese doctor will order a laboratory test such as an X-ray for suspected tuberculosis, a blood test (hepatitis is a constant concern in South China), an electroencephalogram, or an electrocardiogram. Such tests are often ordered at the same time as the herbal prescription is written out. Some younger doctors habitually take the blood pressure of older patients with suspected cardiovascular symptoms, and a few use a stethoscope for auscultation from time to time (slipping it under the patient's outer garments to place it against the chest or back). But these innovations are still little used, especially by the most sought out and renowned older doctors. (If the patient does not plan to return to work because of his illness, he will ask the doctor to fill out and sign a form allowing him to take a specified number of days off from work. These hospital forms are turned in to the work unit.)

The patient then carries the prescription to the cashier's window where the cost is calculated and she pays for the drugs either through a form of insurance or in cash. Once paid for, the prescription is filled at the pharmacy, where herbal medicine specialists assemble the drugs into paper parcels after weighing them, one parcel for each day. If the pharmacy is out of one of the drugs specified in the prescription, the pharmacist will send the patient (or one of his companions) back to the doctor for a substitution. Ordinarily the cost is not recalculated even if the drug substituted is more expensive.

Each day's prescription is decocted one time, although the resulting liquid is usually drunk in two or more doses in the course of the day. Some families reheat or even reboil the medicine each time a dose is taken. Many households have a special ceramic pot for decocting medicines; it has a spout like that of a teapot to allow steam and water vapor to escape while the chopped or ground drugs are being boiled in water that is allowed to reduce several times (with more water added two or three times) to produce a dark and odorous liquid.

Very few people visit a Chinese doctor just once for any illness. Prescriptions are usually made out for three days at a time, and doctors like to see a patient after the medicine has had a chance to produce an effect. They modify and improve the prescription in response to alterations in the symptoms. Patients with chronic conditions may come in to the clinic two or three times a week over a period of months to be seen and checked by the doctor and to have their prescription reissued in the same or modified form.

*   *   *

This description of outpatient clinic practices is based chiefly on observations made in one of the affiliated hospitals of the Guangzhou College of Traditional Chinese Medicine in 1983–1984 and 1988. Within and around this general procedure there is considerable variation. Some practitioners record detailed notes on the patient's condition in the case record booklet, whereas others simply jot down the prescription. Not all doctors attach their names to the record. Some senior doctors often see patients without the assistance of a student or junior colleague, whereas others are almost completely disabled by a temporary lack of assistance. Although patients of this Guangzhou hospital usually keep their own case record booklets, in 1988 at least one clinic within that hospital was asking patients to leave them behind so that they could be coded for a research project. Other clinics I have observed keep these records and reissue them to the patient each time he registers to see a doctor. A walk-in clinic practitioner I have visited in a Shandong county town keeps lengthy records for all his patients on clips arranged on the wall according to surname. Doctors of "Chinese medical gynecology" (*fuke*), many of whom are women, perform a physical examination much more frequently than do doctors of "internal medicine" (*neike*) specialties. Some doctors like to explain a lot to patients and their families, whereas others are remarkably taciturn, allowing their assistants to do most of the communicating and explaining little about the illness or their strategy in treating it.[2] Experimentation with medical and scientific technology has led to some interesting additions; one well-known doctor spent several years practicing alongside a desktop computer as he and students working with

---

2. See my "Speech, Text, and Silence" (Paper presented at the Fifth International Conference on the History of Science in China, San Diego, California, August 5–10, 1988).

him developed a program for syndrome differentiation and treatment determination. Such innovations as pulse-taking machines and "electrogastrography" have also been introduced at times into clinical settings. In addition, practitioners vary widely in their willingness and ability to use Western medicines and diagnostic techniques along with Chinese.

It is impossible to say how diverse the practices of *kanbing* have or will become. But certain features appear to be invariant. The face-to-face, yet not quite opposed orientation of doctor and patient; pulse-taking; tongue examination; and a history interview seem to be irreducible features of clinical work in Chinese medicine. The most immediate result of the encounter, an herbal prescription, is so universal as to be assumed in the practice of attaching the patient's registration number to a prescription form before anyone has started to talk about the illness. No one ever has to completely disrobe, and I suspect that no doctor would move to exclude a patient's companions from participation in the procedure.

The term *kanbing* is used by patients to refer to the act of going to see the doctor and by doctors to refer to the process of treating patients. Its literal meaning is "looking at illness." There is no real ambiguity in this; both doctor and patient look at illness in the clinic. Although they bring different resources to the task (the patient, his experience of the illness and observations of the changes it incorporates; the doctor, his training and experienced clinical judgment), there is (ideally) a sense of partnership between doctor and patient in perceiving and managing the illness's characteristics and course.

Arthur Kleinman has noted that patients in Taiwan do not accord so much decisionmaking power to their doctors as we do in the United States, preferring to take responsibility for primary management of their illnesses within the family.[3] This is a valuable insight that has been supported by my field experience in Guangzhou and Shandong. The patient's own narrative of her illness, her presentation of it to the doctor, plays a major role in delimiting the nature of the illness for both doctor and patient. In a sense the doctor does not have the power to reject any sign reported by the patient; patients, I think, retain a sense of being the experts, the authority of last resort, on their own illnesses. The specialized experience of the doctor enables him to transform signs noted and reported by patients into symptoms that can be channeled through medicine to produce a medical intervention. An understanding of *kanbing* as a technical process in which doctor and patient are engaged together helps account for the centrality of the patient's narrative and for her role as the major definer and presenter of the problem; such an understanding also makes it possible to see why so many illness signs

---

3. Arthur Kleinman, *Patients and Healers in the Context of Culture* (Berkeley and Los Angeles: University of California Press, 1980), p. 66.

seem to be admissable as significant. The discussion of the clinical encounter to follow will focus on medical aspects of *kanbing*—that is, the knowledge and practice of doctors. But until subtler studies are done of the illness-related knowledge and practice of patients and their families, there is no particular reason to place a patient's point of view in opposition to that of the doctor. *Kanbing* is a particular way of looking at and acting on disorder in which doctor and patient are engaged together.

Three Case Histories

A great many volumes of collected case histories have appeared in the burgeoning literature of Chinese medicine in the People's Republic. These anthologies may be the collected cases of one famous physician of the past (the students of a great many late Qing and early Republic period doctors have edited volumes of their teachers' famous cases), of one well-known living physician, or of a group of doctors whose cases are gathered into illness categories.[4] Many working Chinese doctors consider the study of case histories to be an important, even essential, aspect of learning Chinese medicine, and any scholar interested in the work of a famous medical forebear (no idle hobby itself for doctors working in an academic context) will be expected to know and understand his clinical work. Chinese medical journals also publish a great many case reports and very frequently include case histories in more general articles as data.

The usual format of published case histories resembles the notes written in a patient's case record booklet, with the addition (sometimes) of diagnosis and treatment principles and (usually) some commentary indicating why this case was especially interesting, important, or revealing. The exact herbal prescription or acupuncture procedure is always included.

I present three such published cases with the intention of referring to them throughout my discussion of the clinical encounter. I have chosen these cases for the range of issues they can illustrate as the analysis of the clinical encounter proceeds: Case 1, Spring Warm, is of an acute febrile illness in which an unusually nuanced treatment was immediately effective in relieving the symptoms; Case 2, Two Cases of Foetal Death, describes two situations in which foetuses died in utero, the former being easily treated with a classic prescription and the latter becoming a major challenge to Chinese medical methods; and Case 3, Stomachache, which involves an ulcer, demonstrates certain ways in which Chinese medical diagnosis and treatment differ from biomedical methods.

---

4. Yu Yingao and Gao Yimin, eds., *Xiandai Ming Laozhongyi Leian Xuan* (Beijing: People's Health Press, 1983).

Some of the vocabulary and most of the reasoning in this first pass through three cases of illness will appear extremely exotic to most readers. In particular, the lists of drugs will seem to be odd mixtures of romanized Chinese words, English and Latin names of plants, and a few minerals. Achieving a consistent nomenclature for the Chinese materia medica has not been a simple task either in Chinese or English, but the careful scholarship of Professor Shiu-ying Hu has at least provided a reliable guide for comparing names.[5] Herein I use her English names, rather than the Latin pharmaceutical terms she also provides, to convey something of the "mountain herbs" connotations attaching to prescriptions for Chinese patients. Using Latin terms would remove the herbal drugs from the homely evocations they can have in the original Chinese. Citing an authority for drug names does not, of course, remove all the strangeness from texts that can speak of such things as "repletion in the yang visceral systems" and "inadequacy in the active qi sector." Written cases are products of the techniques of reasoning about illness and intervening in it that most of this book will be devoted to clarifying. The relationship between the analytic and the therapeutic processes of the clinical encounter described in the chapters to follow will be explained as Cases 1 through 3 provide examples for points to be made throughout this book.

Three Illnesses: Translations of Case Histories

Case 1 records a brief episode of acute illness with very high fever in a male patient aged eighteen. The treatment used was immediately effective; adjustments to the initial prescription on follow-up examinations responded to symptoms of less and less severity. The text of the case adopts a standard case history format in which commentary and analysis follow notes on the minimal facts of the illness.

Case 1: Spring Warm

[Name] Jiang, M-18: Spring Warm syndrome with high fever, no remission throughout course of illness. Agitation and irritability, dry mouth with excessive thirst, red face and foul mouth odor, tongue and lips dry and parched, occasional delirious speech, no appetite, no bowel movement for eight days, pungent and cooling drugs already administered with no effect. Pulse smooth and accelerated, tongue coating yellow, thick, and dry.

---

5. Shiu-ying Hu, *An Enumeration of Chinese Materia Medica* (Hong Kong: Chinese University Press, 1980). Hu uses Wade-Giles romanization for Chinese words; I have converted these romanizations to Pinyin to be consistent with my usage but have indicated the Wade-Giles spelling in parentheses where it differs from the Pinyin.

Diagnosis. Spring Warm Repletion in the yang visceral systems.

Treatment Principle. Clear above and drain below; use of modified Barrier Cooling Powder indicated.[6]

Prescription 1:

1. Weeping forsythia (capsule)	9 g
2. Black-roasted jasmine seed	9 g
3. Mild skullcap (root)	6 g
4. Wind-weed asphodel (rhizome)	12 g
5. Fresh rhubarb	6 g
6. Mirabilite	4.5 g (brewed)
7. Tricosanthes fruit	9 g
8. Citron (roasted fruit)	4.5 g
9. Four o'clock (root)	6 g
10. Fresh licorice root	2.4 g
11. Dried dendrobium (stem)	9 g (chopped and boiled)

Second Examination. After the prescription above was administered, this morning [the patient] passed a large quantity of dry stools, the high fever was slightly down, he was already able to rest peacefully, and dryness of lips and tongue was not as bad as before. Pulse accelerated, tongue coating yellow; although the repletion in the yang brightness [Stomach and Large Intestine] visceral systems had been cleared, the heat in the [yang brightness] circulation tracts was not yet resolved. Since long fevers affecting yin fluids can bring on major illness, it's still best to nourish yin, clear heat, and drain.

Prescription 2:

1. Fresh gypsum	30 g (ground and boiled)
2. Asphodel	9 g
3. American ginseng	6 g (boiled)
4. Dendrobium	9 g (chopped and boiled)
5. Four o'clock	9 g
6. Fresh rehmannia (rhizome)	24 g
7. Forsythia	9 g
8. Skullcap	4.5 g
9. Licorice root	2.4 g
10. Tendril-leaved fritillary bulb	9 g
11. Tricosanthes	12 g

Third Examination. After administration of the modified Ginseng–White Tiger Decoction [above], the fever suddenly went down, appetite began to

---

6. Herbal prescriptions taken from well-known medical works are usually referred to by standard labels such as this one. The name of the formula does not always refer directly either to its herbal components or to its primary action. Formula names will be capitalized herein to distinguish them from ordinary descriptive terms.

return, the tongue coating was thin and yellow, pulse [was] only a little accelerated, hidden heteropathy had moved to the exterior; appropriate to nourish Stomach yin again to evacuate remaining heteropathy.

Prescription 3:

1. "Large seed" ginseng	6 g	(boiled first)
2. Dendrobium	9 g	(chopped and boiled)
3. Asphodel	12 g	
4. Gypsum	24 g	(ground and boiled)
5. Rehmannia	24 g	
6. Skullcap	4.5 g	
7. Forsythia	9 g	
8. Licorice root	1.5 g	
9. Winter melon seeds	12 g	
10. Fritillary	4.5 g	
11. Yunnan *fuling*	9 g	

After this prescription had been administered two times, the fever had completely subsided, so the skullcap and gypsum were deleted from the prescription and malt added. With two or three more doses the patient gradually recovered. [This case history is reproduced] (from *Cases of Ye Xichun.*)

Commentary [by editors]: There are two kinds of situation that are known as Spring Warm. One kind is hidden qi Warm illnesses, which are cold injuries taken in winter that emerge as acute Heat illnesses when spring comes. The other kind are acute newly contracted Heat illnesses brought about by a Warm heteropathy (*wenxie*) taken in the spring. In the former the following symptoms are usually present before the disease develops: tense limbs and aching body, dry mouth and throat, and reddish and reduced urination with a heat [sensation], among others. After the disease has begun, one is likely to see fever and headache, thirst and nervousness, yellowish red urine, red tongue with yellow coating, pulse small and accelerated, and other symptoms of interior Heat having injured yin [fluids]. In the latter, at the outset of the illness it will manifest as an Interior Heat syndrome, accompanied with cough, little or no perspiration, and usually a floating, accelerated pulse. On the basis of the differing clinical symptomatologies, we would usually use the major therapeutic principles of clearing and draining to expel Interior Heat while protecting and maintaining yin fluids. If Heat is still found to be hidden in the constructive and Blood sectors, or if the yin of Liver or Kidney system has been injured, the treatment principle should be altered appropriately.

This is a case of Spring Warm heteropathic qi stagnating as Heat in the chest cavity, which then manifested as repletion in the yang brightness [Stomach and Large Intestine] visceral systems—hence the use of modified Barrier Cooling Powder to clear above and drain below. In the latter stages cure was achieved with the use of a method that nourished yin and cleared Heat. This reflects Master Ye's skill in grasping temporal factors in treating Spring Warm. . . . As we analyze this [and other similar] case[s], the skill of my teachers in their mastery of the therapeutic principles of our sage forebears becomes evident. Although [these cases] show originality of conception, they also incorporate principles that we can follow.[7]

Case 2 actually incorporates two illnesses. Slightly atypically, it begins with a prefatory commentary that is then enlarged on after both cases have been reported in case history format. In the first instance it was not difficult to induce the dead foetus to descend; descent of the second dead foetus demanded much more time and several revisions in treatment method.

Case 2: Two Cases of Foetal Death

[The process of] diagnosis and treatment determination is one of the essential components of Chinese medicine. Our nation's laboring people through several thousand years of innumerable practices have generalized a set of theories and methods that, when used to guide clinical practice, can attain very satisfactory results. The treatment of the two cases reported below of foetuses dying in the womb is an example in which this can be seen.

Patient I. Deng X X, pregnant seven months, foetal movement having ceased for 20 days, diagnosed as a missed abortion. After admission the following therapies were used: new acupuncture therapy, castor oil enema, quinine injections, high-pressure warm water enemas, injection of pituitarin at an acupoint (30 units/day), foetal membrane decollement, and others. In the course of using these various therapies there were only light contractions; by the time she had been in hospital for 10 days, the situation was rather serious. If surgical treatment was used, there was a danger of contracting infection to be considered. Therefore Chinese herbal therapy was used.

On examination tongue coating was both yellow and greasy white, while the tongue itself was red. Pulse sunken and a little accelerated but vigorous. These symptoms and pulse indicate a repletion condition; thus according to the usual procedure one would use Calming Stomach Powder with the addition of mirabilite (Glauber's salt) and the fruit of trifoliate orange.

Drugs used:

1. *Cangshu*	9 g
2. Magnolia bark	12 g
3. Mandarin orange peel	12 g
4. Licorice root	4.5 g
5. Mirabilite (magnesium sulphate and licorice-radish powder)	12 g
6. Trifoliate orange fruit	12 g

Decocted in water as one dose.

7. Yu and Gao, eds., *Xiandai Ming Laozhongyi Leian Xuan,* pp. 10, 13.

Drug was administered at about 2:00 P.M.; at 6:00 P.M. contractions began, delivery commenced around 9:30, and later in the evening the dead foetus was completely expelled. Patient stated that the cause of the foetus dying was her abdomen having been bumped into by one of the children rushing about.

Patient II. Chen X, pregnant eight months, entered the hospital seven days after foetal movement had ceased. Diagnosed as a missed abortion. No other therapy had yet been attempted since the patient's admission to the hospital.

On examination the tongue was pale and tender with a thin white coating, peeling in the middle; pulse large and accelerated, weak under heavy finger pressure. According to analysis of tongue and pulse images, tender tongue and peeling coating indicate that fluids have been depleted; large, accelerated, and weak pulse indicates inadequacy in the active qi sector; and together these manifestations are classified as qi and fluids both deficient. In the course of asking the patient about her condition, it was determined that she had had a rather extreme reaction to becoming pregnant, having been severely nauseous, which had induced a depletion of fluids and qi. But a foetus dead in the womb is classified as a symptom of the repletion type, i.e., the illness is overstrong while the body itself is weak. In consideration of this it would be unwise to use only a method of the attack type.

First Examination. The treatment principle was to nourish fluids, enliven Blood, cause qi to flow, and lubricate the Lower *Jiao.* Drugs used: adenophora, Chinese angelica, peach kernel, poncirus, and mirabilite. In addition, the *zusanli* [point, V36], *hegu* [point, IG4], and other points were needled as a concomitant treatment.[8] This procedure went on for two days without producing even the slightest uterine movement!

Second Examination. I wondered whether a modified Calming Stomach Powder would be worth a try. So I tried two doses of the prescription used in Case I. The first dose produced two slippery bowel movements after it was administered; the second got no response at all.

Third Examination. Switched to use of Fallen Petals Decoction (Sichuan lovage, angelica, achyranthes root, plantain seed, and cassia twigs) administered in one dose. The foetus still didn't descend.

Fourth Examination. Since I had already used various prescriptions to attack it and it hadn't moved, I switched to a method of replenishing qi and enlivening Blood. Drugs used: Cairo morning glory, *dangshen,* orange peel, angelica, and lovage. But these were also not effective.

Fifth Examination. Realizing that the potency of the previous prescriptions for replenishing and moving qi had been inadequate, I switched to use of modified Opening Bones Powder.

---

8. Acupuncture points are here referred to by the Chinese designations used in the original texts and are followed by the appropriate abbreviations used in Europe. See Lu Gwei-djen and Joseph Needham, *Celestial Lancets* (Cambridge: Cambridge University Press, 1980), pp. 53–59.

Drugs used:

1. *Huangqi*   120 g
2. Angelica   30 g
3. Lovage   15 g
4. Charred human hair   9 g
5. Tortoise shell   24 g (less used due to shortage of drug)
Administered in a decoction.

Drug was administered at about 4:00 P.M., and at about 6:00 P.M. con-tractions began (one approximately every 10–20 minutes). At 8:00 P.M. massage and acupuncture were also used, first on the *sanjiaoshu* point [VU22] and [then on] the *shenshu* point [VU23] to put Triple *Jiao* qi in motion. But after massage the contractions lessened in frequency and be-came slower. Switched to the use of moxa on the *zusanli* [V36] point, a particularly efficacious point for bolstering body strength, after which the contractions accordingly gained in strength, about one every 10 minutes, the systolic being rather strong. Moxibustion was discontinued after half an hour. Acupuncture was continued on the *zhongji* point [JM3], with a rota-tion every 2 or 3 minutes. After needling, the contractions were taking place every 1 to 3 minutes, with extreme force; altogether the needling lasted 15 minutes. When acupuncture treatment was terminated at 11:00 P.M., the dead foetus was expelled; it had been strangled by the umbilical cord.

Notes. A foetus dying inside the mother's body has become an illness-inducing entity—a form of heteropathic qi; and the illness is classified as of the repletion type. Since the Song dynasty [960–1279], in the prescription books of gynecology, Calming Stomach Powder with magnolia bark and magnesium sulphate added has been used to cause the foetus to de-scend. Calming Stomach Powder is an important prescription for strength-ening the Stomach and Intestine systems and moving accumulations of Damp: *Cangshu* is an aggressive strengthening and motivating drug, mag-nolia bark and orange peel are good for moving qi and drying up Damp, and the addition of magnolia bark and magnesium sulphate can lubricate the Lower *Jiao.* Our forebears considered that "if the qi of the Stomach visceral system moves, then the dead foetus will move of itself, and with the addition of magnolia and magnesium sulphate it cannot but descend."

After the Ming dynasty, *The Complete Works of Zhang Jingyue*[9] recom-mended using Fallen Petals Decoction to cause a dead foetus to descend; this prescription is mainly for moving Blood and is used together with plan-tain seed and achyranthes to facilitate downward flow. Calming Stomach Powder treats clogged qi, and Fallen Petals Decoction treats blood stasis.

Opening Bones Powder is made from the Tortoise Shell Decoction of the Song dynasty (for treating difficult delivery, foetal death, etc.) with the addition of lovage. In the Ming dynasty there was also a so-called modified

9. The work cited is Zhang Jiebin, *Jingyue Quanshu,* 1624.

Lovage Angelica Decoction; this prescription relied on Chinese angelica and Sichuan lovage to move Blood, tortoise shell to induce downward motion, and charred hair to induce flow in the channels while stopping [excess] blood [flow, i.e., hemorrhage]. This formula doesn't use drugs of the attack downward or blood beating type; hence it has been widely used since the Ming to treat difficult delivery. Wang Qingren of the Qing dynasty felt that this prescription had both effective and ineffective aspects in the treatment of difficult pregnancy, the reason being that it was only strong with respect to nurturing and enlivening Blood but not specific for replenishing and moving qi; hence he emphasized a heavy use of *huangqi* (120 g) on the foundation of Opening Bones Powder to replenish and move qi, thus refining and heightening the effectiveness of the prescription.

We knew at the outset that the case of Patient II belonged to the class of depleted body with repletion illness, but because our use of drugs was not yet appropriate, we got no results. The use of drugs in the second and third examinations was not consistent with this diagnosis, hence ineffective. The treatment principle in the fourth examination wasn't really wrong, but the drugs weren't strong enough, so there was no effect. At last we used Opening Bones Powder modified with *huangqi,* using large amounts of angelica and lovage to nourish and enliven Blood, [and] a great deal of *huangqi* to replenish and move qi; and although [the formula] was a little short on tortoise shell, which nourishes yin and presses down within, once qi had been restored, Blood was able to flow, orthopathic qi was able to drive out heteropathic qi, and the foetus was able to be expelled. This exactly resembled the advice of our forebears, who said "attack by replenishing," i.e., use replenishing drugs to get the results of an attack drug; this is a typical case [illustrating this principle].

With regard to the acupuncture and moxibustion therapy, we first used moxa on the *zusanli* [V36] to replenish the depletion, then needled *zhongji* (Ren-3 [JM3]) to drain the repletion and lead it downward; this treatment principle was basically the same [as the above], and thus achieved a helpful effect.[10]

The last of these cases is, like Case 1, apparently very simple. The biomedical diagnosis, a duodenal ulcer, is given; a successful treatment is reported; and a brief commentary for Chinese medical readers is attached.

Case 3: Stomachache

Guo X X, M-38, came to the hospital to be examined and treated on June 7, 1976, because of recurrent sharp pain in the epigastric area. Sufferer had begun to have epigastric pain in 1972; barium meal fluoroscopy had diagnosed it to be a duodenal ulcer. The present pain in the stomach and

---

10. Deng Tietao, *Xueshuo Tantao yu Linzheng* (Guangzhou: Guangdong Science and Technology Press, 1981), pp. 284–286.

abdominal cavity was piercing and aggravated by hand pressure, stable in location, and accompanied by heartburn, sour vomitus, black stools, slightly reddened tongue with thin greasy yellow coating, and small strung pulse.

Diagnosis. Qi slowed and Blood static, stagnation of long duration transformed into Heat, giving signs of collateral tract damage.

Treatment Principle. Enliven Blood and transform stasis to stop the pain; regulate Blood to harmonize with qi.

Prescription:

1. Smoke-dried hedgehog skin	4.5 g
2. Stink bugs	4.5 g
3. Buddha hands (fruit)	4.5 g
4. Powdered corydalis (rhizome)	4.5 g
5. Licorice root	4.5 g
6. Meadow rue (rhizome)	6 g
7. Herbaceous peony (root)	9 g
8. Sichuan pagoda tree (fruit)	9 g
9. Citron peel	9 g
10. Calciferous ark shell	12 g
11. Evodia fruit	1.5 g

After six doses of the above formula had been administered, the pain in the abdominal cavity was considerably reduced, sour vomiting had ceased, gastric cavity was still distended and full, and there was not much appetite. Deleted peony, licorice, meadow rue, and evodia from the prescription and added (1) trifoliate orange fruit, (2) amomi fruit, (3) nutgrass flatsedge rhizome, and (4) areca nut shell in order to move qi and relax the center, open the Stomach, and stimulate Spleen function. After three doses were given, stomach cavity pain and swelling were virtually gone, and appetite was increased. After one month, the condition recurred due to alcohol consumption; treated as before with the same effectiveness. [This case history was compiled by] main therapist Zhong Jianhua.

Commentary [by editors]: Stomachache is also called stomach cavity pain. Quite a few classic works of Chinese medicine, which also called it "Heart pain," linked it to the illness syndromes that frequently have stomach cavity pain as a main feature. The most common causes of this illness are [the emotions of] longing, worry, rage, and irritation; loss of regularity in the dispersion functions of the Liver visceral system; lateral backups (*heng ni*) attacking the Stomach; and/or lack of strength in Spleen system transmission, with concomitant loss of orderly descension by the Stomach. It can also be brought about by Fire stagnation or Blood stasis. . . . [This case] is classified as qi slowed and Blood static, stagnation of long duration transforming into Heat and giving signs of collateral tract damage. To treat it, it was necessary to enliven Blood and transform stasis to stop the aching, [at the same time] regulating Blood to harmonize with qi. Although Blood was being treated, the movement encouraged was that of qi, which was assisted with corydalis powder to flow downward; hence this therapy incorporates a courageous insight.[11]

The Temporal Form of the *Kanbing* Process

Figure 3.2 depicts the general temporal form of the process of examining, diagnosing, and treating illness in a contemporary Chinese medical clinic. It can be compared with the descriptive account of the clinical encounter. At the outset the patient brings the various "signs" ($zheng_1$) of his illness to report and present to the doctor; during the description process (A), the doctor notes signs reported by the patient and elicits others through the application of a procedure known as "the four methods of examination" (*sizhen*). The signs of illness are turned into "symptoms" ($zheng_2$) bearing conventional medical labels through the forms of classificatory description incorporated in the *sizhen*.

In the analysis phase (B), symptoms are further classified through the application of one or more classificatory schemes (the figure lists some of them). Symptoms are thereby abstracted and generalized—that is, made amenable to perception as a pattern. This pattern is what I call a "syndrome" ($zheng_3$). The simultaneous discernment of the syndrome and determination of a treatment method (*zhifa*) occupy the apex (C) of the process diagrammed in Figure 3.2. This logical moment is referred to as *bianzheng lunzhi* or *zhengzhi*, and it is thought of as the crux of therapeutic intervention in Chinese medicine. Classificatory analysis (B) and *zhengzhi* (C) are not visible behaviors of the doctor, but they are essential components of the full form of the clinical encounter. (Shortened forms will be discussed in Chapter 7.)

Once the syndrome has been differentiated through classificatory analysis and a treatment method has been determined, a general "formula" for the prescription (*fang*) is usually chosen according to the principles of a subdiscipline called "formulary" (*fangjixue*) (D). As will be seen, formulary begins the process through which the illness analyzed in phases A–C can be materialized in an herbal medicine. In a sense the *fang* is a mirror image of the illness, a remanifestation (D) of it in all its particularity. In addition, formulary classifies *fang* within categories derived from treatment methods, so the formula may be chosen from the set of those *fang* that follow logically from the determination of the treatment. In the final phase of the clinical encounter, classical formulae are modified by adding or deleting individual drugs; these are selected on the basis of their qualities as classified in

---

11. Du Huaidang, ed., "*Tantan Zhiliao Weiwantongde Jingyan,*" *Xin Yiyao Zazhi* 10 (1977):15; cited in Yu and Gao, eds., *Xiandai Ming Zhongyi Leian Xuan,* pp. 198, 200.

56

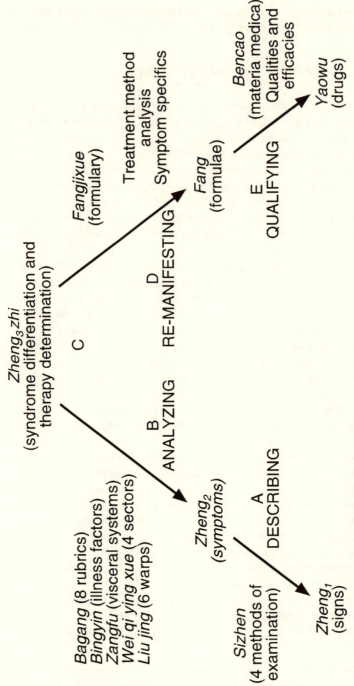

FIGURE 3.2 The *kanbing* and *bianzheng lunzhi* process

the subdiscipline of materia medica (*bencao*), further qualifying (E) the drug formula with reference to the symptoms specific to this patient. Thus, the treatment principle allows the generation of a general formula (a remanifestation of the illness pattern that has been perceived through analysis), which is then qualitatively customized to the symptoms with the addition or deletion of individual drugs. The full written formula guides the assembling of the proper collection of herbal drugs in the pharmacy, where specialists may make minor substitutions depending on supplies and quality-control considerations.

The terms *sign* (*zheng$_1$*), *symptom* (*zheng$_2$*), and *syndrome* (*zheng$_3$*) appearing in Figure 3.2 are technical terms of Chinese medicine.[12] *Zheng$_1$* is the least used in medical discourse, simply denoting manifestations arising from a certain condition. I use the word *sign* for this term in the same sense that we say that smoke is a sign of fire or that heat lightning is a sign of a storm in another place. It is a manifest part indicating the existence of a less-manifest whole. All the discomforts reported by a patient at the beginning of a clinical encounter (e.g. the anxiety and nervousness, low appetite, and constipation of the patient in Case 1) as well as those observed and elicited by the doctor (such as the red face and excessive thirst of the same patient) can be signs in this sense. But the word is little used medically because these manifestations of illness are quickly transformed into symptoms with conventional medical terms attached to them.

Zheng$_2$ therefore overlaps referentially with *zheng$_1$* but is seldom confused with it because the former has strictly medical uses. If we look, for example, at symptoms presented in Cases 1 and 3, we can see them as signs of illness, but some are noted only because the process of medical elicitation and examination has drawn attention to them and attached conventional labels to them (i.e., turned them into symptoms). Examples are excessive thirst and pulse and tongue images in Case 1 and pain aggravated by hand pressure, black stools, and tongue and pulse images in Case 3. In one sense all symptoms are also signs, but some signs attract notice only at the "medicalized" symptom level. In other words, the two words are chiefly distinguished by being on two sides of the point of entry into the medical world. Since some illness manifestations are first noted only in the clinical encounter, not being articulated or observed by the patient (unless he is very experienced at

---

12. I use the English terms in a sense somewhat different from that of Western medical dictionaries, partly to suggest literary and anthropological uses of the word *sign* and partly to preserve a bit of the punning usage that is evident in Chinese. See Tadashi Yoshida, "Some Problems in the Analysis of Manifestations of Sickness," in Yosio Kawakita, ed., *History of Diagnostics* (Osaka: Taniguchi Foundation, 1987), pp. 210–214, where the author discusses various approaches to defining the usage of the English words *sign* and *symptom* in medicine. He indicates the centrality of a distinction between objective (signs) and subjective (symptoms) for most usages, which distinction is not useful for Chinese concepts of *zheng$_1$* and *zheng$_2$*.

being a patient), the realm of signs overlaps but does not completely encompass that of symptoms.

$Zheng_3$ is a pattern of symptoms recognized as a recurrent form in medical experience (e.g., the Spring Warm of Case 1). A syndrome in medical English need not be caused by a known disease process; rather, syndrome can be used to characterize a group of symptoms or signs typical of a particular condition or disturbance. In Chinese medicine, the typicality of a grouping of manifestations is one of the conditions referred to whenever a $zheng_3$ label is given to an illness. But this is not a typical expression of a known underlying body state; rather, it is (as Hans Agren's translation of "manifestation type" for the same term suggests) a recurrent form of illness manifestation known to doctors as recurrence because they have seen it often in the course of their medical experience.[13] The reference of $zheng_3$, in other words, is more to patterns of history than to structures of the body and disease.

The word I translate as syndrome is sometimes used in a longer form, *zhenghou, hou* being a word for a period of time of unspecified length. The compound emphasizes the temporal quality of this central concept of Chinese medicine; the syndrome is a pattern in and of time rather than an atemporal structure with symptoms as its atoms. The significance of $zheng_3$ as a term and as a pivotal locus in medical practice will be explored in Chapter 5, as will the nature of syndrome differentiation, or diagnosis (etymologically a most inappropriate word). Note, however, that the syndrome, by virtue of being relevant at a higher level of generality, does not overlap in meaning with either sign or symptom.[14]

Phases A, B, and C of the clinical encounter diagrammed in Figure 3.2, then, transform mundane complaints ($zheng_1$) into symptoms of a medically understandable illness ($zheng_2$), then organize these symptoms into a recognizable syndrome ($zheng_3$). Once this logical work has been done, it becomes possible to mirror or remanifest the illness in a drug formula (Figure 3.2, D) and qualify it with modifications targeting particular symptoms with the specific efficacies of drugs (Figure 3.2, E).

---

13. Hans Agren, "Patterns of Tradition and Modernization in Contemporary Chinese Medicine," Arthur Kleinman et al., *Medicine in Chinese Cultures* (Washington, D.C.: John E. Fogarty International Center, 1975), pp. 37–59. In writing practice, $zheng_2$ and $zheng_3$ are sometimes used interchangeably. It is usually easy to determine which notion is intended, and my efforts to check my understanding of specific passages where the "wrong" character had been used with teachers and students corroborated my sense of the linguistic range of the terms. Usually I was told that a questionable appearance of one or the other character was "just sloppy usage."

14. Another term to be used herein is also pronounced *zheng*. It refers to the healthful order of bodily qi that engages in struggle with "heteropathic qi" (*xie* qi) to prevent disease occurrence and development. This $zheng_4$ is traslated as "orthopathic qi." Relationships between heteropathic and orthopathic qi are discussed in Chapter 4.

All the processes of transformation, reduction, and generation briefly summarized here will be discussed in detail in Chapters 4, 5, and 6. The general point is that this basic temporal sequence organizes and puts into play a wide variety of explanatory principles, accumulated lore, subdisciplinary and factional perspectives, and practical methods of Chinese medicine. In this active processual core of Chinese medical practice, classified knowledge and classificatory techniques are brought to bear on illness in a process that, while maintaining the hierarchical structure diagrammed, can produce numerous perceptual and strategic alternatives.

4

Description and Analysis
in *Kanbing*

IN THE NEXT THREE CHAPTERS I will explore in detail the practical logic of the clinical encounter.[1] I will separately discuss each of the phases of the *kanbing* process (marked A–E in Figure 3.2) as a moment in the process of syndrome differentiation and treatment determination (*bianzheng lunzhi*). Unlike the textbooks from which I have drawn to clarify this process, I do not attempt a thorough discussion of terms, categories, and commonly encountered situations in medical practice.[2] Instead I focus on forms immanent in practice and on modes of deploying knowledge and techniques. In

---

1. Pierre Bourdieu has developed the notion of practical logic in *Outline of a Theory of Practice* (Cambridge: Cambridge University Press, 1977) and in *The Logic of Practice* (Stanford: Stanford University Press, 1990). His discussion of the play of coherent principles of practical activity is very suggestive for understanding modes of knowing in a social world that "takes practice as its guide." I have adopted the term to refer to regularities and forms that seem to be immanent in Chinese medical practice. In speaking of the logic of the clinical encounter, I want to indicate modes of classification and inference that are common to the work of a great many doctors and that could constitute a Chinese medical method as well as constrain it—that is, principles of classifying effects and inferring a dynamic situation can be well or badly applied, and experienced practitioners can distinguish between skilled and unskilled practice. Some of the principles informing Chinese medical practice have been carefully articulated and explored in recent theoretical writing in China; others remain more implicit.

2. For systematic explications of Chinese medical knowledge and its clinical applications, see Liu Yanchi, *The Essential Book of Traditional Chinese Medicine*, 2 vols. (New York: Columbia University Press, 1988). The latter half of Nathan Sivin, *Traditional Medicine in Contemporary China* (Ann Arbor: Center for Chinese Studies, University of Michigan, 1987), is a shorter but clearer translation of a similar 1972 text. Other studies that aim at a comprehensive description are Manfred Porkert, *The Theoretical Foundations of Chinese Medicine* (Cambridge, Mass.: MIT Press, 1974); and Ted J. Kaptchuk, *The Web That Has No Weaver* (New York: Congdon and Weed, 1983). These latter two are noticeably influenced by the ways in which textbooks published in the PRC organize knowledge.

accord with the advice of my doctor-teachers in Guangzhou, this is a way of taking practice (rather than collected and systematized knowledge) as our guide for the study of contemporary Chinese medicine. These chapters, then, will show how illnesses are specified and differentiated and how an appropriate therapy is generated through classification at several levels of abstraction.

Describing: The Four Examinations (*Sizhen*)

The *sizhen* are methods of examining disease. The methods of examining disease in our fatherland's medicine are of four main types: looking, listening/smelling, asking, and palpating, known for short as the four examinations. The four examinations are extremely important; they are a crucial component of Chinese medical diagnosis, providing an objective basis for clinical syndrome differentiation and disease treatment. In any disease whatsoever, whether it be slight or serious, difficult or easy [to treat], to do a correct diagnosis and achieve the desired therapeutic effectiveness, it is necessary to thoroughly understand the illness situation, comprehensively collect every kind of objective material relating to the disease, and gain a detailed grasp of every aspect of the characteristics [*neirong*] of the emergence, development, shifts, and therapeutic situation—this process must depend on the method of the four examinations.

Ancient scholar-doctors, in their long period of practical therapeutic activity doing battle with disease, depended on their own sense organs to conduct careful and meticulous direct examinations of sick people, advancing a comprehensive understanding of the sick person's signs and symptoms with respect to the state of their whole body; they created many kinds of methods and they accumulated rich experience, which they summarized as the four examination methods of "looking, listening/smelling, asking, and palpating."[3]

The four examinations are discussed in detail in basic textbooks, usually occupying a separate chapter with four sections. They are, as the preceding passage explains, looking, listening/smelling (one term, *wen*), asking, and palpating. These four modes of medical elicitation, the first stage in the transformation of illness manifestations into a named syndrome, involve well-trained clinical sensitivities. The subtle discrimination of bodily manifestations is a capacity that a doctor should continue to refine throughout life. Many senior doctors are respected by students and sought out by patients because of their ability to discern fine differences in pulses, in hues of the tongue or face, and in the timing of symptom appearance.[4]

---

3. Liu Yanchi, Song Tianbin, Zhang Ruifu, and Dong Liantong, eds. *Zhongyi Jichu Lilun Wenda* (Shanghai: Shanghai Science and Technology Press, 1982), p. 71.

4. See Shigehisa Kuriyama, "Pulse Diagnosis in the Greek and Chinese Traditions," in Yosio Kawakita, ed., *History of Diagnostics* (Osaka: Taniguchi Foundation, 1987) pp. 43–67, on ancient pulse discriminations.

Although the four examinations are logically, discursively, and practically separable from later stages of the clinical encounter (a junior doctor may perform most of the examination before the supervising doctor becomes involved with an illness, for example), experienced doctors seldom clearly divide the methods of examination from the techniques of diagnosis and therapy. Clinicians may pursue parts of an examination with particular care on the basis of a suspicion that a certain illness mechanism is at work and may neglect others for the same reason. In addition, they often repeat a pulse reading or a tongue examination while tinkering with the drug formula.

The four examinations are heavily emphasized in textbooks and in clinic teaching. This is partly because the process by which diffuse signs ($zheng_1$) are transformed into medically significant and organizable symptoms ($zheng_2$) is considered to be basic to medical perception and action. The four examinations, taught in classrooms as a protocol but practiced more like a checklist, should constrain the doctor to remain alert to every evidence that could influence his perception of an actionable pattern. As the following quote argues, these skills of sensitive discrimination organized into a method should prevent him from lapsing into "one-sidedness":

> The real spirit and essence [*jingshen shizhi*] of the four examinations is "syndrome differentiation and treatment determination" [*bianzheng lunzhi*]. Because disease is expressed on the outside of the body, and is extremely complex, it has both quite ordinary situations and special variations; both of these have their normal and altered, genuine and bogus [expressions]. Therefore, clinically it is necessary to use the four examinations in very close connection with each other if one is to fully grasp [the condition], discriminate doubtful appearances, and discern similarities and differences, thereby making an exactly proper diagnosis. This is an important link in the work of diagnosis. If the spirit of a holistic viewpoint is neglected, the mistake of one-sidedness will be made.[5]

In the four examinations, lists of physical signs that are noted for presence/absence, quality (e.g., color, slipperiness), and degree of severity are loosely organized under the four headings of looking, listening/smelling, asking, and palpating. Under each of the four textbook headings is a series of small sets of contrastive relations. Examples are the thickness/thinness and yellowness/whiteness of the tongue coating, constipation or diarrhea, and the redness/paleness/darkness/grayness/yellowness of facial color. Awareness of these contrastive sets allows the doctor to structure his activities in the first stages of the examination and enables him to perceive and record the symptoms present in this particular instance.

At this stage, then, he is not classifying signs into any kind of interrelated network; he is merely classifying them as one symptom or another. For

---

5. Zhao Fen, ed., *Zhongyi Jichu Lilun Xiangjie* (Fuzhou: Fujian Science and Technology Press, 1981), p. 388.

example, a pulse rate of seven beats for each of the doctor's own in-and-out respirations is classified as an accelerated pulse, and avoidance of drafts and dislike for cold liquids are lumped together as "intolerance of cold." In Figure 3.2 the four examinations are a descriptive level that feeds into the analytic level above it. They reduce the complexity of the illness-as-presented very little. Symptoms that have resulted from use of the four examinations are often referred to as "materials" (*cailiao*) on which diagnosis can work. This can be seen in the long excerpt that opens this section as well as in discussions devoted specifically to diagnosis, as in a theoretical appendix to an introductory textbook of Chinese medicine entitled "Relations Among Several Kinds of Diagnostics": "Diagnosis is a process of taking the materials collected through looking, listening/smelling, asking, and palpating and, according to their intrinsic organic connections, further generalized and abstracted, inferring a diagnosis."[6]

A reading of the four examinations section of any introductory Chinese medicine text impresses one with the range of phenomena admissible as symptoms in Chinese medicine. Not only anxiety, excessive dreaming, wild talk, and other discomforts that we might regard as psychological, but also such phenomena as dislike of drinking cold water, a sour taste in the mouth, or sleeping under a great many quilts may be considered symptomatic. The foul mouth odor and dry lips of Case 1, for example, and the sour flavor of the vomitus in Case 3 are not elements usually cited as symptomatic in biomedicine; here, however, they are presented as facts of equal status with pulse images, constipation, and stomach pain. As the examining doctor begins to perceive a familiar pattern, he takes some signs less seriously than others; once he is sure of his diagnosis, he does not consider many details of the condition as pivotal and thus does not record or specifically treat them. In general, however, the transformation of signs into symptoms through the application of the four examinations is less a reduction in the amount of information than it is a medicalization of it, a reorganization of the patient's perception of his illness and the signs he presents on his body surface into a list of symptoms that are conventionally labeled and more well defined in their content than illness terms used in ordinary-language discourse.

Cases 1 and 3 incorporate typical symptom lists as they would have appeared in the case record booklets of those patients:

> Case 1: Agitation and irritability, dry mouth with excessive thirst, red face and foul mouth odor, tongue and lips dry and parched, occasional delirious speech, no appetite, no bowel movement for eight days, pungent and cooling drugs already administered with no effect. Pulse smooth and accelerated, tongue coating yellow, thick, and dry.

---

6. Office of the 1977 Physicians of Western Medicine Class in Chinese Medicine, ed., *Zhongyi Jichuxue* (Guangzhou: Guangdong College of Traditional Chinese Medicine, 1977), p. 164.

Case 3: Recurrent sharp pain in the epigastric area. Sufferer had begun
to have epigastric pain in 1972; barium meal fluoroscopy had diagnosed it
to be a duodenal ulcer. The present pain in the stomach and abdominal
cavity was piercing and aggravated by hand pressure, stable in location,
and accompanied by heartburn, sour vomitus, black stools, slightly reddened tongue with thin greasy yellow coating, and small strung pulse.

The symptoms named in Case 1 are not in order according to the four
examinations, but it is easy to see which of the four elicitation techniques
produced each symptom and where these techniques probably overlapped.
Thus, in Case 1 anxiety and restlessness were undoubtedly clear from the
patient's account of his illness (elicited by asking) and possibly in his manner
of speaking with the doctor (listening); "occasional delirious speech, lack
of appetite, [and] no bowel movement for eight days" emerged from the
patient's or his family's account in response to the doctor's asking. Red face
was noted by the doctor as a result of looking and foul mouth odor as
a result of examining the patient's tongue—hence it was a result of the
listening/smelling examination. The tongue image itself (coating yellow, thick,
and dry) is a result of the looking examination, and the pulse image (smooth
and accelerated) is the only symptom usually recorded as a result of palpating.

In Case 3 most of the symptoms reported were incorporated in the patient's own account. We can assume that in the course of asking, the doctor
inquired whether the pain was aggravated by hand pressure (he probably did
not test this himself) and whether its location shifted, and he no doubt
accepted the patient's description of the color and quality of his stools. The
looking examination resulted in a tongue image ("slightly reddened with
thin greasy yellow coating"), and palpating produced a pulse image of
"strung and small." Thus, it appears that in this case the listening/smelling
examination was not relevant. Since it is confined mainly to foul odors and
nonlinguistic sounds such as hoarse voice or moist coughing, listening/
smelling is often unnecessary in clinical work.

The four examinations are the first step in a general move from the apparent illness, as reported and presented by the patient, to the inferred active
processes that produce illness signs. An intense focus on "examination"
(*guancha*) of certain indicative body surfaces, followed by "inference"
(*guina*) from these outer surfaces to the "inner" processes that have given
rise to these images, is much discussed as a fundamental characteristic of
"our fatherland's medicine" in contemporary theoretical writing in the
PRC.[7] The relation of the surface to a presently invisible interior (not neces-

---

7. See, for example, Liu Changlin, *Neijingde Zhexue he Zhongyixuede Fangfa* (Beijing: Science Press, 1982); Hou Can, "*Cong Kexue Fangfalun Kan Woguo Yixue Keyande Xuanti*," *Yixue
yu Zhexue* 83, no. 3 (1983):4–6; Xu Chengzu, "*Cong Renshilun Tan Zhongyi Fenxing Lunzhi*,"
Yixue yu Zhexue 83, no. 2 (1983):9–11; and Huang Jitang et al., eds., *Zhongyixue Daolun* (Guangzhou: Guangdong Higher Education Press, 1988). This last work includes a description of an

sarily coterminous with the body interior, an issue that will be taken up shortly) is in keeping with the metaphysics of sources and manifestations discussed earlier. It is also a relationship that is frequently referred to in connection with the four examinations, as can be seen in a text edited by the Beijing College of Traditional Chinese Medicine:

> The human body is an organic whole, local illness changes can extend their influence to the whole person [*shen*], and illness changes in inner organs can in many respects ramify outward in the sense organs, the limbs, and the body surface. It is just as the *Danxi Xinfa* states: "He who would know its interior should do it by observing its exterior; he who examines the exterior can thereby know the interior." Thus, by means of the techniques of looking at colors, listening to sounds, asking about symptoms, and palpating pulses, [thereby] examining the symptoms and signs of disease manifestations in every respect, one can understand the causes, character, and internal connections of disease and provide a basis for syndrome differentiation and treatment determination.[8]

Here illness signs are explicitly seen as manifestations arising from "local changes" and "inner organs," and the four examinations are the means by which these manifestations are read; they also provide a basis for analysis and intervention.

Lists of symptoms elicited during the clinical encounter need not go in any particular order, and the relative orderliness of the four examinations evident in introductory texts is never reproduced in the clinic.[9] In a sense the four examinations are not so much a feature of clinical Chinese medicine as of the teaching of medicine, being important as a protocol only at a

---

order of examination somewhat different from that I describe here, which "takes the location or symptomatology as its basis and the four examinations as its method" (pp. 58–59). Huang sees this alternate method as a way in which "certain scholars" seek to more fully generalize and unify the four examinations.

8. Beijing College of Traditional Chinese Medicine, ed., *Zhongyixue Jichu* (Shanghai: Shanghai Science and Technology Press, 1978), p. 66. The *Danxi Xinfa* (New Methods of Zhu Danxi) referred to in the quote is by Zhu Zhenheng (1281–1358), revised by Cheng Chongxiao and published in 1481.

9. The discontinuity between the formal presentation of the four examinations in textbooks and the mode in which they are put into play in the clinical encounter argues for caution in the use of textual materials to make cross-cultural points about Chinese medical practice. Often the very doctors who serve on textbook committees and labor to achieve a greater systematicity in didactic presentations of Chinese medical knowledge are those who in their own practice deviate most noticeably from all textbook versions. As a formal system the four examinations have a relatively short history; late imperial scholars such as Li Yanwen of the Ming period and Lin Zhihan, the compiler of the *Sizhen Juewei* (Selection of Subtleties in Diagnostic Technique) (1723), dealt with the four examinations at length, but some of the systematicity evident in contemporary textbooks has not been found earlier than the late nineteenth century (Sivin, *Traditional Medicine,* p. 175).

stage when doctors are developing their own sense of the features that must be looked for in the treatment of illness. The first years of clinical practice are also formative in this respect since young doctors examine patients according to the procedure used by their supervising clinic teacher. At best the checklists provided by textual material on the four examinations remind practitioners of the phenomena that could inform their analysis of the illness in question. Insofar as widely used texts keep such seldom-used diagnostic techniques as abdominal palpation in the awareness of academic doctors, they may function to prevent too narrow an emphasis on any one technique. The four examinations are a constraint on the clinical examination, but they do not appear to be its inner organizing principle.

This is partly because so much of the preliminary stage of the clinical encounter depends on the patient's own account of her illness; most doctors are able to jot down the symptom names of the signs that interest them while the patient talks more or less freely about the history and characteristics of her illness. In addition to what the patient perceives as the significant features of her condition, only a few elicitations are generally seen as essential; these are looking at the tongue and palpating the pulse as well as asking after bowel movement and urination, appetite and digestion, and sleep.

Just as *kanbing* names the clinical encounter from both the doctor's and the patient's point of view, so the material generated through the four examinations consists of both doctor's and patient's experiences and perceptions of the illness. They collaborate in looking at the illness.

There is other evidence beyond the centrality of the patient's own narrative for a strongly collaborative quality in the *kanbing* process. Most practicing doctors attach great value to pulse-taking, in which the patient's pulses are counted against the doctor's breathing; indeed, the important pulse image is generated wholly in the relationship of doctor and patient, without reference to abstract time. The rich vocabulary of modern Chinese language for describing physical sensations (pain, aching, oppression, heaviness, agitation, etc.) makes it possible for patients to report and doctors to record (in an almost-as-rich and generally similar medical language) a wide variety of symptoms for which no "objective" measure is appropriate. And only the patient and his family are in a position to note the times at which symptoms appear, disappear, or change. Authority for the "truth" of symptoms, or at least for their character and relevance, seems to be distributed among all participants in the clinical encounter. The voices and experiences of patients and their families are especially crucial at the description stage in which the four examinations are used.

The four examinations are not meant to be mutually exclusive. The asking and listening/smelling examinations clearly overlap since the latter focuses on speech patterns (e.g., delirium, irritability) as much as the former does. The history elicited by asking incorporates the patient's own observations of her condition, including symptoms usually generated through the other three examinations. Since all four examinations are put into play at the same time, and there is no set order in which they must be used, they strongly inform one another. A report of irritability or nervousness from the patient or a relative will prompt the doctor to listen for agitated speech patterns; a face that looks swollen, or a report of an earlier swelling, will prompt examination by palpation; and sweaty palms detected by palpating or looking when taking the pulse suggest a line of questioning regarding fevers and dryness in the mouth.

The interdependence of the four examinations is acknowledged in a frequently cited maxim, *Sizhen hecan*, "The four examinations work jointly." Indeed, some recent works assert this maxim as one of the fundamental features of "our fatherland's medicine."[10] A strong contrast with biomedicine is embodied in the notion that the four examinations work jointly; many Chinese medical people see an overreliance on discrete and highly focused laboratory tests to be one of the defining characteristics of Western medicine. Perhaps the prominence of this idea is also an acknowledgment that the four examinations as protocol and as somewhat artificial categories have a limited role at the same time that the sensitivities and self-discipline that they require are fundamental features of clinical skill.

In spite of much recent systematizing of Chinese medical practice, and frequent textual insistence that careful practitioners will explore many avenues to achieve "a comprehensive understanding" of the illness condition, a popular image of the great traditional doctor who achieves a full grasp of the situation with one pulse reading or one quick look at the patient's face persists. Such legendary skill is not mystical, and it is not, I suspect, thought of in opposition to the more pedestrian skills of a schoolbook practitioner; it is more likely to be seen as having been achieved through a lifetime of clinical experience, much of which could have been spent practicing the four examinations in quite literal-minded ways. A senior doctor who has looked at many illnesses begins to embody a rich knowledge of the paths along which illness manifestations usually run. In a sense he performs a complete examination with a pared-down method: One pulse reading for him may entail findings from looking, asking, and listening/smelling examinations. (On "shortcuts" of this kind, see Chapter 7.)

---

10. See, for example, Deng Tietao, *Shiyong Zhongyi Zhenduanxue* (Shanghai: Shanghai Science and Technology Press, 1988), pp. 81–83; Deng Tietao, ed., *Zhongyi Jichu Lilun* (Guangzhou: Guangdong Science and Technology Press, 1982), p. 61; Liu et al., *Zhongyi Jichu Lilun Wenda*, p. 71; and Zhao, *Zhongyi Jichu Lilun Xiangjie*, p. 298.

Several processes of transforming signs to symptoms have been described here. One process is renaming: Illness signs reported in ordinary language by patients are recorded in case record booklets using conventional medical labels. This practice is in part a deployment of professional authority since it enables direct comparison of the patient's symptoms with those reported in earlier medical literature and locates the experience reported by the patient within medical (as opposed to, e.g., family or village) discourse.

A second process is a shift of temporal forms from the idiosyncratic personal concerns of the patients to the conventionalized patterns that interest the doctors. Patients often report their illnesses in long narratives, to which doctors attend carefully because the timing of the appearance of symptoms (e.g., the appearance of sweating before or after fever or the appearance of fevers only at night) influences their perception of the illness process at work. But doctors note only certain medically significant temporal patterns, which they pick out from the patients' narratives through asking; doctors have a bias toward symptoms expressible in "body-time," whereas patients may see their illness, and report it, as more socially and emotionally complex than the doctors see it.

A third process is reduction through generalization: Although the patient may see that all his complaints are noted in his record, the fact of their being transformed into conventional medical language begins to assert the perceptions of medical experience over the quality of his experience. For example, a woman's report that she can no longer hold a knife handle tightly enough may be noted as "weakness in the hands, difficulty making a fist," a linguistic shift that shrinks her complex experience of limitation in the accomplishment of family duties inward toward a generalized debility located in her own body.

In spite of the important constituting role that the patient plays as presenter of the illness for inspection, the quality of the doctor's perception is different from the patient's. His view of illness endows it with a medical quality presumably unseen by the patient. It becomes a condition similar to illnesses that have been previously treated in the world of Chinese medicine and is expressed in terms that can be found in the clinical language and vast literature of medicine. The doctor is not so much discovering an illness essence hidden within the body (a process for which the penetrative clinical testing employed in biomedicine is better suited) as he is recasting the illness into a mode of discourse that can link it with prior therapeutic experience. The four examinations are the initial procedure through which the illness presented by the patient is transformed into a medical event. The patient allows his experience to be cast in a medical mold in the hope that in this form the experience of the doctor and of his medical forebears can bring about an improvement.

Analyzing: The Major Classificatory Methods

The task of the clinical encounter is the differentiation of a syndrome and the determination of a therapy (*bianzheng lunzhi*).[11] To this end it is necessary to see the relationship of the symptoms to each other; it is *patterns* of symptoms from which illness dynamics can be inferred. Individual symptoms mean little in themselves, as the following demonstrates:

> In differentiating syndromes of the Heart visceral system, take palpitations as an example: When the person has heart palpitations and agitation, at the same time showing a preference for cool and avoidance of heat, red tongue with little coating, pulse small and accelerated, and other symptoms of Yin-Depletion Inner Heat, this can be diagnosed as palpitations of "Depleted Heart Yin," with a therapeutic method that takes nourishing Heart yin as its central component. If the palpitations are severe, along with sudden episodes of spontaneous sweating, intolerance of cold with cold extremities, pale tongue, slightly weak pulse, etc., this is classified as "Depleted Heart Yang," and the therapy should take warming and replenishing Heart yang as its central component. In addition, if heart palpitations are accompanied by bright white facial color, shortness of breath, and heavy breathing on exertion, the palpitation is one of Heart Qi Depletion.[12]

Clearly, it is a particular array of symptoms, rather than the presence of heart palpitations alone, that enables syndromes such as Depleted Heart Yin and Heart Qi Depletion to be differentiated from each other.

Groups of symptoms are perceived as a syndrome through the operation of a primarily classificatory logic. The underlying dynamic of an illness becomes clear when symptoms are characterized in terms of several classification schemes, referred to in textbooks as "syndrome differentiations" *bianzheng*. Since these are methods of characterizing illness in general analytic terms, I translate them loosely as "diagnostics". The most commonly used diagnostics are the eight rubrics (*ba gang*), illness factors (*bingyin*), the visceral systems of function (*zangfu*), the four sectors of the

---

11. The *lun* in this term refers to "discourse." *Lunzhi* could be translated (somewhat more vaguely than is desirable in English) as "discoursing on treatment." *Bianzheng lunzhi* is a term that is often used as a summation of the central characteristics of Chinese medicine as opposed to Western medical "diagnosis" (*zhenduan*, a word that incidentally preserves some of the etymological content of diagnosis, or knowing apart, with its attachment of *duan* [break, judge] to *zhen* for medical examination.)

Bianzheng lunzhi is fascinating in that it focuses on differentiation of syndromes, or patterns of manifestation, and on a social and linguistic approach to choosing a therapeutic intervention. Its very use in contemporary discourse seems to insist on a very deep epistemological divide between "Western" structural, essentialist and representational biases and the practical, collective, and relativistic biases characteristic of Chinese medicine.

12. Office of the 1977 Physicians, *Zhongyi Jichuxue,* p.164.

Warm Illnesses school (*wei qi ying xue*), and the six warps of the Cold Damage school (*liu jing*).

Once symptoms have been abstractly characterized with reference to the categories of these schemes, certain stable relationships holding among the categories themselves can reveal the connections among symptoms. As will be seen, for example, the relationship of complementarity, struggle, and intertransformation between the seventh and eighth terms of the eight rubrics, yin and yang, is strongly analogous to the relationship between the first two terms, Cold and Hot. Many symptoms are easily classified as Hot or Cold and are therefore entered into an explanatory and predictive model, that is, yinyang dynamics, at the moment that they are classified. The diagnostics are most often used in combinations of two or more to develop a multifaceted picture of the illness, on the basis of which a treatment plan is developed. Thus, each symptom may be multiply classified both within and among the diagnostic methods.

As with other forms of Chinese medical classification, the diagnostics focus on likenesses and differences in quality. Such likenesses and differences enable classification.[13] As will be seen most clearly in the discussion of eight rubrics analysis to follow, classification is done to reveal the dynamic relations presently obtaining among the manifestations that have been read and described by a clinician. The relations thus revealed are subject to formal and substantive shifts at any time. This kind of classification is not a method of determining or fixing the essential nature of each symptom or locating the structural substrate of the disease; nor does it sort each "item" (a symptom) into only one exclusive category. Chinese medical classification is not, in other words, a taxonomic procedure of the Linnaean or Baconian type in which the likeness of things enables a fixing of the unique and permanent essence common to the elements of each class. Like the myriad phenomena (*wanwu*) of classical Chinese philosophy, symptoms are manifestations of an invisible and constantly shifting active source. (See Chapter 2.) Chinese medical classification characterizes an illness condition by specifying its presentation and inferring the dynamic state of its source condition from this specification. The image generated is always temporally limited, subject to fundamental change with any superficial shift.

Consider the operations of the eight rubrics diagnostic method, which classifies symptoms as Cold or Hot, interior or exterior, depletion or repletion, and yin or yang. A determination that a sharp stomach pain arises from excessive Heat is important because a cooling therapy is indicated as a conse-

---

13. Comparison and classification and their relationship in the methodology (*fangfalun*) of Chinese medicine are discussed in Huang et al. *Zhongyixue Daolun,* pp. 72–74. Also see Liu, *Neijingde Zhexue he Zhongyixuede Fangfa,* pp. 326–349; and Xu, "*Cong Renshilun Tan Zhongyi Fenxing Lunzhi,*" pp. 9–11.

quence. A combination of Heat qualities and repletion in a specified Inner location, as in Case 1 (the yang visceral systems of Stomach and Large Intestine), suggests an intervention that cools, reduces the repletion, and localizes the therapy in specific visceral systems. The eight rubrics into which symptoms are classified thus must work in parallel with similarly classified components of therapy. And because Heat and repletion are usually associated with yang effects, other symptoms of the yang type should be looked for among the illness manifestations (while obvious symptoms of the yin type would suggest a more complex situation requiring closer analysis). The focus of interest is not so much on the inherent nature of the classificatory terms, or the contents of each class, but on the nature of the relationships between classes.

A full analysis of symptoms should provide at least two dimensions of classification, the qualitative and the spatiotemporal.[14] "The qualities" (*xingzhi*) of the symptoms (i.e., those that have been generated through the application of the four examinations) can be classified most effectively by means of the eight rubrics (e.g., Hot, Cold, depletion, repletion) and the illness factors (e.g., Wind, Cold, Heat, Moisture, Dryness, and Fire).[15] And the spatiotemporal locations of the illness process can be well characterized through visceral systems, six warps, or four sectors diagnostics. In other words, the functional systems affected by the illness process and the direction and speed of development of disordered states through them are specified by means of the latter three analytic methods, whereas the former two methods (especially the eight rubrics) are well suited to characterizing the general kind of disorder that is involved. Diagnosis almost always involves, then, "one from column A and one from column B"—qualities and locations are not separate hierarchical levels of perception, one coming first and the other after it; rather, they are cross-cutting dimensions of an illness process that is revealed and characterized by the methods of analysis to be described.[16]

---

14. A third important dimension of analysis is that of substance, with its appropriate classification method of "qi, Blood, *jing,* and dispersed body fluids." See Sivin, *Traditional Medicine,* pp. 237–247, for a translation of a textbook discussion of these substances and their clinical significance. In addition, a tract-based diagnostic, *ziwuliuzhu,* that emphasizes temporal shifts in symptoms, efficacies, and vulnerabilities was revived in the 1980s; see Zhong Weichen, *Ziwu Liuzhu Paoyaofa Chutan, Shandong Zhongyi Zazhi* 83, no. 5 (1983):6–7.

15. Office of the 1977 Physicians, *Zhongyi Jichuxue,* p. 164. The appendix on "Relations Among Several Kinds of Diagnostics" characterizes the eight rubrics diagnostic method as essentially about qualities (*xingzhi*) and ascribes the prominence of this method to the necessity of talking about qualities in all diagnosis.

16. Kuriyama has argued in his comparative study of Greek and Chinese pulse lore that qualities and spatiotemporal locations vary together for classical Chinese medicine; he shows that the hexagrams of the *Book of Changes* (*I Jing*) and the Five Phases "express directions of transformation. [They] remind us (for in the Chinese context this is not a matter of debate) that positions in

The qualities that can be perceived (in description by means of the four examinations and in analysis by means of the eight rubrics and the illness factors) are not direct unmediated sense perceptions. They are degrees of variation that as they are perceived are classed in conventional ways—a "red" (*hong*) tongue is only relatively more red than healthy "pink" (*danhong*), and "crimson" (*jiang*) is more extreme than red. Subtle variations in pulse quality are theoretically classifiable under twenty-eight named "images" (*maixiang*), although only twelve are commonly encountered in clinical practice. The virtue of such conventional classifications of the manifest qualities of an illness is that they can link up by means of conventional correspondences with higher-order classifications (Heat, depletion, Wind, etc.), which then lead directly to a highly compressed image of the dynamic state of the illness as a whole, that is, the syndrome. (This sequence of entailments will become clearer in the remainder of this chapter.) But they are arrived at strictly by means of a judgment on the part of the doctor; until recently, no attempt was made to render the means by which symptoms are evaluated and recorded impersonal or objective.[17]

The spatiotemporal characterization of illness manifestations by means of such diagnostics as visceral systems, six warps, and four sectors involves a specification of space in a somewhat unfamiliar sense. Although the visceral systems, for example, are named with reference to an internal organ, they are not bounded or discrete subterritories of an anatomically structured body. They are not, for example, livers that are homogeneously liver tissue from edge to edge or hearts that can be removed and replaced with a mechanical organ that can be held in one hand. Rather, they are interpenetrating systems of related functions that have a definite spatial dimension. One can (indeed must) talk of up and down, in and out while describing Chinese visceral physiology; but Spleen and Liver visceral systems extend throughout the same bodily space with their differing domains of responsibility. Similarly, the six warps and four sectors diagnostics differentiate degrees of internality of a disease process without reference to a measurable depth inside the body. The concern of these two diagnostics is the space-time of an illness process; they evaluate the seriousness of the patient's condition according to the relative interiority of the systems affected. For example, the final phase of a Warm illness, analyzed according to the four sectors, if it persists, is likely

---

space are not just abstract points in an isotropic coordinate system but rather gradients of change. Each site in the universe, and, by correspondence, each site on the body is engaged in a specific network of responsiveness by virtue of nothing other than its position. Place, not form, determines function" ("Pulse Diagnosis," p. 56).

17. See Hu Qingyin and Wang Wande, "*Maizhen Qiantan*," *Heilongjiang Zhongyiyao* 83, no. 2 (1983):15–20; 83, no. 4 (1983):10–15. One senior Chinese doctor in Guangzhou often insisted to me that pulse images and tongue qualities were scientific measures because they were "objective" (*keguan*). "I can feel it, you can feel it, so it's not subjective" (*zhuguan*).

to involve the Kidney system; this system is the chief physiological source of "true" or "original" qi, so damage to it is more serious, more "inner" in the special spatiotemporal sense being developed here, than damage to any other visceral system.

I have argued that even the simplest illnesses are seldom dealt with using only one diagnostic method. Yet there seems to be no obvious principle or level of medical reality to which all are reducible such that there is no contradiction among them. Simply by virtue of being one of a set of six terms, rather than two, for example, the Heat of the six external illness factors little resembles the (more generalizing) Heat of the eight rubrics; and the six warps diagnostic (*liu jing*) deploys the notion of "circulation tracts" (*jing*) quite differently than acupuncturists do, who even count them differently (usually as twelve, *shier jing*).

The relationships among the various diagnostic methods must be sought in an understanding of how they work together in practice, as is argued in an appendix to a 1977 foundations text:

> These methods of syndrome differentiation [*bianzheng fangfa*] each have their own special characteristics, and they are selectively used in the clinic according to their strong points in differing diseases. But among themselves they can also relate to each other and supplement each other. For example, the eight rubrics are the general categories for every kind of syndrome differentiation method, and the visceral systems are the foundation of every kind of syndrome differentiation method; the six warps and four sectors diagnostics are syndrome differentiation methods that mainly target exogenous Heat illnesses, but they can't depart from eight rubrics and visceral systems diagnostics and exist autonomously. Thus, there is no contradiction among them; rather, they are used together, taking the strengths of one to bolster the shortcomings of others. Only in this way can we be helped to better and more correctly recognize diseases and select appropriate therapeutic methods.[18]

It is interesting that this somewhat polemical essay was appended to a chapter in a committee-edited foundations text rather than incorporated into the body of the text. Perhaps its argument for a unified view of the various diagnostic methods was a minority view or was felt to be something better left to practical clinic training to convey. In any case it seems clear in this excerpt and throughout the essay that no ideal ground of compatibility can be found for the various diagnostics—their arena of coexistence is the ever-new and very concrete challenges of the clinic.

The unifying and systematizing urge reflected in this appendix is motivated in part by recent controversies in the teaching contexts and professional literature of Chinese medicine, as discourse proceeds along such newly formulated paths as "theoretical foundations" (*lilun jichu*), "dialectics

---

18. Office of the 1977 Physicians, *Zhongyi Jichuxue,* p. 164.

of nature" (*ziran bianzhengfa*), "methodology" (*fangfalun*), "episte-mology" (*renshilun*), and "systems theory" (*xitonglun*). Although the rela-tionship among the major diagnostic methods may be more troubled or less smoothly theorized than the essay always acknowledges, there is never-theless an element of practical interlock in their use that is essential to the syndrome differentiation and treatment determination process of the clinical encounter.[19]

Consider Cases 1 through 3. Although the first case of foetal death in Case 2 mentions only the eight rubrics classifications of the condition, this is because visceral system involvement is self-evident, the condition being a gynecological one requiring treatment of the Kidney visceral system and the Uterus (an "auxiliary" hollow organ closely governed by the Kidney visceral system) as well as the auxiliary *Chong* and *Ren* circulation tracts. Gynecolog-ical practice assumes the special relevance of these visceral systems and circu-lation tracts; hence they need not be explicitly stated. Only Case 1 refers directly to one of the conventional illness factors, external Warm or Hot heteropathic qi. (As with most determinations of the illness factor involved, this understanding is not crucial in this case to the *bianzheng lunzhi* pro-cess.) Nevertheless, the illness factors involved in all the cases cited here can be reasoned out of the case histories. All three cases can be characterized in terms of any of the diagnostics, but these classificatory procedures are quite differently emphasized in each case.

Although the diagnostic methods are applied with considerable flexibility and variation, a narrowing focus can be seen in the movement from the eight rubrics and illness factors (classification of qualities) to the more

---

19. "Relationships Among Several Kinds of Diagnostics" was added to the diagnostics sec-tion of a 1977 foundations textbook as a special didactic gesture, a response to conditions per-ceived to be problematic within professional discourse. The authors were responding to an increas-ing tendency to theoretically compare the various systematic methods of Chinese medicine with each other in an attempt to reconcile them into a single body of self-consistent theory and practice.

Such a project is riddled with difficulties; but it has taken on considerable importance under current conditions in the PRC, where Chinese medicine is under great pressure to epistemo-logically describe and characterize itself, delineating its areas of strength in opposition to Western medicine. This systematizing effort has not yet found any easy formulae in terms of which the eight rubrics, illness factors, visceral systems, six warps, and four sectors diagnostics can be articulated into a coherent overarching structure within which any given symptom could be economically, correctly, and reproducibly classified into only one cell. If such methods are seen, however, as modes of analysis that are selectively deployed in practice in response to concrete conditions, rather than as aspects of a unitary body of systematic knowledge, contradictions and redundancies recede in importance. Thus, this essay asserts the mutually supplementary role played by the various analytic methods in practice, each being brought to bear where it will be most clarifying. The essay claims that there is no contradiction among them.

I suspect that much of the systematizing activity that has been recently undertaken in Chinese medicine is chiefly for pedagogic purposes. Systems to facilitate memorizing, which are then brought into question in practice, are perhaps not quite the same thing as systematic knowledge.

complex and specific visceral systems, six warps, and four sectors diagnostics (classification of locations). The eight rubrics not only classify the quality (Hot/Cold, repletion/depletion) of symptoms but also make a first pass at spatially locating the illness (exterior/interior). From such determinations certain probable directions of change can be predicted following the dynamic regularities of the yinyang relationship. Similarly, the conventional illness factors have both qualitative (e.g., Hot, Damp, changeable) and spatial (e.g., Dryness readily harms the Lung system; Cold is dangerous to the Kidney system) components. Thus, although the eight rubrics and the illness factors diagnostics are primarily concerned with qualities of the illness, they open the question of location by (at least) distinguishing inner from outer. They are more broadly but more grossly analytic than the visceral systems, six warps, and four sectors diagnostics.

Visceral systems diagnosis is much more complex, locating the illness in an elaborate network of physiological relationships and functions. This network is partly analyzable in terms of the abstract relations obtaining in the classificatory system of the Five Phases, as at least one authority has shown, as well as in yinyang terms.[20] The six warps and the four sectors are used mainly to place the illness in time (which incorporates an evaluation of its mildness or seriousness). Thus, whatever classificatory analytics are employed, it is the specific interlock of *quality* (Hot/Cold, repletion/depletion, changeability or tendency to clotting) and spatiotemporal *location* (exterior/interior, the five yin viscera, the four sectors, the six warps) in an illness process that can adequately characterize symptoms and enable the differentiation of a pattern nameable as the syndrome. Each of the major diagnostic methods can now be considered in turn.

Eight Rubrics (*Ba Gang*) Analysis

Eight rubrics diagnostic—one of the basic methods of syndrome determination. Uses the eight rubrics of yin and yang, exterior and interior, Cold and Hot, depletion and repletion to advance analyses and inferences about an illness syndrome and provides a basis for deploying therapy. Exterior and interior differentiate the shallowness or depth of the illness location; Cold and Hot differentiate the quality of the illness syndrome; depletion and repletion differentiate the strength or weakness of heteropathy and orthopathy; and yin and yang are thus the general rubrics that permeate the other six. Exterior, Heat, and repletion belong to yang, and interior, Cold, and depletion belong to yin. The contradictions of the four dyads of the eight rubrics are relative,

20. Beijing College, *Zhongyixue Jichu*, pp. 10–28, 112–127; Denq Tietao *Xueshuo Tantao yu Linzheng* (Ghangzhou: Guangdong Science and Technology Press, 1981), pp. 4–15.

interconnected, and intertransformative. The many complex and various clinical syndromes can all use them as a basic method of analysis and inference.[21]

All the diagnostic analytics to be taken up here provide a systematic pattern of abstracted relationships that can be mapped over symptoms to develop a coherent (if partial) picture of the illness process. Because these relationships entail certain forms of interaction and produce general tendencies on which prognosis can be based, they can guide therapy. As the foregoing dictionary definition indicates, the eight rubrics are simple, basic, and relevant to nearly every illness. They are almost certainly the most widely applied diagnostic method, and they appear to have much in common with nonmedical thinking about health and illness.[22] In addition, the eight rubrics are an elegant example of the dynamic classification characteristic of the traditional Chinese sciences.

A typical chapter on the eight rubrics in a theoretical foundations text opens as follows:

> Eight rubrics refer to eight types of syndrome: yin, yang, exterior, interior, Cold, Hot, depletion, and repletion. On the basis of the materials obtained through the four examinations, a comprehensive analysis is conducted that infers these eight types of syndrome according to the depth or shallowness of the illness's location, the character of illness changes, and the waxing and waning vicissitudes of [the relationship between] heteropathic and orthopathic qi—this is the eight rubrics diagnostic. Because the eight rubrics are summarized from all the diagnostic methods, they are the general categories of all the kinds of syndrome differentiation. In the process of differentiating syndromes, they have the function of simplifying complexities and bringing out the essentials.
>
> Although disease expressions are infinitely variable and complex in the extreme, the eight rubrics can basically be used as a means of inference in all of them. For example, the type of disease can be classed as a yin syndrome type or a yang syndrome type; the depth or shallowness of an illness location can be classed as an exterior syndrome type or an interior syndrome type; the character of the disease can be classed as a Cold syndrome type or a Heat syndrome type; [and with regard to] the strength or weakness of heteropathic and orthopathic qi, when heteropathy is overstrong, it is a repletion syndrome type, and when orthopathic qi is depleted, it is a depletion syndrome type. This way, using the eight rubrics diagnostic, we can cope with extremely

---

21. Editing Committee of the Unabridged Dictionary of Chinese Medicine, *Zhongyi Dacidian, Jichu Lilun Fence* (Beijing: People's Health Press, 1982), s.v. *bagang bianzheng*.

22. See Marjorie Topley, "Chinese Traditional Etiology and Methods of Cure in Hong Kong," in Charles Leslie, ed., *Asian Medical Systems* (Berkeley and Los Angeles: University of California Press, 1976), pp. 243–265; Eugene N. Anderson, Jr. and Marja L. Anderson, in Kwang-chih Chang, ed., "Modern China, South" *Food in Chinese Cultures* (New Haven: Yale University Press, 1977), pp. 317–382; and Katherine Gould-Martin, "Hot Cold Clean Poison and Dirt: Chinese Folk Medical Categories," *Social Science and Medicine* 12B (1978):39–46.

complicated clinical manifestations, which are basically divided into the four paired classificatory syndrome types of exterior-interior, Cold-Hot, depletion-repletion, and yin-yang and are used to guide clinical therapy. Among these, yinyang is the general rubric that can summarize the other six; thus, exterior, Hot, and repletion are classed as yang syndrome types, and interior, Cold, and depletion are classed as yin syndrome types.[23]

The eight rubrics system is structured by relations of contrast and of commonality. The yinyang relation, a "unity of opposites" (*duili tongyi*) characterized by mutual struggle, interdependence, and the capacity of active and structive positions to transform into each other, typifies and summarizes these two kinds of relationship. Functioning as classificatory rubrics, yin and yang allow manifestations that have qualities, properties, or positions in common to be classed together: Active aspects of an effect can be called yang, and structive aspects can be called yin. Diverse effects can be compared in terms of their abstract yinyang characterizations. Functioning as a dynamic relationship, yin and yang summarize the kinds of relationship that are possible among manifestations classed as contrasting. The most general medical relationship that follows this logic is that between herbal drugs and symptoms: A yin drug can engage in "struggle" with pathological conditions classed as yang, or it can supplement and bolster body processes (e.g., fluid production) associated with yin.

The relationship between yin and yang is the general form of relations of contrast in the indigenous Chinese sciences. Given the pervasive transformativity of things, a strong contrast can only be a dynamic relation. The struggle of opposites and their capacity to transform into each other are features of the very existence of things and effects in time and space, yin and yang in this sense being distinct moments in a continuous flux. ("When heat reaches an extreme point, then there will be cold," is a frequently heard proverb reflecting the yinyang relational form of the eight rubrics.) It follows that definition of each polar quality is possible only relative to the other. And the recognition that any dyad or relation of contrast depends on a common ground of comparability is consistent with the assumption that yin and yang are interdependent because of their source in the one qi that moves through the world. That is, the unity of the active source of all manifestations is both a metaphysical assumption and a logical necessity. This unity is revealed in relations of contrast of the yinyang type and expressed in the notion of the mutual dependence of yin and yang.

The qualities associated with each great class of things are relative, however, and the relations of commonality or contrast established through classification are not taken to be permanent or essential. Thus, anything hot,

23. Deng, *Zhongyi Jichu Lilun*, p. 97.

fast, bright, and outer is yang only by comparison with and in relation to things that are cooler, slower, dimmer, or more inner *under the specific conditions obtaining at the time of observation.* This space-time specificity of classifications and relationships of the yinyang type cannot be overemphasized. The eight rubrics sorting of manifestations into yin and yang classes generates contingent and relative commonalities among things while at the same time producing a pattern of abstract qualities. This is seldom a homogeneous pattern. As textbooks constantly emphasize, and as will be seen in the case analyses to follow, illnesses are complex and an eight rubrics analysis is rarely uncontradictory in practice. Deng Tietao explains this situation carefully:

> The eight rubrics respond to several important aspects of every sort of contradiction [that can develop] in the process of illness changes, but in clinical use they are both connected to each other and inseparable from each other. If one distinguishes exterior from interior, this must be related to Cold and Heat, depletion and repletion, and if one distinguishes depletion from repletion, this must be related to exterior and interior, Cold and Heat. This is because disease changes are so seldom pure or simple; rather, they commonly manifest a complex situation of exterior and interior, Cold and Hot, depletion and repletion mingled together. In addition, there are also exterior syndromes progressing inward and interior syndromes coming to the surface, Cold syndromes transforming into Heat, and Heat syndromes turning to Cold, and depletion and repletion turning into each other as well as a distinction between genuine and bogus Heat and Cold [symptoms]. When using the eight rubrics diagnostic, one must not only skillfully grasp the individual characteristics of each of the eight syndrome types but also attend to their interconnections and use them adeptly before the disease can be correctly and completely understood. The eight rubrics are conceptual categories of syndrome differentiation and therapy deployment appropriate for use in every clinical discipline.[24]

The skill and adeptness Deng mentions are required both to achieve the correct classification of each symptom in terms of three dyads and to interpret the pattern that emerges once this classification has been accomplished.

The fourth dyad, yin-yang, being the "general rubric" for the other three dyads, operates more as a tool of interpretation than as a preliminary classificatory rubric for symptoms. It is frequently emphasized that Hot, repletion, and exterior symptoms are usually classed as yang and that Cold, depletion, and interior symptoms are classed as yin. Thus, the first three dyads of

---

24. Deng, *Shiyong Zhongyi Zhenduanxue,* p. 171.

the eight rubrics can be reduced to the fourth dyad, yin-yang, in most cases producing a more simplified and more powerfully dynamic image of the relational pattern of the illness.

Each of the four dyads of the eight rubrics relates to a different aspect of the illness phenomena to be classified; all four dyads are used for direct classification of symptoms, but the fourth, yin-yang, is also used to infer the dynamic relationships holding among the symptoms thus classified. Therefore, the Cold-Hot dyad describes the basic *character* of the illness, the depletion-repletion dyad describes the *force* of its movement (heteropathic qi too strong or orthopathic qi too weak), and the interior-exterior dyad describes the *location* of the illness.

Each of these is a dimension of a state, a total situation that becomes visible in the clinical encounter. But because this moment is necessarily caught up in a dynamic process that must be perceived to be manipulated, and because the future of an illness must be inferred from its present, the yin-yang dyad can be applied to place the illness in a specific *temporal* process. Since the first three dyads are subsumed in relations of commonality by the categories of yin and yang, the symptoms can first be differentially affiliated to the six categories and then classified as dynamically yin or yang. On the basis of the temporal yinyang relation, drugs can be deployed to attack a pathological preponderance of yin or yang symptoms (the struggle attribute of yin and yang) or to supplement orthopathic processes in a yin or yang direction. And predictions can be made about the potential for shifts into other manifestation forms, either as the illness takes its natural course or as it responds to intervention (the mutual dependence and mutual transformability attributes of yin and yang). Eight rubrics classification is thus both descriptive at a higher level than the description accomplished by the four examinations (i.e., a more general classification of manifest qualities) and analytic in a grosser way than some of the diagnostic methods to be discussed (i.e., it is a dualistic predictive model).

Tables 4.1–4.4, taken from a text on diagnosis, summarize the classification of many common symptoms according to the eight rubrics method. Each of these tables is devoted to one of the four dyads, and the dual contrasts involved are organized according to the four methods of examination (Tables 4.1 and 4.4) or some other convenient general set of classes. Although repletion and depletion are revealed here as the most complex of the four dyads, all these tables display the yinyang contrast well.

Most experienced academic doctors emphasize that tables of this kind have limited usefulness since in practice symptoms can be only relatively and contingently classified. Tables tend to reify the qualities that a good clinician should perceive in an illness; if the clinician relies too heavily on such tables, they could blind him to the dynamic relations (e.g., between Cold hetero-

Table 4.1 Symptoms Classifiable as Cold or Hot

	Symptoms	
Examinations	*Cold*	*Hot*
Looking	Shrinking and clenching of body and limbs, withdrawal; facial color pale white, eyes greenish, closed or averted; lips pale white or greenish purple; nails greenish purple; no tongue coating or white coating, coating slippery or moist, tongue color pale, tongue wide and tender; mucus usually fine and white	Stretching and extending of body and limbs, body light and easy to move; agitation and restlessness; face and skin around eyes red, eyes wide open and staring; lips dry and parched or red and swollen; nails reddish purple; tongue coating rough, dry and yellow showing thorn-prick macules, or black and dry; tongue surface toughened and rough; mucus thick and yellow
Listening/ smelling	Quiet, unwilling to talk	Agitated and talkative
Asking	Not thirsty, likes warm food, sleepy, urine clear, urination prolonged, diarrhea	Thirsty with dry mouth, likes cool drinks, insomnia, urine reddish, urination brief, constipated
Palpating	Pulse sunken, small, moderate, with little force	Pulse floating, swollen, accelerated, forceful

SOURCE: Adapted from Guangdong College of Traditional Chinese Medicine, ed., *Zhongyi Zhenduanxue* (Shanghai: Shanghai Science and Technology Press, 1982), p. 107.

pathic qi and a Hot response in the body) that have given rise to illness manifestations. The necessity to remain alert to the occasional appearance of bogus Hot symptoms, mentioned in Dr. Deng's previous cautions on complexity, is a good example. Classification of symptoms under the eight rubrics can be guided by reliable rules of thumb, such as these tables, but it

Table 4.2 Symptoms Classifiable as Exterior or Interior

	Exterior	*Interior*
Place	Skin, hair, circulation tracts	Visceral systems
Symptoms	Intolerance of cold and fever, head and body aches, stuffed nose, pain in limbs	High fever, emotional agitation, thirst with dry mouth, chest or abdominal pain, constipation or diarrhea, reddish urine, reduced urination
Pulse	Floating	Sinking
Tongue coating	Fine, white	Yellow or gray-black

SOURCE: Adapted from Guangdong College of Traditional Chinese Medicine, ed., *Zhongyi Zhenduanxue* (Shanghai: Shanghai Science and Technology Press, 1982), p. 103.

Table 4.3 Symptoms Classifiable as Resulting from Depletion or Repletion

Type/Site	Depletion	Repletion
Qi	Lung qi depleted: short and hard breathing, spontaneous perspiration, spiritless speech Middle *Jiao* qi depleted: weak and cold extremities, intermittent abdominal swelling, aching eased by hand pressure, no appetite, diarrhea Source qi depleted: depletion Yang floating upward, cheeks splotchy red-white and tender, ringing in ears and deafness, dizziness and palpitations, hand tremors, irregular breathing	Lung qi repletion: stuffy chest, dizziness, blurry vision, excessive mucus, difficulty breathing when reclining Stomach qi repletion: abdominal fullness, heartburn and upset stomach, foul-smelling eructations, sour taste when swallowing, nausea, vomiting Intestinal qi repletion: lower abdomen distended, umbilical area pain, constipation or excessive urination (reddish or clear), hectic fever and delirium Liver qi repletion: headache and dizziness
Blood	Lips pale, face white, agitation and instability, weak nerves, depleted fluids, night fevers and sweats, muscular twitching and cramps, limb convulsions in extreme cases	Stasis in muscles and tendons: local swelling and pain Stasis in tracts: body aches and clenched muscles Stasis in Upper *Jiao*: pain on rotating trunk Stasis in Middle *Jiao*: acute abdominal pain Stasis in Lower *Jiao*: distension and acute pain in lower abdomen In all these blood stasis pains, location unstable, black stools
Five Visceral Systems	Heart depletion: tendency toward melancholy Liver depletion: blurry and reduced vision, contracting testicles, cramps, anxiety Spleen depletion: reduced use of extremities, poor digestion, full abdomen, sorrow and worry Lung depletion: short breath, shallow breathing, lusterless hair and skin Kidney depletion: dizziness and blurry vision, lower back pain, constipation, irregular urination or dysuria, nocturnal emission, early morning diarrhea	Heart repletion: personality abnormalities, hysterical laughter Liver repletion: aching sides, anger Spleen repletion: abdominal fullness and distension, constipation, edemas Lung repletion: cough, difficulty breathing Kidney repletion: blockage of Lower *Jiao*, aching or distension

SOURCE: Adapted from Guangdong College of Traditional Chinese Medicine, ed., *Zhongyi Zhen-duanxue* (Shanghai: Shanghai Science and Technology Press, 1982), p. 111.

Table 4.4   Symptoms Classifiable as Yin or Yang

	Yin	*Yang*
Looking	Facial color white, dark, or pale; body sluggish and/or clenched, no strength or vigor in stance, listless and spiritless; tongue pale, wide, tender; coating moist and slippery	Facial color all red or blotchy red, fever (seeking coolness), delirium, agitation, restlessness; mouth and lips cracked and dry; scarlet tongue or tongue black with thorn-prick macules; tongue coating yellow or coarse and yellow
Listening/smelling	Voice low and weak, quiet and unwilling to talk; short breath and shallow breathing	Loud strong voice, agitated excessive speech; obstructions in breathing, cough with phlegmy noises; delirium and sudden cries
Asking	Passes foul smelling gas; low appetite, no taste in mouth; not agitated and not thirsty or likes hot drinks; urine clear and plentiful or reduced	Hard or foul-smelling stools or constipation; no appetite; dry mouth, agitation and thirst; brief urination and reddish urine
Palpating	Lower abdominal aches (eased by hand pressure); body and extremities cold; pulse sunken, swollen, small, rough, halting, retarded, weak, or without force	Lower abdominal aches (aggravated by hand pressure); fever and warm extremities; pulse floating, accelerated, large, smooth, forceful

SOURCE: Adapted from Guangdong College of Traditional Chinese Medicine, ed., *Zhongyi Zhen-duanxue* (Shanghai: Shanghai Science and Technology Press, 1982), p. 99.

cannot become completely automatic; hunches about the underlying disease process and a quick grasp of the total pattern of symptoms must inform the classification. Although tables of correspondence are widely used in teaching today, they do not appear to be advanced as objective and invariant protocols. Once memorized by students, they become mnemonics for the skilled and adept practitioner rather than rules that determine his practice.

The clinical focus shifts as eight rubrics classification proceeds; the symptoms that were named in the four examinations are put to one side as an abstract characterization of them emerges and is deployed to guide treatment. In other words, a specific pattern of relations is generated by the application of eight rubrics classification; for the time being it is this pattern, rather than the list of the symptoms themselves, that is the focus. Most of the symptoms recorded in Cases 1 through 3 can be conventionally classified according to the eight rubrics.

Case 1

When seen in the later stages of an exogenous febrile disease, as here, these symptoms are classified as follows:

Unremitting high fever	Interior, yang
Agitation and irritability	Interior, yang, Hot
Dry mouth with excessive thirst	Interior, Hot, yang
Red face	Hot, yang
Foul mouth odor	Hot
Tongue and lips dry and parched	Hot, yang
Delirious speech	Hot, repletion
Lack of appetite	Yang
Lack of bowel movement	Interior, Hot, repletion, yang
Smooth pulse	Yang
Accelerated pulse	Hot, yang
Tongue coating yellow	Interior, Hot, yang
Tongue coating thick	Hot, yang
Tongue coating dry	Hot, yang

Case 1 thus presents a simple picture of an extreme yang Hot syndrome. This is a general but unequivocal diagnosis. Although it is refined in this case with six warps and four sectors analysis, which discern some interesting spatial and temporal complexities of the illness, the eight rubrics affiliations remain important in the management of the case and in the design of the herbal prescription.

Case 2

Patient I

Tongue coating yellow	Hot
Tongue coating also greasy white	(Damp) Hot
Tongue color red	Hot, yang
Sunken pulse	Interior
Slightly accelerated pulse	Slightly Hot, repletion, yang

Patient II

Tongue pale	(Qi and Blood both) depleted
Tongue tender	Depletion, Cold
Tongue coating thin and white	Cold
Coating peeling in the middle	Depletion, yin
Pulse accelerated and large	Interior, Hot, repletion
Pulse weak under heavy pressure	Interior, depletion
Severe nausea in early pregnancy	(Spleen-Stomach) depletion

The first of these two cases shows a consistent picture of interior Heat repletion, which would be predominantly yang in character. A common classical formula only slightly modified could thus be used to attack and break up the Damp-Heat repletion that was preventing expulsion of the foetus. The second case was more complicated, however, since there were mixed repletion and depletion, Cold and Hot symptoms; a more subtle implementation of alternative treatment principles and classical formulae was therefore required based on further analysis using other methods.

Case 3

Pain piercing	Repletion, interior, yang
Pain aggravated by hand pressure	Repletion, yang
Heartburn	(Qi) repletion
Sour vomitus	(Qi) repletion
Black stools	(Blood) repletion
Tongue slightly red	Hot
Tongue coating greasy	Cold
Tongue coating yellow	Interior, Hot
Pulse strung and small	Cold, yin

The mixed yin and yang character of this condition suggests that both Cold and Hot elements are involved in the illness process. The consistent picture of repletion symptoms and the interior location indicate the possibility of an interior Cold repletion giving rise to some Hot effects.

Each of these cases has certain complex features that place its full pattern beyond the reach of any one analytic method. But Cases 1 and 3 are unequivocal enough to show how the eight rubrics can clearly characterize the important features of the illness and help the doctor see whether it is dominantly yin or yang. Whatever further analytic methods are employed, the eight rubrics analysis has already considerably narrowed the range of therapeutic options. Case 1, for example, is strongly yang in type and Hot in character; since the illness has already gained a foothold in the interior of the body, its heat is undoubtedly damaging fluids and impairing the capacity of orthopathic processes to reverse the advance of yang heteropathies. Treatment will (at least) have to emphasize cooling, draining, and replacing fluids. As the doctor analyzes the symptoms in other terms, the characteristics elucidated by means of the eight rubrics and the therapeutic responses they have made obvious remain an important dimension of all the other patterns that emerge.

Illness Factor (*Bingyin*) Analysis

> *Illness factor diagnostic*—one of the methods of syndrome differentiation. Investigates illness factors and pathological changes according to the differing disease expressions, providing a basis for therapeutic drug use. For example, dizziness, tremors, and convulsions are all classed as Wind; and fever, agitation, mania, and coma are all classed as Fire. This kind of analytic method is known as seeking the cause when differentiating the syndrome [*bianzheng qiu yin*]. Clinically it is often used together with the eight rubrics diagnostic such that they supplement each other. In the nineteen passages on the courses of illnesses preserved in the *Basic Questions, juan* 22.74, illness factors and illness courses are used with many kinds of symptoms to provide a general inference; this is an example of the study of illness factors.[25]

The preceding dictionary entry characterizes the illness factor diagnostic method as one of "seeking the cause" and translates as "cause" the same word, *yin,* that I have translated as "factor" in the *bingyin* compound. The structure of this catch phrase is interesting, mirroring the form of the much more widely applicable phrase, "When treating illness, trace the root" (*Zhibing qiu ben*). The factors that induce illness under certain conditions, such as the "six excesses" and the "seven emotional states," are not, however, the root of illness; a distinction must be made between the limited importance of knowing what external or internal factor has contributed to the onset of the illness and comprehending the dynamic root condition that is giving rise to the manifest illness. The illness *root* is always a specific relationship among forces or tendencies; in modern usage, at least, the illness *factor* is only one of these contributing tendencies.[26]

Illness factor analysis as it is deployed in the clinical encounter is best understood in the context of the struggle between heteropathic and orthopathic qi (*xie qi* and *zheng qi*).[27] In explaining Chinese medicine's theoretical foundations, Zhao Fen describes this struggle as follows:

> So-called orthopathic qi indicates an organism's physiological [*shengli*] mechanisms and its capacity for resisting illness, also known as nutritive essence [*jingqi*], true qi [*zhenqi*], and primordial qi [*yuanqi*]; so-called heteropathic qi generally designates all kinds of illness-inducing factors. Chinese medicine

---

25. Editing Committee, *Zhongyi Dacidian, Jichu Lilun Fence,* s.v. *bingyin bianzheng.*

26. I have chosen not to translate *bingyin* as "illness cause," although the precedent set in Sivin, *Traditional Medicine,* is sensible and the most direct and accurate translation of *yin* is "cause" or "reason." This deviation is necessary partly to clarify the process of tracing the root, from which so much of the clinical encounter takes its coherence, and partly because the notion of cause has been so central in our own scientific history that it could only be confusing to assign it a less than central position in the quite different history of Chinese medicine.

27. See Sivin's discussion of heteropathy and its relation to a "language of possession," *Traditional Medicine,* pp. 100–106.

considers that, although reasons for the onset of illness are many, it is mainly determined by the strength or weakness of the organism's orthopathic qi. Thus, we take the growth and diminution of the [relative] strength of orthopathic and heteropathic qi to explain the occurrence and progress of disease. But after heteropathic qi invades the body, orthopathic qi is sure to resist it— this is what is known as the "struggle of orthopathy and heteropathy with each other." Therefore, the occurrence of disease is none other than an expression of the struggle of orthopathy and heteropathy; and the symptoms of disease are simply a response to the relative increase and decrease of orthopathy and heteropathy in the course of their struggle. Thus, when treating illness, one must not only expel heteropathic qi but must also correspondingly support and assist orthopathic qi as well. In the whole scholarly system of Chinese medicine, which is permeated with the holistic viewpoint of the unity of inner and outer and the unity of body and spirit, speaking of the person and discussing [his or her] illness are never done in isolation from each other.[28]

This excerpt not only makes the wide applicability of the orthopathy-heteropathy struggle clear; it also indicates the relative meaninglessness of the struggle apart from concrete illness situations. Because it is so highly contingent, the illness factors listed in textbooks cannot be considered an exhaustive account of heteropathic forces.

As Sivin has explained, and as the foregoing quote suggests, pathological process is disorder; medical intervention aims to restore healthy order.[29] Heteropathy can refer to whatever attacks a healthy physiological order, whereas orthopathy refers to the many ways in which heteropathic forces can be physiologically resisted, neutralized, or transformed. Because good health is a state in which orthopathic processes are vigorous and ongoing, the mere existence of a potentially heteropathic condition of the external or internal environment cannot "cause" illness. Rather, one of the six excesses or the seven emotional states can induce pathological disorder only in a person whose health is already suffering, perhaps invisibly, an insufficiency.

Like other dyads discussed herein, the practical meaning of these terms— heteropathic and orthopathic qi—is situation-specific; the terms are defined

---

28. Zhao, *Zhongyi Jichu Lilun Xiangjie*, p. 253.

29. Sivin, *Traditional Medicine*, pp. 96–99. This discussion emphasizes the strong sense in which health is a state of order, illness (*bing*) is disorder, and treatment (*zhi*) is a form of management intended to restore order. Sivin's explanation is important for any sociological consideration of Chinese medicine because it enables one to perceive bodily health and healing in continuity with the self-cultivation of the "superior man" and the management of family, local, and state affairs. Perhaps it hardly needs to be added that where the universe is known to be constantly changing, where transformation is the only unalterable condition, healthful order is highly contingent. In other words, if health is conceived as a stable order, neither people nor states can be said to be "naturally" healthy. Rather, order must be produced and continually reproduced. One could say that in the Chinese sciences, in direct contrast to modern (but perhaps not "postmodern") Western science, stability is what must be constructed because change is a given.

relative to each other under specific conditions of time and space. Thus, when severe weather conditions prevail, some people will fall ill in response to one of the six excesses—Wind, Cold, Summer-Heat, Damp, Dryness, or Fire; the external illness factor is the heteropathy in such illnesses, and the defensive (*wei*) qi that moves through the outer part of the body is orthopathic against it. If *wei* qi is strong enough, the illness will remain superficial, and the patient will recover quickly. In another situation, heteropathic qi may be internal, as in the dead foetuses in Case 2; in this case the forms of orthopathic qi concerned were probably the primordial qi (*yuanqi*) associated with the Kidney visceral system and the genetic qi (*zongqi*) ruled by the Lung system as well as numerous allied physiological functions. They were clearly not strong enough to expel the heteropathy embodied in the foetuses without medical supplementation.

Neither weather conditions, such as heat, cold, or damp, nor extreme internal states of excess, such as pregnancy, are malignant in and of themselves. The illness factors, then, are not powerful causes. They are, rather, common forms of heteropathy, reifications of some of the complex factors that influence an ailing physiology toward overt illness.[30] They are defined as heteropathic qi only after illness has appeared and it becomes important to understand the nature of the physiological struggle giving rise to symptoms. Moreover, although illness factor analysis is particularly concerned with classifying forms of heteropathic qi, there are more forms that a heteropathy can take than are considered in textbook *bingyin* theory. Because heteropathic qi becomes a reality only in the context of an illness occurrence, this overflow of illness factors does not constitute much of a problem; in a sense all analytic methods, not just illness factor analysis, concern themselves with the nature of the specific struggle between forces designated as heteropathic and functions designated as orthopathic. The precipitating illness factor, or *bingyin,* need not be part of any preordained series.

As a classification of forms of heteropathy, the illness factor diagnostic, then, is quite partial and noticeably unsystematic in comparison with the other diagnostics. These days the *bingyin* are divided into external factors (the six excesses, or *liu yin*), internal factors (mainly the seven emotional states, or *qi qing*), and factors neither external or internal (unbalanced diet, exhaustion, excesses in alcohol consumption or sexual activity, traumatic injuries, etc.). But this tripartite breakdown has varied considerably even in recent years.[31]

In a few types of illness the textbook illness factors are very important; such conditions are primarily characterized with reference to the factors that

---

30. Ibid., p. 100.
31. Ibid., p. 274.

have precipitated them. Wind and Damp-Heat illnesses, for example, are frequently encountered and have unique qualities deriving from the nature of the external heteropathy that has induced them. Thus, Wind-induced illnesses show yang qualities, being mobile in location but mainly attacking the upper and outer parts of the body; they are also prone to frequent shifts in illness manifestations. There are a number of drugs that are specific in combating Wind; hence no other form of diagnostic analytic will characterize or treat a Wind illness as fully as the illness factor diagnostic. Damp-Heat symptoms, because they involve signs of stasis and internal congealment more often associated with Cold conditions, are sometimes difficult to correctly characterize through the application of other analytic methods. Seasonal considerations can in such a situation be important; knowing that patients have been much exposed to Summer-Heat (*shu*, a form of Heat showing a particular affinity for Damp qi) can prevent misdiagnosis and the utilization of warming therapies that could only worsen the patient's condition. Moreover, there are a number of herbal specifics designed to dispel Damp-Heat.

Other applications of illness factor analysis are important only at a preliminary stage of syndrome differentiation and treatment determination. If a patient reports that he fell ill after a fit of rage, or if he is normally prone to be moody and withdrawn, this information will help the doctor locate the visceral system most likely to be involved. (Anger has an affinity with the Liver system, and excessive thought affects the Spleen system. Because I was far from home while in China, and undoubtedly because of personal idiosyncracies, I was often warned by Chinese doctors that I would make myself sick from thinking too much.) But once that step has been taken, eight rubrics and visceral systems analytics are much more useful in diagnosis and therapeutics. Most of the *bingyin*, in fact, play no great part in guiding therapy, and they are seldom given more than lip service in discussions of the *bianzheng lunzhi* process.

Of the cases translated in Chapter 2, for example, only in Case 1 is the illness factor a major consideration, and even there it is doubtful that the identification of the *bingyin* had much influence in guiding therapy. The commentary on the case points out that Spring Warm can be induced by Cold qi (one of the six excesses) taken in the winter or by a Heat excess taken in the spring. In this case the heteropathy was identified as springtime Heat, but this determination was irrelevant to the choice of therapeutic strategies in the case. Other diagnostic methods (eight rubrics, visceral systems, four sectors, and six warps diagnostics) yielded a clear picture of the illness condition (the locations of the Heat repletion, the degree of severity in temporal terms) and provided adequate guides to therapy. The illness factors are identifiable in Cases 2 and 3—the internal factor of dead foetuses and the neither internal nor external factor of excessive eating and drinking, respectively—but in neither case were they crucial to the therapeutic strategies employed.

The idea of illness factors is not new in Chinese medicine, as the dictionary entry cited previously attests. But as it also suggests (when it refers to illness factors and mechanisms together providing for general inferences in a classical source), the relative autonomy of the illness factors as a diagnostic method appears to be quite recent.[32] All basic textbooks now have a chapter on the *bingyin,* where the factors that can induce the appearance of illness are listed and linked up with clinical manifestations and therapeutic techniques. This textual prominence is not matched, however, by much attention to illness factors in clinical work. Doctors in hospital and clinic practice seem to attend very little to the factors that have stimulated the first appearance of symptoms since they have much more powerful analytic methods for the characterization of the illness state and the underlying processes in which pathology has appeared. When I asked doctors in Guangzhou about the *bingyin* in specific cases, they frequently said that I should ask the patient; they had not bothered to inquire since it made no practical difference in the management of the illness.

Possibly the recent elevation of illness factors to a mode of diagnostic analysis prominent in textbooks reflects a comparison with Western medicine, in which action is often organized around the identified cause of the illness. The six excesses and seven emotional states as well as the "epidemic diseases" referred to in the *bingyin* chapters of textbooks can be thought of as causes parallel to the bacterial agents, viruses, and "stressors" of biomedical explanation. But Chinese medical modernizers have yet to organize much practice around these identifiable causes. Some of them see suggestive resemblances between the notion of orthopathic qi and the functions of the immune system, which they emphasize in various larger polemics on the scientificity of traditional medicine. Although this latter approach may seem a more promising route toward the systematic incorporation of the *bingyin* into a modernized Chinese medical theory and practice, for the time being illness factors remain interesting in only a restricted number of syndromes. In other words, only where such illness factors as Wind or Summer-Heat are the most elegant notions with which to characterize a continuing feature of the illness process, and where therapies can be found that are specific against these heteropathic forces, are causes of this kind clinically interesting.

Teachers and textbooks of Chinese medicine constantly emphasize the principle "In treating illness, trace the root." But the casual approach of Chinese doctors to the identification of the *bingyin* in most illnesses reminds us that the root of an illness is not the pathogenic agent that initially triggers it. One difference between illness factors and the illness root is temporal:

---

32. Ibid., p. 274n.

Illness factors can induce symptoms and may become relevant from time to time as heteropathic factors during the course of a long illness; but all illnesses always manifest themselves from a root or source condition. And that condition is always a dynamic relationship among a variety of factors. If we adopt the point of view of the textbook cited previously (not, of course, the only possible view of illness roots), the struggle between orthopathic and heteropathic qi could be seen as the root of an exogenous Heat factor illness such as that of Case 1, whereas the *bingyin* is simply one of the six excesses in evidence for a while shortly before the patient fell ill. The root of an illness is the state of play between yin and yang forces that gives rise to its symptoms. In such a formulation, the yinyang condition exists at the same moment in time with the manifestations it produces. It is not a temporally or mechanically prior factor inducing an illness sequence; rather, it is the hidden condition that continually generates the perceptible forms of the moment.

Illness factor analysis thus takes its place as a limited, not very systematic, and mostly retrospective view of an aspect of the illness course. In a few cases it can strongly influence the doctor's perception and ability to act on the illness; but in general it is more helpful to analyze symptoms through classificatory methods that can elucidate a present root condition or state of play.

Visceral Systems (*Zangfu*) Analysis

> *Visceral systems diagnostic*—one of the basic methods of syndrome differentiation. Taking characteristics of the physiology and pathology of the visceral systems as its foundation, by means of the four examinations and the eight rubrics it differentiates the changes in yin and yang, qi and Blood, depletion and repletion, Cold and Hot, etc., of the five yin visceral systems and the six yang visceral systems to provide a basis for therapy.[33]

The yin and yang visceral systems of function (the *zang* and the *fu*) are a complex of processes that when functioning wholesomely produce the living body. These processes are referred to as physiology (*shengli*). "Pathology" (*bingli*) comprises patterns of disorder that develop in this interdependent array of functional systems, among which the yin and yang visceral systems are preeminent. Both physiology and pathology are immensely complex. Awareness of their common and less common manifestations is fundamental to Chinese medical understanding, and an ability to intervene appropriately in their dynamic relationships is crucial to therapy.

One of the central modern specialties of Chinese medicine, *neike*, or internal medicine, is held to be essentially the same as the teachings on the visceral systems. But analysis of visceral systems functioning is not confined

---

33. Editing Committee, *Zhongyi Dacidian, Jichu Lilun Fence*, s.v. *zangfu bianzheng*.

to internal medicine specialists. It figures prominently in almost every medical college course, not only forming the total content of courses in internal medicine but also filling many pages of foundations texts.

Even so, comprehensive and systematic explanations of how normal physiology might work as a whole are notable for their absence in the literature of Chinese medicine. Rather than an image of "the functional body," for example, organized analogously to the structural body of anatomy (from head to toe, macrofunctions to microfunctions), we get (at best) lists of systems and subsystems, each with its characteristic functions. These are supplemented by discussions of the relations obtaining between pairs of *zang* or *fu*. In spite of a pervasive insistence on the holism of Chinese medicine in general and of visceral systems physiology in particular, no describable whole corresponding to "the body" emerges from the contemporary literature.[34] If such an entity is mentally assembled by Chinese doctors as they develop their skills in practice, none of them appears to have found a means or felt a need to represent it in prose or diagrams. This situation naturally supports the overall point being made here—that practice is more fundamental and comprehensive than written knowledge in the world of Chinese medicine. But it is worth bearing in mind that clinical work always starts from somewhere and that the work of Chinese medicine suggests that strategy need not be planned with a comprehensive "map." As will be shown in this section, symptoms implicate specific visceral systems, each visceral system has explicit relations with functionally "adjacent" systems, and an infinite number of therapeutic paths can be traced using these connections.

Especially because discourse emphasizes the materials needed for forging strategies against pathology over any comprehensive description or representation of normal physiology, I cannot hope to convey much of the complexity of this area of knowledge and practice here.[35] After considering some of the textbook knowledge that well-trained physicians nowadays take to their clinical work, I will discuss the visceral systems dimension of Case 3 in some detail to illustrate the way in which the visceral systems diagnostic can work.

The visceral systems are classified and correlated in Table 4.5. The Triple *Jiao*[36] is sometimes correlated with a sixth "yin visceral system,"

---

34. I explore the apparent absence of a unitary body in Chinese medicine in "Body Contingency and Healing Power in Traditional Chinese Medicine," *Discours Social/Social Discourse* 3, nos. 3–4 (1990–1991):53–70.

35. See Porkert, *Theoretical Foundations,* for an extensive and sophisticated discussion of classical visceral systems imagery, which he translates as "orbisiconography."

36. To help readers recall that anatomy is not at issue in the visceral systems, I capitalize the names of the anatomical organs by which the visceral systems are named (Heart, Lung, etc.). Contemporary explanations of the Triple *Jiao* are discussed in footnote 41 of this chapter; *jiao* is defined in dictionaries as "burning" or "scorching" and has consequently been translated as

Table 4.5 *Zang* and *Fu* Affiliations

Yin Visceral Systems of Function (Zang)	*Yang Visceral Systems of Function* (Fu)
Heart	Small Intestine
Lung	Large Intestine
Spleen	Stomach
Liver	Gallbladder
Kidney	Urinary Bladder
	Triple *Jiao*

the Pericardium, but this is more for numerical symmetry than because the Pericardium has physiological significance parallel to the more conventional list of five *zang*.

Knowledge about the *zang* and *fu* does not simply label and functionally correlate discrete anatomical organs; as has by now been established in the English language literature on Chinese medicine, the visceral systems are functional complexes linking all parts of the body in processes of producing normal and pathological effects. It is these effects (wholesome activity such as growth and expression of emotion as well as illness symptoms) that are rendered comprehensible with reference to the functioning of whole body systems through time and the extension of such functions in space.

In spite of a long-standing reference to anatomical organs in the names of the visceral systems, little confusion between anatomy and Chinese medical physiology (*shenglixue*) is encouraged in the Chinese literature. A recent influential work of theory, *Neijingde Zhexue he Zhongyixuede Fangfa* (The Philosophy of the Inner Canon and the Methods of Chinese Medicine) makes this important dictinction very clear in a passage immediately following a discussion of early Chinese anatomical knowledge:

> In the very distant past, at the same time as people were doing dissections of animal and human bodies, they were also using another kind of research method: This was to holistically observe living bodies, coming to understand, through analyzing the different responses of bodies to differing environmental conditions and external stimuli, the physiological and pathological principles of the human body. The *Inner Canon* mainly relies on this kind of method, at the same time connecting it with knowledge gained from dissections to form the teachings on visceral systems imagery and the circulation tracts.

"burner" by Kaptchuk, among others. Following Sivin, I find the word untranslatable since its physiological function has nothing to do with burning and since it is not one thing, not really an object at all. In addition, its functions and characteristics have varied over the centuries, perhaps more than those of other visceral systems, so a translation reflecting contemporary thinking (e.g., watercourse processing loci) would be very misleading for older uses of the term.

Why does the *Inner Canon* call its study of body physiology and pathology "visceral systems imagery" [*zangxiang*]? Wang Bing of the Tang dynasty explains: "*Xiang* means what can be seen on the outside; it is what we can apprehend" (Wang Bing annotations to *juan* 3.9 of the *Basic Questions*). Zhang Jiebin of the Ming dynasty also considers that "*xiang* is manifest form. Viscera are located on the inside, forms are visible on the outside, thus [the method] is called visceral systems imagery" (*The Classified Canon, juan* 3.2). This tells us that *zang* refers to organs that are concealed [*yincang*] within the *living* body, whereas *xiang* are the functions of inner organs that are manifest on the outside of the body and can be grasped through direct observation. Dead people's inner organs have ceased their activity and have lost their manifest form on the outside of the body. Thus, one can speak of visceral systems imagery only with respect to living organisms; essentially it is relevant only to dynamic states and has nothing to say about dead people. The research emphasis of the teachings on visceral systems imagery of the *Inner Canon* is really the means by which the principles of activity of the human body's inner organs can be inferred from the external signs of the living organism and by which the relationship between images and inner organs can be defined.[37]

The dynamic and relational quality of visceral systems analysis is evident in this text in spite of a modern tendency to reify the organs as discrete anatomical entities. Given the pivotal role that a valorization of anatomical knowledge based on cadaver dissection has played in Western medical history, this author's emphatic distinction between a medicine of living organisms and a structural understanding of dead bodies is not morbid. Rather, it is a central difference that renders the knowledge of Chinese medicine very difficult to translate into biomedical terms. The phenomena investigated in the two sciences are fundamentally different.

This text also provides a clear example of the source-manifestation relationship discussed in Chapter 2 as it is instantiated in visceral systems imagery.[38] The text cites several authoritative sources to the effect that the viscera are invisible sources of forms manifest on the outside of the body; these forms, or *xiang*, can be read for an understanding of internal dynamics. Since symptoms often change throughout the course of an illness, it is evident that neither symptomatic manifestations nor visceral sources are inherently fixed.

Table 4.6 (very simplistically) summarizes visceral systems physiology. Tables of this kind may be designed by teachers for use in introductory

---

37. Liu, *Neijingde Zhexue he Zhongyixuede Fangfa*, p. 144.

38. Liu Changlin is not alone in presenting visceral systems imagery as a means of reading manifestations arising from invisible sources. See also Huang et al., *Zhongyixue Daolun*, pp. 45–46; Zhao, *Zhongyi Jichu Lilun Xiangjie*, pp. 42–43; and Wang Qingqi and Qian Chenghui, eds., *Zhongyi Zangxiangxue* (Shanghai: Shanghai College of Traditional Chinese Medicine, 1987), pp. 1–3.

Table 4.6   The Five Visceral Systems of Function

Governs	Stores	Unfolds In	Affiliated To
HEART SYSTEM			
Blood	*Shen* (vitality)	Vessels Manifests in face Vents at tongue	Small Intestine (which digests and assimilates; separates pure from impure)
LUNG SYSTEM			
Qi Breathing		Skin and body hair Clears away Regulates water-course Vents at nose	Large Intestine (which transmits and carries residues downward)
SPLEEN SYSTEM			
Transmission and transformation Elevates clear fluids Governance of blood flow		Flesh Four limbs Vents at mouth Manifests in lips	Stomach (which receives food)
LIVER SYSTEM			
Dredging and draining Dispersion upward and outward	Blood	Sinews Vents at eyes Manifests in nails	Gallbladder (which stores gall bile)
KIDNEY SYSTEM			
Fluids Marrow Accepts qi	*Jing* (semen)	Bones Manifests in hair Vents at ear, genitals, anus	Urinary Bladder (which stores and excretes urine) Triple *Jiao* (which controls water-course functions)

classes, or students may produce them to review for exams; but less reductive methods of explaining the differing functions and multiple relationships among the visceral systems are much more important. Even a table of this kind, however, impresses one with the complexity of visceral systems physiology.

This summary of visceral systems functions should demonstrate the systemic and functional emphasis of Chinese medical physiology. Perhaps the most clear evidence of the holistic nature of each of the five great systems is in the "unfolds in" column, where each system incorporates parts of the body quite remote from it and stretching from head to toe.[39] No neat symmetry among the systems can be found in tabular presentations of this kind. Although the yin visceral systems (Heart, Lung, Spleen, Liver, and Kidney) are often announced as "solid organs" that store substances, only three have some form of storage listed as a primary function. The yang visceral systems (Small and Large Intestine, Stomach, Gallbladder, Urinary Bladder, and Triple *Jiao*), although reputed not to store substances, do act as reservoirs for gall bile and urine. Other parallels are equally difficult to make. The Heart and Lung, high in the body, are affiliated to the Intestines, low in the body; but the Spleen, Liver, and Kidney systems are affiliated more horizontally to the Stomach, Gallbladder, and Urinary Bladder, respectively. Visceral systems knowledge lacks the symmetrical elegance we would expect from a pure intellectual technology (e.g., Five Phases theory) or from a symbolic or mythic construct. Rather, some complex and deeply historical mix of speculation, experience, inscription, and faithfulness to classic sources can be seen at work.

Each of the five yin systems and the six yang systems that make up the *zangfu* is related to all the others in networks of mutual influence. A disorder appearing in one system can quickly ramify into others and produce symptoms implicating additional visceral systems or even masking the role of the visceral system that is its primary source. Visceral systems analysis in syndrome differentiation must be informed by an awareness of the normal physiological relationships among the systems.

One approach to these relationships takes the ancient form of the Five Phases as its organizing principle. Deng Tietao has argued that relations

---

39. The term *unfolds in* is inspired by observations made by John Hay in an article exploring relationships between Chinese calligraphy theory and medicine ("The Human Body as a Microcosmic Source of Macrocosmic Values in Calligraphy," in Susan Bush and Christian Murck, eds., *Theories of the Arts in China* [Princeton: Princeton University Press, 1983], pp. 74–102). Hay suggests that the verb usually translated as "rules," "dominates," or "governs" (*zhu*) refers to hierarchical relations among the viscera that are not imperiously causal. Thus, "the heart rules the blood and vessels" might be better translated as "the heart is chief among the viscera with respect to Blood and the vessels." In this work Hay explores a logic of dense centers and dispersed peripheries that is very suggestive for medicine. Such a model of interlinked physiological systems, each with its own dense generative core, would not demand that a final decision be made between viscera as anatomical organs and viscera as functional systems, for example.

What is required to understand the semantic range of the verb *zhu* is a full grasp of the physiological and pathological relationships among the visceral systems as well as a social and historical investigation of such topics as Chinese rulership. For approaches to the latter, see James Hevia, "Guest Ritual and Interdomainal Relations in the Late Qinq" (Ph.D. diss., University of Chicago, 1986); and Angela Zito, "Grand Sacrifice as Text/Performance" (Ph.D. diss., University of Chicago, 1989). No single translation will do for the range of meanings of *zhu* in Chinese medicine. I have kept the conventional translation "governs" where control of some kind is meant and have used "unfolds in" where ramification is obviously involved.

among the visceral systems can be analyzed quite meticulously in Five Phases terms. He shows how the correlations of Liver to Wood, Heart to Fire, Spleen to Earth, Lung to Metal, and Kidney to Water involve the visceral systems in concrete interactions of the "production, conquest, accroachment, and violation" types. This ancient technology of Five Phases dynamics thus provides a powerful tool for analyzing pathology as well as for predicting the direction that pathological changes will take.[40]

The five yin visceral systems are functionally superior to the five yang visceral systems with which they are correlated in the sense that they are relatively active and dominant with respect to the passive and subordinate activity of their yang partners. The one additional yang visceral system, the Triple *Jiao,* is held in contemporary thinking to coordinate some of the activities of these five dyads, especially those relating to movement of nutrients and fluids in a vertical direction (the watercourse, *shuidao*) through the body.[41]

The conventional yinyang classification of the *zang* and *fu* is said to derive from their relative positions in bodily space. The yin viscera are classified as yin because they are more "inner" than the yang viscera. They are also relatively solid because they "store nutritive essences [*jingqi*] but don't drain; hence they fill but cannot be too full." The yang visceral systems, by contrast, are hollow; they "transmit and transform things but don't store them, hence they can be too full but they do not [normally] fill up."[42] Obviously these maxims are more a reference to the general proclivities of the two types of visceral system than to their concrete functions, as has been seen in Table 4.6.

---

40. See Porkert, *Theoretical Foundations,* pp. 50–54, for the physiological and pathological relations among the Five Phases; and Deng Tietao, *"Zhongyi Wuxing Xueshuode Bianzhengfa Yinsu"* (Dialectical Factors in Chinese Medicine's Teachings on the Five Phases); and *"Zai Lun Zhongyide Wuxing Xueshuode Bianzhengfa Yinsu"* (Another Consideration of Dialectical Factors in Chinese Medicine's Teachings on the Five Phases), both essays reprinted in his *Xueshuo Tantao yu Linzheng.*

41. Unlike the other visceral systems, the Triple *Jiao* is not named after an internal organ recognizable in anatomical terms. Of course, this is not much of a problem for a purely functional approach to the visceral systems since the physiological role of the Triple *Jiao,* at least in contemporary thinking, is quite clear—it governs the movement of fluids downward through the body and is divisible into three regions of fluid management, the Upper, Middle, and Lower *Jiao.* The first patient mentioned in Case 2 benefited from an analysis involving the Triple *Jiao*—she was treated with a formula that ordinarily facilitates bowel movements by treating Stomach and Intestine systems, with the addition of "magnolia bark and magnesium sulphate, [which] can lubricate the Lower *Jiao.*" For Western commentators who like to think in terms of a single "material substrate" for every named group of functions, the Triple *Jiao* is a troubling anomaly. If, however, visceral systems physiology is looked at from the point of view of those who understand the Triple *Jiao* as a diagnostically coherent complex of *functions,* it is rather surprising that the rest of the visceral systems should each be named after only one organ.

42. These formulae from the *Basic Questions (juan* 3, sec. 11) for differentiating *zang* from *fu* are often cited in general textbooks. Cf. Beijing College, *Zhongyixue Jichu,* p. 10.

A 1978 national textbook describes their relationship as follows:

The main relationship between the yin visceral systems (*zang*) and the yang visceral systems (*fu*) is an internal-external relationship. The *zang* are yin; the *fu* are yang. Yang dominates the outside; yin dominates the inside. One *fu* and one *zang*, one yang and one yin—they are coordinated with each other and are woven together through their circulation tracts to form an interior-exterior relationship.[43]

The relationship between any yin visceral system and its yang partner—for example, that between the Spleen and Stomach systems—is hierarchical. In a manner somewhat counterintuitive for dynamic yinyang logics, the yin partner is more active and initiating than the yang partner; if Stomach system functions show a disorder, a prior pathology of the Spleen system should immediately be suspected. Even though this hierarchy of powers is consistent with the innerness of sources relative to (external) manifestations, it seems to reverse the relationships in which yang, "the active aspect," initiates and yin, "the structive aspect," completes.[44] This reversal suggests that the Chinese medical body, despite all its dynamic temporality, still has a certain bias toward solidity and structiveness. Emerging from visceral systems descriptions is an image of physiology in which the solid yin viscera are produced and reproduced by the processing activities of the hollow yang viscera, yet they become the "dense centers" that govern and unfold in those same processes as well as in many others. That functional systems classed as yin have a greater claim to medical interest, and a greater role to play in normal physiology, than the more external yang systems suggests that the human body may enjoy a rather stolid and conservative mode of being compared to, for example, the "wind and water" of the Chinese science of siting[45] or the relation of ruler and ministers posited in Confucian literary theory.[46]

When visceral systems diagnosis is used, both spatial and temporal dimensions of clinical problems are involved. Indeed, visceral systems analysis presents an elegant example of a complex analytic method that does not separate time from space. The temporal and spatial qualities of a pattern of symptoms are talked about together, and time and space are not idealized into abstract dimensions. Each of the "five great systems" has a certain spatiotemporal character. For example, the Lung system is relatively high and external, and its illnesses are (generally speaking) short and not life

43. Ibid., p. 21. In this extract yin and yang are used both as conventional labels (the yin visceral systems) and as clarification of the dynamic relationship between *zang* and *fu* systems as well as between the interior and exterior. These usages sound similar but are logically distinct.

44. Porkert, *Theoretical Foundations,* pp. 13–31.

45. Stephen J. Bennett, "Patterns of the Sky and Earth," *Chinese Science* 3 (1978):1–26.

46. Liu Hsieh, *The Literary Mind and the Carving of Dragons* (New York: Columbia University Press, 1959). This is a sixth-century work of literary theory.

threatening. The Kidney system, by contrast, is relatively low and internal; it is often responsible for serious chronic illnesses that are very difficult to cure. Because the functions belonging to each visceral system are spread throughout the body, their spatial quality is not simply a result of the placement of what Porkert calls the "material substrate," the anatomical organ from which the system takes its name. Rather the time and space qualities attributed to each system derive from the assumption that with time a disorder will move inward and downward. Thus, late-stage inner illnesses are by definition serious ones.

Physiological patterns of influence through time move along certain dimensions—in and out (floating, *fu,* and sinking, *chen*), up and down. Specific forms of transformation accompany these movements: generation, distribution, storage, and conversion of substances (*jing,* qi, Blood, fluids, *shen*).[47] Many introductory medical texts take up the question of bodily substances under the broader heading of the visceral systems. In one case, *jing,* qi, Blood, and fluids are called the "material basis of the functional activities of the visceral systems."[48] In another, they are defined as "important substances for the maintenance of the human body's life activities."[49] The relationship between substances and the locations at which they are transformed is not simply one of contents to vessel. Indeed, it is doubtful whether the visceral systems could be said to have any significant existence for Chinese medicine apart from the substances that transform through them. Huang Jitang hints at this (at least as far as qi is concerned) in one of his discussions of the philosophical roots of Chinese medical knowledge:

> Chinese medicine insists on the doctrine that qi is the one source. Qi is the world's root, heaven and earth and the myriad things are all made from qi, and human bodily life is also a product of the movement and development of qi. The *Basic Questions* (*juan* 8.25) says, "Heaven and earth mingled qi, bounded it and called it human" [*Tiandi he qi ming zhi yue ren*]. . . . The human body depends on the nurturance of the natural world and obeys natural principles for its life. "Living qi pervades the Cosmos." Thus, in medicine it is necessary to explore the principles of the body's physiological and pathological changes following the principles of change in Heaven, Earth, and the myriad things. . . .

---

47. See Sivin, *Traditional Medicine;* and Porkert, *Theoretical Foundations,* for extensive discussions of the denotative and connotative range of these medical terms. The substantial nature (or the material base) of these physiological entities is a major issue as Chinese medicine modernizes. Here and in other general contexts I tend to call all these entities substances, not because they have an unproblematic material nature, but because I wish to emphasize their physiological reality within the idiom of Chinese medicine. Their relative degrees of presence or absence, force or yielding, produce concrete healthy activity or illness. In Chinese medical discourse they are not, or at least not yet, "mere" theoretical constructs, spirits, or abstract functions.

48. Office of the 1977 Physicians, *Zhongyi Jichuxue,* p. 118.

49. Zhao, *Zhongyi Jichu Lilun Xiangjie,* p. 100.

The unceasing motion and changes of qi are called "qi transformation" [*qihua*]. Qi transformation produces the myriad things and the human body. The *Basic Questions* (*juan* 3.9) says, "Qi mingles and form emerges." Effects [*shiwu*] that have form all come into being through a gathering together of subtle qi. But not only is the orderliness of effects that have form relatively transient, their material form [*xingti*] can also disperse as qi transforms, or they can transform into a different effect. The *Basic Questions* (*juan* 19.68) says, "Elevation and descension, inward and outward movement are never without their thing (*qi*); thus, the thing is the place of generation and transformation. If the thing disperses, they are divided; generation and transformation cease." A "thing" is an effect with a form; it is the site of the generation and transformation of qi. Elevation and descension and inward and outward movement are the manifest form of qi transformation. The thing dispersing refers to a dispersion of the original gathered state of qi, and its process of generation and transformation thereby comes to an end, turning into a different form of gathered qi. Thus it says, "The generation of effects comes from transformation; the expansion of effects comes from change. When [generative] transformation and [expansive] change both become attenuated, this is what maturation and decay come from." The human body is also a "thing" [in which] "qi mingles and form emerges." In the course of life there is continuous qi transformation, continuous elevation and descension, inward and outward movement. The study of the human body, this process of up and down, inward and outward qi transformation, is Chinese medical physiology. If the qi transformation of the body loses its regularity and elevation and descension, inward and outward movement are disordered, its steady state is injured, and a stable equilibrium cannot be maintained, so disease occurs. The study of these processes of losing regularity is Chinese medical pathology.[50]

This description of Chinese medical physiology and pathology could hardly be further from anatomy. The viscera are highly contingent sites at which regular transformations of qi take place. Thus, the Lung system has a certain responsibility for combining the clear qi of breathing with the refined nutritive essences derived from food and the primordial qi sent upward from lower visceral systems to produce defensive qi, which maintains a barrier against invasive heteropathies. From one point of view, the "lungs" are not more than the locus of responsibility for this complex of functions.

This being the case, it is easy to see how pathological changes in physiological relationships can affect the wholesome interdependence of visceral positions. That is, one system may become overactive and unduly stimulate activity in the visceral systems "downstream" from it; or a visceral system may become depleted and allow overactivity in systems that under normal conditions are subject to its constraint. Forms of heteropathic qi such as

50. Huang et al., *Zhongyixue Daolun*, pp. 43–44.

Heat, Cold, Fire, and Wind tend to move along lines of normal physiological influence among the viscera and must be attacked with an awareness
of these more or less stable dynamic relations.

Each of the *zang* and *fu* pairs is, then, located along the dimensions of
in and out, up and down, and manages certain modes of substance transformation. In general, each visceral system can be differentiated from the
others with reference to these characteristics. If we compare, for instance,
the Spleen system of functions with that of the Liver system, the following
summaries are typical: "The Spleen is located in the Middle *Jiao*. Its main
functions are to be in charge of transmission and assimilation, elevate clear
[substances], and govern [the flow of] Blood fluid."[51] "The Liver is located
in the sides. Its main physiological function is to be in charge of dredging
and draining and to store Blood."[52]

The locations cited refer to more than the anatomical position of the
organs. Location in the Middle *Jiao* implies a relationship to the watercourse aspects of physiology managed by the Triple *Jiao* and hence an intimate involvement with up and down motion of fluids. Location in the sides,
by contrast, implies a "reservoir" position not central to alimentary up and
down motion.

The activities of the Spleen and Liver denoted by the terms transmission
and assimilation (*yunhua*) and dredging and draining (*shuxie*) are not self-
evident even in Chinese; the words have a specialized physiological reference. An examination of more detailed accounts of the functional roles of
these two viscera shows that the Spleen system concerns itself with nutritive
fluids such as Blood, whereas the Liver system disseminates qi and other
relatively yang substances such as *shen* (vitality) or, in pathology, Fire and
Wind. Thus, these two terms show the Spleen and Liver to be similar in
the direction of movement they govern (outward throughout the whole
body rather than solely up and down) but different in the substances they
disseminate.[53]

The Liver nevertheless has a relationship to Blood as its reservoir,
whereas the Spleen has a relationship to the qi that functions to control the
flow of Blood within the vessels. The yinyang logic of these relationships
belies any sense of paradox in this. The Liver system can be yang relative to
qi (active and initiating) and yin relative to Blood (providing a passive recep-
tacle for fluid substance). And the Spleen can be yin in that it has a strong
relationship to "moist" Blood and fluids while being yang in that it remains

---

51. Beijing College, *Zhongyixue Jichu*, p. 12.

52. Ibid., p. 13.

53. But note that the Spleen also has an important role in the up-down movement of digestion,
giving its cyclic transformative function a different emphasis in terms of its whole system than the
"dredging and draining" activities of the Liver.

"dry" itself and acts like qi (in the classic Blood/qi relation) as it impels them outward through the body.

The Spleen's involvement in the watercourse functions is specified here; it elevates clear substances. This stands in parallel to one of the major functions of the Stomach, its yang partner in an interior-exterior relation. The Stomach governs descension of turbid substances. The two visceral systems together are crucial to both the up-down and the outward digestion and distribution of food and nutritive essences.

Both the interdependence of visceral systems and the way in which they are explained as a system of differences are important for the process of diagnosis. The differences among visceral systems enable doctors to find the locus of an illness, the functional position of the root of a disorder. This locus of disorder is operationally defined as the visceral system or systems that should be most aggressively treated to effect a thorough recovery. It follows that the manifold forms of possible physiological interdependence must be understood if the whole illness and all its actual or possible pathological effects are to be controlled.

This is not to say that diagnosis does not concern itself with causal origins of illness within the body. Sources operating in the present are a major concern in syndrome differentiation. But all such evaluation orients itself first and last to therapeutic action. Unless the symptomatic manifestations of an illness are very acute, necessitating an interim intervention at a more superficial level, the visceral system root of a disorder is not other than the system (or relationship between systems) that should be treated. And successful treatment demonstrates that the visceral system the doctor singled out was indeed the one most responsible for producing the illness.

The richness of explanations, metaphors, and images arising from (and no doubt informing) visceral systems physiology cannot be overstated. The relationships that are realized in physiology and verified in effective practice are a form of technical knowledge; although they are fully understood only by Chinese medical clinicians, they are very suggestive as models for reading other domains of Chinese knowledge and practice. In this book, however, these possibilities will go unexplored. Instead this section will conclude with a consideration of the way in which a doctor traces the root in the practical process of syndrome differentiation through the application of visceral system analytics to specific illnesses.

Any such method must rely on simplifying mnemonics and rules of thumb that can reduce the wilderness of influential relationships known as physiology to a manageable set of frequently seen connections between effects. Table 4.7 is an example of such a simplification from a specialized internal medicine text.

The relationships summarized in a table such as this are helpful only for the commonly encountered clusters of effects; greatness in clinical work

Table 4.7   Syndrome Differentiation and Therapy Use in Heart Illnesses

Symptom Categories	Depletion Syndromes		Repletion Syndromes		
	1	2	1	2	3
Illness mechanisms	Heart yang depleted / Heart qi insufficient	Heart yin depleted / Loss of Heart Blood	Mucus heteropathy / Mucus Fire harrying inside, bypassing Pericardium	Retained fluids heteropathy / Retained fluids back flowing upward, obstructing Heart yang	Blood stasis / Blood stasis blocking reticular tracts
Mental state	Calm, tired / Body cold / Dislikes moving / Face puffy	Emotionally hypersensitive / Suspicious / Face lusterless	Dementia / Speech lacks sense to the extent of raving	Avoidance of Cold / Ticcing / Or expectorating mucus	Sporadic pain / Restlessness / Nails purplish green
Palpitations	Hollow palpitations	Palpitations when agitated	Agitation when palpitating / Heat agitation in chest	Depression and palpitation / Or difficulty breathing	Intermittent palpitations with aching
Sleep	Prefers bed rest	Excessive dreaming / Little sleep	Sleepless / Disturbing, confused, or even manic dreams	Sleeplessness from difficult breathing	Sleeplessness from aching
Perspiration	Frequent spontaneous perspiration	Frequent night sweats			Perspiration when pain acute
Tongue, tongue coating	Pale white	Tongue pink or scarce, coating on tip of tongue	Tongue red / Coating dry and yellow	Tongue moist / Coating white and greasy	Tongue dark red, with purple macules / Coating scarce
Pulse image	Empty and weak or large with hollow center	Small and accelerated	Smooth and accelerated	Sunken and rough or small and smooth	Rough
Therapy	Supplement Heart qi / Warm Heart yang	Nourish Heart yin	Clear Heart of accumulated mucus	Transform retained fluid / Expel mucus	Enliven Blood / Move stasis / Harmonize reticular tracts
Formulae	Cultivate Heart Decoction / Four Backflows Decoction	Lord of Heaven Bolster Heart Pills / Cinnabar Spirit-calming Pills	Clear Qi—Transform Mucus Pills / Mica Rollaway Mucus Pills	Chinaroot-Cassia-Baishu-Licorice Decoction / Lead Away Mucus Decoction	Blood Site Drive Out Stasis Decoction

SOURCE: Adapted from Shanghai College of Traditional Chinese Medicine, ed., *Zhongyi Neikexue* (Shanghai: Shanghai Science and Technology Press, 1982) p. 7.

consists in being able to refer partly anomalous situations back to general physiology for a fuller understanding of atypical symptom clusters. In foundations texts, then, chapters on visceral systems diagnostic analysis tend to present a lengthy discussion of the general physiological character of each visceral system, along with lists of symptoms often associated with that visceral system.[54]

A typical foundations textbook entry on syndrome differentiation in Spleen and Stomach system illnesses begins with a brief review of the differentiating features of this *zang-fu* dyad:

> The Spleen is in charge of [*zhu*] transmission and assimilation [*yunhua*] as well as the governance of Blood [flow]. The Stomach is in charge of the acceptance and decomposition [of food]. The Spleen and Stomach are in an exterior-interior relation to each other. The Spleen elevates [substances], and the Stomach causes [them] to descend. The two systems are Dry and Wet in a relation of mutual assistance, together accomplishing the ingestion, digestion, and distribution of [nutrients from] food and drink. They are a source of the generation and transformation of qi and Blood and the root of the "latter heaven" [the environmental element in growth and development].[55]

The passage goes on to list classes of symptoms often found in Spleen-Stomach disorders: (1) Damp swelling and distension resulting from obstructions in digestive processes; (2) nausea, vomiting, and diarrhea resulting from loss of regularity in ascension and descension functions; and (3) hemorrhages resulting from inadequate qi and Blood.

A useful rule is then offered: The Spleen system suffers more often from depletion syndromes, and the Stomach system is more often afflicted with repletion. Spleen-Stomach depletion is often seen as a loss of yang qi and yin fluids; repletions in these paired systems are most often brought about by attacks of Cold, Damp, Dryness, Heat, or accumulations of food. These generalizations having been made, ten major syndromes primarily attributable to Spleen or Stomach system dysfunction are listed and described, with an enumeration of their characteristic complexes of symptoms.

This is a typical format for an introduction to a visceral system diagnostic; it indicates clearly the way in which rules of thumb and short lists of commonly seen syndromes can be generated from a review of Spleen and Stomach system physiology. The doctor is warned to consider these systems when he encounters digestive obstructions, swellings, nausea, diar-

---

54. Internal medicine texts for specialists, in contrast, are often organized according to syndrome name, suggesting that syndrome differentiation can be done in a preliminary way before the real technicalities of visceral systems analysis are engaged. See Shanghai College of Traditional Chinese Medicine, ed., *Zhongyi Neikexue* (Shanghai: Shanghai Science and Technology Press, 1982).

55. Beijing College, *Zhongyixue Jichu,* p. 116.

rhea, and internal hemorrhage. He also receives advice on how the pathological roles of Spleen and Stomach can be differentiated from each other
along depletion/repletion lines.

Actual diagnosis, of course, involves constant critical evaluation of the
visceral processes that produce symptoms. It is far from being a static classification procedure requiring only the location of the appropriate cell in a vast
taxonomic table of illnesses. Thus, in Case 3, Stomachache, the symptoms
would seem to have been generated from the Stomach or Small Intestine
since it was known when the patient walked into the clinic that he had a
duodenal ulcer. Dr. Zhong's commentary, however, implicates the Liver
system, and analysis of the first prescription used also shows an emphasis on
treatment of the Liver. (Nine of the eleven drugs used were specific in their
ability to affect the Liver. Six were directed at the Stomach, and four affected
the Spleen. Many of the drugs used are known to target more than one
visceral system, hence the overlap.)

It must be remembered that the Stomach is a yang visceral system (*fu*).
The first step when encountering symptoms in such hollow organs is to
trace the illness back to the yin visceral system, the *zang*, that rules the *fu*
involved. In Stomach illnesses this would be the Spleen. But since none of
the key symptoms implicating the Spleen system were remarked in this case
and even though the Spleen was necessarily involved, the true *zang* source
of the illness could well be elsewhere. Thus, there were only minor problems with swelling and distension or nausea and diarrhea and no sign of
hemorrhage. In addition, recall the eight rubrics analysis of these symptoms
cited previously:

Pain piercing	Repletion, interior, yang
Pain aggravated by hand pressure	Repletion, yang
Heartburn	(Qi) repletion
Sour vomitus	(Qi) repletion
Black stools	(Blood) repletion
Tongue slightly red	Hot
Tongue coating greasy	Cold
Tongue coating yellow	Interior, Hot
Tulse tense and thready	Cold, yin

This is a picture in which interior repletion is the major consistent impression given; and we have seen that the Stomach has an affinity for repletion syndromes. There is no marked sign of Spleen depletion to match the
obvious Stomach repletion present, but it would be safe to assume some
form of depletion in the Spleen system simply because its proper function of
transmission and transformation has failed to prevent Stomach repletion. It
remains to determine whether another yin visceral system has been a source
of the disorder of the Spleen.

An important factor is that the pain was stable in location and of long duration. This suggests that Stomach symptoms might have been produced through a relationship less spatially and temporally immediate than that between the Spleen and Stomach. This relationship would most likely be between yin viscera since they functionally govern the (relatively passive) activities of the yang viscera; the Liver system is immediately implicated. Foundations texts emphasize that the clearing and draining action of the Liver has two main aspects: One is emotional, in pathology involving deviations of the seven emotional states, and the other is digestive, through the production from excess Liver qi of the bile stored in the Gallbladder visceral system and used in Stomach digestive functions. Given the commentary in this case, Dr. Zhong considered both aspects to be involved in producing the long-term stasis of which the duodenal ulcer was only a symptom. In addition, the pulse image (strung, small) is one strongly associated with Liver system disorders.

Since the differences among the visceral systems depend in large part on the body substances they process, it was necessary in this case to determine which of several possible substances—for example, Blood, qi, food matter, Mucus (*tanyin*)—had slowed and collected to produce the area of pain. In deciding that both Blood and qi were stagnating, Dr. Zhong was no doubt influenced by the long duration of the illness (no matter which stoppage came first, the other substance would soon be influenced because of the intimate dependence of Blood and qi on each other) and by the mixed Blood and qi repletion symptoms discernible through eight rubrics analysis. He treated both Blood and qi stagnation in this case by using a number of drugs specific for moving and regulating qi (nine out of eleven in the first prescription), most of which also targeted the Liver. Thus, the Liver's function of dispersing qi (matched by its characteristic of abhorring stagnation) was being improved in an effort to influence all the visceral systems involved toward more vigorous activity in moving fluid substances.[56] In the words of the commentators on the case, "Although Blood was being treated, the movement encouraged was that of qi."

Whether Stomach, Spleen, or Liver became ill first is not the main point here. As already argued, the root of the illness is not a temporally prior cause; rather, it is the locus where intervention promises to have the most far-reaching beneficial effects. Consequently, yang viscera are seldom treated alone, being relatively passive; the dominant yin partner of the yang visceral system that is manifestly affected, or another yin visceral system having important relations with the yinyang visceral pair directly involved, is dealt with. In this case Dr. Zhong may not have considered the Liver system to be ill at all; its usual physiological activities simply may have been inadequate

---

56. Ibid., pp. 13–14.

to break up the area of stasis that developed (for whatever reason) in the Stomach system. This suggests another sense for the notion of tracing the root, one in which pathological phenomena are traced back through normal physiological relationships to a point where intervention in an essentially wholesome system can produce therapeutic results in disordered viscera that are physiologically downstream from it.

Here I have suggested that visceral system analytics rely on a masterful grasp of the whole array of physiological processes while making use of a few rules of thumb that direct attention toward key symptoms (swelling, hemorrhage) and ruling relationships (such as that between the Spleen and Stomach or among the five yin visceral systems). Quite likely, however, a great many other considerations come into play. I suspect, for example, that Dr. Zhong looked for Liver system involvement in Case 3 not so much because of textbook relations between the Liver and the Spleen-Stomach systems but because the Liver is particularly involved with the emotions. He may have been influenced by popular Chinese attitudes linking eating, commensality and ritual food exchanges with family and community emotional life or by Western notions transmitted through medical comparisons about the relationship of ulcers to stress.

Many well-known doctors habitually emphasize the role of one or another visceral system in producing a wide variety of symptoms. Quite possibly Dr. Zhong considered the Liver system to be more central and more powerful in general than other visceral systems, and this conviction was reflected in most of his therapeutic strategies. This is not seen as an illegitimate bias in medical knowledge; since all visceral systems are functionally connected, action on one will eventually embroil all the others. Therefore, if a doctor continues to get good results by "blaming" one system for most illnesses, this is an interesting and admirable approach even if it contradicts the careful evenhandedness of committee-generated textbooks.

Four Sectors (*Wei Qi Ying Xue*) Analysis

Four sectors analysis: a method of syndrome differentiation in Warm illnesses originated by Ye Tianshi [Ye Guitiao, 1667–1746] of the Qing dynasty. It divides the pathological process by which exogenous Warm illnesses go from shallow to deep or from slight to serious into the four stages of defensive qi sector [*wei qi fen*], active qi sector [*qi fen*], constructive qi sector [*ying fen*], and Blood sector [*xue fen*], each having its corresponding syndrome characteristics. Illnesses that gradually develop according to [the sequence] *wei, qi, ying, xue* are a "following" type of transmission; those that rapidly develop from the defensive sector to the constructive and Blood sectors [thus skipping the active qi sector] are an "opposing" type of transmission. Among these, syndromes that manifest at the same time in two sectors are called "simultaneous" illnesses. The defensive qi sector is the stage of exterior syndromes [as determined by the eight rubrics], and [its] various illness factors [*bingyin*] should thus be clearly distinguished. The active qi sector is the stage of dominant Heat, so one should determine whether Heat heteropathy is concentrated there or not; if [the heteropathy] is classed as Damp Heat, it is necessary to distinguish the relative weighting of Heat and Damp. If the illness heteropathy is even more deeply settled into the constructive qi or Blood sectors, this is the stage of injury to yin and inducement of internal obstructions or hemorrhages, and one must clearly distinguish the illness changes of the various visceral systems, for example, Heart, Liver, Kidney. Therefore, the meaning (*neirong*) of this diagnostic method is established with reference to illness factors, stages, positions, transmissions, and degrees of illness change.[57]

The four sectors diagnostic described in this dictionary entry is that emphasized by the Warm Illnesses school of thought, which is an active scholarly faction in contemporary discourse. Warm Illnesses scholars set themselves off from, and sometimes attempt syntheses with, the teachings of the Cold Damage school. Both schools of thought adapt their methods particularly to febrile diseases induced by external heteropathies, but they differ on more than the quality (Hot or Cold) of the heteropathies concerned. Although the historical relationship between these two groups of scholar-doctors will not be explored here, aspects of it can be glimpsed in their parallel categories of knowledge and modes of practice: four sectors and six warps diagnostics.

The modes of analysis discussed up to this point have already revealed qualitative, spatial, and temporal dimensions in the characterization of illness. Each of the methods considered combines qualitative classifications with inferences about the functional location and the stage of development of the disorder. Arguably, eight rubrics and illness factors analysis are strongly qualitative, whereas visceral systems analysis emphasizes the position of the disorder in a dynamic network. Although a temporal component is taken for granted in these three methods, many clinicians prefer to think in terms of four sectors analysis and six warps analysis when they need a finer articulation of the stage, progress, and prognosis of an illness. Both of these latter methods rely on characterizations generated through eight rubrics and visceral systems analysis, and they cannot really be used independently of these qualitative and spatial judgments.[58]

The temporal emphasis of four sectors analysis is evident in the definition just provided from *Zhongyi Dacidian, Jichu Lilun Fence* (Unabridged Dictionary of Chinese Medicine, Theoretical Foundations Volume), which privileges the centrality of "stages" of illness in its rather wide-ranging

---

57. Editing Committee, *Zhongyi Dacidian, Jichu Lilun Fence*, s.v. *wei qi ying xue bianzheng*.
58. Office of the 1977 Physicians, *Zhongyi Jichuxue*, pp. 164–165.

characterization of the method. These are stages of a pathological process particularly characteristic of exogenous illness, and "each [has] its corresponding syndrome characteristics." Thus, as foundations textbooks also point out, "*wei, qi, ying,* and *xue* are the general categories for the four syndrome types of Warm and Hot illnesses, and they also represent four different stages of superficiality or depth, slightness or severity in the developmental processes of such illnesses."[59] These careful definitional statements emphasize the categorical function and the temporal reference of the four sectors. But the four sectors also have a spatial dimension and a substantive reference that are more complex. A lengthier description from a Warm Illnesses text introduces the method in more detail:

> Four sectors syndrome differentiation was originated by Ye Tianshi. In the course of a long period of clinical experience, Master Ye discovered that the whole developmental course of illnesses of the Warm type had a certain regularity [*guilu*], such that their pathological changes were mainly manifested as loss of functional regulation or damage to the substance of defensive qi, active qi, constructive qi, or Blood. In the different developmental stages of the illness process, because the locations of these pathological injuries were different, their manifestation as syndromes also varied. In Warm illnesses, the entire development and evolution of the illness process amounted to the mutual influence of pathological changes in defensive, active, and constructive qi and Blood [substances and sectors] and concrete responses to their transmission [from sector to sector] and transformation [of substances] into each other. Hence Master Ye's theoretical categories of defensive qi, active qi, constructive qi, and Blood are used in Warm Illnesses analysis to guide the process of differentiating syndromes and deploying therapy.[60]

Although the "locations of . . . pathological injuries" are claimed here to determine the clinical manifestations of the syndrome, there is no detailed way to focus on discrete locations using the four sectors. Of the four, only defensive qi is sometimes strongly associated with a "part" of the body (i.e. its surface): "At the outset of a Warm illness, the disorder is in the superficial exterior, where it produces a syndrome of the defensive sector. As it progresses it generates a syndrome in the active qi sector, then one in the constructive qi sector, finally producing a syndrome in the Blood sector."[61] Yet in other contexts defensive qi substance is not confined to the superficial exterior; rather, it functions throughout the body "flowing outside the vessels,"[62] and it is therefore hard to conceive of a discrete location for

59. Beijing College, *Zhongyixue Jichu,* p. 131.

60. Nanjing College of Traditional Chinese Medicine, ed., *Wenbingxue* (Shanghai: Shanghai Science and Technology Press, 1979), p. 10.

61. Guangdong College of Traditional Chinese Medicine, *Zhongyi Zhenduanxue* (Shanghai: Shanghai Science and Technology Press, 1982), p. 140.

62. Editing Committee, *Zhongyi Dacidian, Jichu Lilun Fence,* s.v. *weiqi.*

"injuries" to defensive qi. Active and contructive qi and Blood are even less easy to anatomically localize than defensive qi. In addition, when the four sectors are thought of as substances (as the preceding extract quite explicitly suggests they can be), rather than types of function, they are thoroughly interwoven throughout the body.[63] In spite of these apparent contradictions, a language of spatial distinction and substantial quantity is quite important to the practical use of the four sectors. Very little sense can be made of contemporary four sectors analysis as a whole unless the functional, substantive, spatial, temporal, and categorical possibilities built into the four terms *wei, qi, ying,* and *xue* are all considered.

Perhaps the broadest sense of these terms is as category headings under which symptoms (*zheng₂*) can be filed. Because the workings of these categories cannot be grasped except as they function in a whole analytic system, the "meaning" of each category heading is nothing less than a contingent position within the whole set of analytic and practical understandings associated with it in the Warm Illnesses school. For this reason, definitions of these terms can be only partial and preliminary. The categorical, temporal, and symptomatic affiliations of each sector as well as key indices for differential diagnosis are summarized in Table 4.8. An introductory textbook that is widely used in college-level Warm Illnesses courses first characterizes the sectors in these terms and then differentiates them and explores their physiological dynamics with reference to the character of *wei, qi, ying,* and *xue* as vital substances.[64]

Defensive qi is a yang form of qi that moves throughout the body outside the circulation tracts and has the specialized function of protecting against invasion by heteropathic qi. Contemporary discourse assigns a relatively superficial location to defensive qi:

> The *Divine Pivot, juan* 7:47, says, "*Wei* qi is that which warms the interstices of the flesh, tones the skin, fills out the gaps of the muscles, and manages opening and closing." And the *Plain Questions* [*juan* 1.3] [says], "Yang is that which protects the outside so it will be solid." So we know that *wei* qi mainly spreads out over the body's muscular exterior and has such functions

---

63. Nanjing College, *Wenbingxue,* p. 11. See Sivin, *Traditional Medicine,* pp. 147–164, for a helpful introduction to the history of qi and other vital substances. For the purpose of understanding the early sources, he remarks, "The difference [between Blood and qi], like that of other vital substances, is aspectual, not material" (p. 153). The modern transformation of the functional forces aspectually described in the medical classics as qi, Blood, *jing,* and so on into material substances theoretically conformable with anatomy is by no means easy or complete. Contradictions have continued to emerge, and many of these are particularly evident in the Warm Illnesses specialty.

64. Nanjing College, *Wenbingxue,* p. 11.

Table 4.8   Preliminary Characterization of the Four Sectors

Sector	Illness Stage	Clinical Expressions	Key Symptoms
Defensive qi	Initial	Fever; slight intolerance of cold, and wind; headache; little or no perspiration; cough, dry mouth, and thirst; thin white tongue coating, tip and sides of tongue red; pulse floating and accelerated	Fever with intolerance of cold
Active qi	Pursuant to defensive qi sector syndromes	Heat dominant in yang brilliance systems, whole body feels hot, intolerance of heat rather than cold; much perspiration; thirst with a desire for cool drinks; tongue coating dry and yellow; pulse floating and accelerated or swollen and large	Fever; lack of cold intolerance; thirst; yellow tongue coating
Constructive qi	After defensive and active sector illnesses or an original illness	Whole-body fever worse at night; dry mouth but no thirst; restlessness and agitation; occasional delirium; Heat macules, red to crimson tongue; pulse small and accelerated	Fever worse at night; crimson agitation and delirium
Blood	Developed from constructive qi sector illnesses	Whole body fever, hyper-irritability; mania; tongue deep crimson; vomiting blood, nosebleeds, blood in urine and stools; draining ulcerations	Deep crimson tongue and bleeding

as warming and nourishing muscle and skin, regulating the opening and closing of sweat pores, and repelling external heteropathies.[65]

---

65. Ibid. The almost perfect correspondence between defensive qi and the bodily exterior is a modern simplification of what was once a more complex situation. Cf. Sivin, *Traditional Medicine,* pp. 147–164. In contemporary medical writing efforts are made not to contradict the structural features of a more or less Western anatomical body. Although everyone knows that qi cannot be reduced to the anatomical categories of Western medicine, some appear to be feeling a pressure to coordinate its functional distributions with the structural features of a body that, although its history is Western, is increasingly seen in China as scientific, natural, and universal.

The defensive sector therefore involves the earliest and most superficial stages of illness since the Warm Illnesses school concerns itself chiefly with illnesses induced by external heteropathies (i.e., the six excesses). And because defensive qi is the body's primary orthopathic function, symptoms can often be analyzed as resulting from the struggle between orthopathic and heteropathic qi.

The active qi sector is the first point of entry for external heteropathies to the "body interior" (*li*); it has a special relationship to the Lung and the Upper *Jiao* visceral systems. By virtue of ruling the qi that is breathed in and out, managing the preliminary stages of digestion, and being located in the upper part of the body, these systems are relatively exterior. Consequently, the active qi sector is also relatively yang, and active qi can be thought of as a very general (i.e., whole body) motive force:

> The *Divine Pivot, juan* 6:30 says, "The Upper *Jiao* opens and expands, sends down the flavors [i.e., nutrients] of the five grains, disseminates vapors to the skin, fills out the whole frame, and imparts moisture and shine to the hair like irrigation with fog and dew—this is called qi." [Active] qi is the material basis that safeguards the body's life activity, and at the same time it is the motive force of the physiological activity of the whole body and of each visceral system.[66]

Constructive (*ying*) qi is that form of qi that moves throughout the body in circulation tracts, also driving the Blood and carrying nourishment. (This definition differentiates it from the more generally circulating active qi.) Consequently, constructive sector illnesses are more interior and severe than those of the defensive or active qi sectors. Illnesses in this third sector threaten the regular functioning of the visceral systems. Constructive qi can be distinguished from other vital substances as follows:

> The *Plain Questions, juan* 7:43 [says], "Constructive qi is the nutritive essential qi of food and drink, harmonized and regulated through the five yin visceral systems, overflowing into and dispersed through the six yang visceral systems." The *Divine Pivot, juan* 8:12 [says], "That shallow and floating qi that doesn't follow the paths of the circulation tracts is classed as defensive qi, whereas that refined qi which flows with the circulation tracts is classed as constructive qi." Hence we know that constructive qi originates in the refined essences of food and drink, is transported inside the circulation tracts, and has the function of nourishing the whole body in tandem with Heart qi.[67]

Constructive qi has an intimate relationship with Blood, and illnesses classified as belonging to the constructive sector communicate readily to the Blood (*xue*) sector:

---

66. Nanjing College, *Wenbingxue,* p. 11.
67. Ibid.

The Divine Pivot, *juan* 10:71, says, "Constructive qi secretes its fluids, concentrates them in the vessels [*mai*], and transforms to become Blood." Hence we know that Blood is something transformed from constructive qi that flows in the vessels, circulating without ceasing. When heteropathy is in the constructive sector, if in due time it doesn't emerge into the active qi sector, then it will necessarily go deeper and enter the Blood sector, thereby inducing diminution or disturbance of blood [*haoxue dongxue*].[68]

Disorder in the Blood sector is the most severe state of illness, in which permanent damage of some kind becomes almost inevitable. Both the constructive qi and Blood sectors are relatively yin in quality.

When the four sectors are thought of strictly as classificatory rubrics under which symptoms can be organized and correlated with an illness stage and a predictable course of exogenous illness, they form a clear and internally coherent method. Certainly it becomes easier to accommodate a wide variety of textual materials, both historical and contemporary, if they are thought of in this way. But one receives the strong impression from contemporary Chinese doctors that the sectors have a more substantial reality than any mechanically classificatory approach can accommodate. We have seen that definitions of the sectors include reference to the nature of their namesake substances. And a popular use of the sectors as if they were levels—that is, relatively inner and outer bodily strata—makes it possible to assert, for example, that Spring Warm is an illness of the active qi sector in more or less the same sense that one can say that Depletion Cold (*xu han*) is an illness of the Kidney visceral system.[69] The inward penetration of external "evils"—another sense of heteropathic (*xie*) qi—leads to a mounting concern as disorder moves inward; this is an actual material process, not a dry intellectual undertaking. Thus, although it could be argued that an overliteral spatialization or substantialization of *wei, qi, ying,* and *xue* distorts classical sources and introduces contradictions into discourse, something is nevertheless gained by broadening the reference of the four sectors in this way.

Table 4.9, translated from the college textbook *Wenbingxue* (Warm Illnesses), summarizes the relationship of symptoms to illness processes characterized in terms of locations and substances affected. It is more comprehensive than Table 4.8, in which I have merely summarized the correlations of the four sectors, and more suggestive for diagnostic analysis.

Like all such mnemonic devices, this representation is a simplification; but four sectors analysis, by correlating the symptoms characteristic of a stage of illness with an illness course understandable in terms of visceral

---

68. Ibid.

69. A recent textbook by Deng, *Shiyong Zhongyi Zhenduanxue,* p. 199, uses the term *level* (*cengci*) as his modern equivalent of the word *fen,* translated here (following Sivin) as "sector."

Table 4.9   Four Sectors Syndrome Differentiation

Illness Process	Symptoms	Diagnostic Essentials
Defensive qi (early, slight)		
Warm heteropathy lodged at exterior; Lung and defensive qi fail to flow.	Fever; mild intolerance of cold and wind; headache; little sweat; throat blockage, cough, thirst; tongue coating fine and white, tongue sides and tip red; pulse floating and accelerated	Fever with mild intolerance of cold and wind; slight thirst; pulse floating and accelerated; tongue coating thin and white
Active qi sector (intermediate, severe)		
Heteropathy enters active qi level; Heat steams body interior.	Whole-body fever; no intolerance of cold but avoidance of heat; copious sweating; thirst and desire for cool drinks; tongue coating yellow and dry; pulse smooth and accelerated or large	High fever; no intolerance of Cold; thirst; yellow tongue coating
Constructive qi sector (late, dangerous)		
Heat scorches constructive yin (i.e., fluids); mental state is disturbed.	Fever worse at night; mouth dry but no marked thirst; agitation and restlessness; occasional delirium; Heat ulcers appear on skin; tongue crimson; pulse small and accelerated	Fever worse at night; agitation; tongue crimson; pulse small and accelerated
Blood sector (very late, difficult to cure)		
Dominant Heat disturbs Blood; mental state is disordered.	Whole-body fever; extreme agitation, confusion, and mania, wild speech; spitting blood, nosebleeds, blood in urine and stools; draining ulcerations; tongue deep crimson	Fever and extreme agitation; ulceration and hemorrhage symptoms; deep crimson tongue

SOURCE: Adapted from Nanjing College of Traditional Chinese Medicine, ed., *Wenbingxue* (Shanghai: Shanghai Science and Technology Press, 1979), p. 12.

systems and vital substances, can become a very rich tool of diagnostic and therapeutic thinking. On the basis of a thorough grasp of the dynamics of Warm Illnesses, clinicians can deviate from the interventions made obvious by conventional classifications in inspired ways while still using a four sectors terminology to articulate their practice.

One kind of complexity that the Warm Illnesses school has particularly explored is deviations in the regular movement of heteropathy from outside to inside, from slight symptoms to severe ones. Warm illnesses cannot be assumed to take a unidirectional or inevitable course. Medical management of the illness involves drawing disorders that have entered the "deeper" and later sectors outward such that increasingly slight symptoms are manifested. Moreover, every textbook emphasizes that many complicated illnesses can involve two adjacent sectors at once or can move back and forth between sectors. Some can even originate in an internal sector.

The unity of time, space, and qualities in physiology is what makes prognosis and management of the illness possible in the Warm Illnesses approach.[70] The doctor is enabled through this analytic method to read symptoms (e.g., via eight rubrics qualities) in a way that tells him immediately which visceral systems (i.e., systems of spatial extension) are likely to be most affected and which require the most immediate protection from invasion as the illness develops (in time). In an interdependent physiology of constant motion and transformation, this is obviously important; a heteropathy that severely disrupts or penetrates the outer barrier of defensive qi is apt to travel quickly through the body via the circulation tracts (*jingluo*) and attack the major visceral systems.

Four sectors analysis, then, renders the illness and the body coterminous and comparable by locating the disorder in bodily space and time. This reminds us that the Chinese medical body is "naturally" as thoroughly temporal as the illness is; both physiology (*shenglixue*) and pathology (*binglixue*) are processes, rather than structures, patterned sequences of manifestations that are a much more prominent focus of Chinese medical interest than the body as anatomy. Tangible bodily masses are the manifest products of underlying dynamic processes, just as the liquid blood that flows in the vessels is transformed from (invisible, intangible) constructive qi.

This understanding of the body as a set of processes moving through time provides an important reminder about the relations of heteropathic and orthopathic qi. The unfixity of physiological relations evident in Chinese medical usage is what enables the body to shift fairly readily into an escalating sequence of pathological changes in response to the influence of

---

70. Kuriyama's exploration of the conjunction of time, space, and quality in classical Chinese pulse lore has influenced my discussion of both the four sectors and six warps diagnostics. See note 16.

an equally unfixed outer situation. Heteropathic qi is not, in other words, an autonomous microbial body that moves through an otherwise benign outer environment to attack a solid human body. Rather, heteropathy is a condition of excess (Wind, Heat, etc.) obtaining for a time in the environment as a whole and inimical to the orthopathic processes that operate to maintain the continuity of wholesome physiological activity. It is evident here, as elsewhere, that causation on the mechanical model, in which structured objects physically collide to produce effects, is not at issue, not because the body is immaterial, but because it is observed in time and its spaces are understood in temporal and qualitative terms rather than being theoretically lifted out of time to become a physiology of structural relations. As Nathan Sivin has pointed out, the classificatory analytics of Chinese medicine were "names for the types of *ch'i* [qi] responsible for change. Looking at it the other way round, the usefulness of these concepts encouraged physicians to think of the body as an ensemble of processes carried out in functional systems by *ch'i*, rather than as a structure of tissues that grow and maintain themselves and are susceptible to lesions."[71] Such a body must be cultivated and nurtured with care if its wholesome integrity is to be maintained; an old term for medical knowledge, "the cultivation of life" (*yangsheng*), reminds us that Chinese medicine has always been continuous with mundane practices of diet, exercise, and self-regulation—practices that are now referred to under the depressing name of "prevention" (*yufang*).

In Case 1, Doctor Ye relied heavily on Warm Illnesses analysis. Part of the interest of the case lies in the way the outer to inner spatial arrangement of the four sectors is supplemented by an emphasis on up-down physiological relationships analyzable in terms of Triple *Jiao* functioning.[72] Given the phrasing of the case history, Doctor Ye probably recognized immediately that this acute febrile illness was Spring Warm syndrome; it was no doubt spring at the time, and particularly if Ye (a resident of Zhejiang Province) allies himself to the "southern" tradition, he would be inclined to classify any markedly febrile illness immediately in terms of Warm Illnesses teachings.[73] Spring Warm is one of the seven major syndrome types covered in *Warm Illnesses* and demonstrates considerable variation in its forms of clinical manifestation:

---

71. Sivin, *Traditional Medicine,* p. 91.

72. Triple *Jiao* diagnostic analysis is an aspect of Warm Illnesses teachings that I will not take up here. The therapeutic principle deployed in Case 1, clear above and drain below, is probably a reference to the Triple *Jiao* tripartite division of watercourse functions.

73. Warm Illnesses doctrine is nowadays popularly associated with a southern medical tradition, whereas Cold Damage doctrine, with its analysis according to the six warps, is felt to be more popular in the north. A review of 1983 Chinese medical journals from all provinces generally supported this division of emphasis.

Spring Warm is an acute Heat illness induced by Warm or Hot heteropathic qi contracted during the spring season. The initial stage of the illness has high fever, agitation, and thirst; in extreme cases confused mental state or convulsions; and other interior heat symptoms as its main characteristic signs. It mainly occurs in the spring or in the transition between winter and spring, generally coming on suddenly and acutely, [manifesting as] a rather severe illness state showing frequent shifts.[74]

It is characteristic of the febrile illnesses of the spring season that they bypass the defensive sector and manifest suddenly as serious disorders in the active qi or deeper sectors.

Both classic Spring Warm and the illness described in Case 1 are rather severe afflictions induced by a heteropathy of the Warm-Hot type; the commentary to Case 1 makes clear that penetration of Heat to the constructive sector has already occurred. The most specific mode of determining which sectors are affected is through classification of the symptoms, many of which are affiliated clearly to each of the sectors. The symptoms listed in Case 1 can be conventionally analyzed as follows:

High fever without remittance [no intolerance of cold]	Active qi sector
Agitation and irritability	Constructive qi sector
Dry mouth with excessive thirst	Active qi sector, yang brilliance viscera (Stomach and Large Intestine) affected by fluid damage
Red face	Interior Heat
Foul mouth odor	Interior, Stomach visceral system
Tongue and lips dry and parched	Stomach affected by fluid damage
Occasional delirious speech	Constructive qi sector, Heat repletion in the closing yang visceral systems
No appetite	Interior, Stomach repletion
No bowel movement for eight days	Repletion in the yang brilliance visceral systems
Pulse smooth and accelerated	Active qi sector
Tongue coating yellow, thick, dry	Active qi sector, Stomach Heat

"Yang brilliance" refers to the circulation tract system and to the categories of six warps analysis. Two of the twelve major tracts, those affiliated to the Stomach and the Large Intestine, are classified as yang brilliance tracts. It is interesting that in his analysis of this case of Spring Warm, Dr. Ye distinguishes between the viscera classified as belonging to the yang brilliance

---

74. Nanjing College, *Wenbingxue,* p. 42.

tracts and the tracts themselves; he notes that the affected visceral systems were cleared of pathology before their corresponding tracts.

Heat repletion affecting the yang brilliance visceral systems of Stomach and Large Intestine is recognized in Warm Illnesses thinking as an illness chiefly appearing in the active qi sector. But in this case the patient's excessive agitation and irritability and occasional delirium indicate a movement of the illness toward the later and more inner constructive sector.

This is also clear in the commentary, where the fact of yin fluids having already been damaged implicates the constructive and Blood sectors. Once an illness involves the constructive sector, therapeutic action must be aggressive to avoid quick transmission and transformation (*chuanhua*) to the Blood sector. (The term *chuanhua* neatly combines the notions of transmission of a heteropathy from one sector to another and transformation of disordered constructive qi into, presumably, disordered Blood.)

Apparently fluids had been injured only in the Stomach and Large Intestine systems, both relatively outer (they are both yang visceral systems and hence classified with the exterior [*biao*]) and both directly concerned with watercourse functions. The commentary refers to the possibility that Liver or Kidney systems might be injured (yin viscera classified with the interior [*li*]), but these were not treated in the case at hand.

By determining that this illness was in the active qi sector and beginning to invade the constructive sector, Dr. Ye demonstrates why a different doctor's previous procedure of using pungent and cooling drugs had shown no effect. The therapeutic methods of "using pungent and cooling drugs to flush Heat from the exterior" (*xinliang jie biao*) would have been effective only if the illness had been in the defensive sector; illnesses in the active qi and constructive qi sectors require "clearing and draining" of Heat (*qingxie*). Once properly treated, the changing symptoms (peaceful sleep indicating an end to agitation and delirium, reduced fever, bowel movement, evidence of fluid regeneration) indicate outward progress away from the inner and later sectors toward the shallower defensive qi sector.

I have already pointed out that space, time, and quality are a physiological unity. The practice of four sectors analysis illustrates clearly that movement through time entails movement through space, and vice versa, and that space-time positions are textured with predictable qualities. But four sectors time and space are not abstract dimensions apart from concrete physiological and pathological processes. The stages of a Warm illness may pass quickly or slowly and are discernible as stages only with respect to the pathological qualities that characterize them. The sectors are not discrete territories that carve up a structural body; rather, they are thoroughly interpenetrant functional domains.[75] In the case of illness, symptoms are non-

75. See Sivin, *Traditional Medicine,* p. 379n, on the translation of *fen* as "sector." In this note he makes a useful comparison of Warm Illnesses sectors with sectors of an economy.

arbitrary manifestations of certain spatiotemporal situations, and they can be described in the qualitative language of the eight rubrics. In the case of treatment, drugs and named therapeutic measures have qualitative (e.g., Warmth and Coolness), spatial (e.g., visceral system and tract affinities), and temporal (differing degrees of efficacy) potencies. Every act of medical classification has complex entailments; space, time, and quality are practically and theoretically inseparable. The mutual entailment of these dimensions of illness is reflected in the term *chuanhua,* which in Warm Illnesses theory refers to movement between the sectors. Similarly, it is often pointed out that syndromes (*zheng₃*) are not diseases (*jibing*) since their whole nature changes as they progress through the body and are reversed in therapy.[76]

Six Warps (*Liu Jing*) Analysis

Six warps diagnostic—the syndrome differentiation method of the *Treatise on Cold Damage.* The six warps are mature yang [*taiyang*], yang brightness [*yangming*], immature yang [*shaoyang*], mature yin [*taiyin*], immature yin [*shaoyin*], and attenuated yin [*jueyin*]. They are six categories of syndrome differentiation that were summarized by Zhang Zhongjing [Zhang Ji, second century A.D.] from the combined transmission situations of exogenous Heat illnesses on the basis of the six cardinal circulation tract dyads of the *Inner Canon;* they are also the six general syndrome types [derived from] the depth [of penetration] and stage [of development] of exogenous illnesses. The six warps are connected among themselves and can manifest corresponding illnesses [*hebing*], simultaneous illnesses [*bingbing*], double infections, and transmission of illness among themselves; they cannot be sharply divided.[77]

The six warps diagnostic method is similar in many respects to the four sectors diagnostic. The two are historically closely linked: Warm Illnesses teachings are an eighteenth-century revision of the classical Cold Damage approach from which the six warps diagnostic is drawn. Many Chinese medical workers today see the two methods as parallel in application even if constrasting or contradictory in theory, and the problem of the relationship

---

76. Contemporary Chinese medical texts do not often emphasize the temporality of the syndrome as compared with the fixity of the concept of disease, partly because time contingency is so widely taken for granted in Chinese medical practice and discourse. The centrality of transformation through time in the four sectors and six warps methods will be expanded on, but see Liu et al., *Zhongyi Jichu Lilun Wenda,* p. 97, for a discussion of syndrome differentiation that emphasizes a time dimension.

77. Editing Committee, *Zhongyi Dacidian, Jichu Lilun Fence,* s.v. *liujing bianzheng.* I follow Sivin (*Traditional Medicine,* p. 80) in translating the *jing* of *liujing* as "warp," though I tend to refer to "warp classes" rather than warps. As he points out, the word basically refers to the lengthwise threads in weaving and is the same as the *jing* meaning one of the twelve cardinal circulation tracts.

between the Warm Illnesses and Cold Damage schools of thought has been the subject of numerous articles in the recent professional literature.[78]

The definition of the six warps method to be found in a 1977 text emphasizes the way in which the method is (like the four sectors method) a specification of the temporal course of an illness:

> The *Treatise on Cold Damage* by Zhang Zhongjing takes the six cardinal circulation tract dyads as its rubrics and *divides the developmental process of exogenous Heat illnesses into six syndrome types* according to illness location, symptom characteristics, and relations of transmission among them, advancing a mode of syndrome differentiation and treatment determination that is called the six warps diagnostic for short.[79]

Statements of this kind display the functional similarities of the six warps and four sectors methods well and also suggest why there is sometimes a sense of conflict or competition between their proponents. The two schools of thought are differing approaches to the characterization of phases in the "developmental process of exogenous Heat illnesses" and to the design of interventions in such illness processes; they do the same job in rather different ways. Obviously, the rubrics they use to classify the effects observed in the course of Heat illnesses are not the same or are not easily conformed to one another. Four sectors analysis names its categories after four types of body substance (or four bodily manifestations of qi), whereas the six warps are named with reference to the twelve cardinal tracts familiar in acupuncture (e.g., the hand mature–yang Small Intestine tract, the foot yang–brightness Stomach tract). And rather different points of view on physiological dynamics can be inferred from this categorical and substantive divergence.

Having explored phase logic in regard to four sectors syndrome differentiation, I now wish to go beyond that logic and discuss how Cold Damage thinking differs from the four sectors method of the Warm Illnesses school.[80] I will illustrate this distinction with a discussion of Case 1 at the end of the section.

Following are two passages from the *Treatise on Cold Damage* attributed to Zhang Ji:

---

78. Cf. Wan Yousheng, *Han Wen Tongyi Lun* (Shanghai: Shanghai Science and Technology Press, 1988); Huang Meilin, "*Tongyi Waigan Rebing Bianzheng Ganglingde Yanjiu Gaikuang,*" *Guangxi Zhongyiyao* 83, no. 5 (1983):44–48; Shan Shujian, "*Shilun Wu Zhitong dui Zhongjingde Jicheng he Fazhan,*" *Jilin Zhongyiyao* 83, no. 2 (1983):4–7; Wu Dingbang, "*Shanghan Wenbing Shaoyang Zheng Yitong Chuan,*" *Hubei Zhongyi Zazhi* 83, no. 1 (1983):51–52; and Yuan Baoting, "*Shilun Zhang Zhongjing zhi Wen Xueshu Chengjiu,*" *Henan Zhongyi* 83, no.5 (1983):10–12.

79. Office of the 1977 Physicians, *Zhongyi Jichuxue*, p. 145; emphasis added.

80. This procedure is historically backward but logically more convenient since (in theory at least) six warps analysis is more complicated than four sectors analysis.

Cold damage: pulse floating and slippery, Heat in both exterior and interior. White Tiger Decoction rules it. ([maxim] 181). . . . Cold damage: pulse floating but attenuated Heat in the interior. White Tiger Decoction rules it. ([maxim] 350).[81]

These passages show the typically cryptic and epigrammatic style of this work, which was organized and compiled from fragments after Zhang Ji's death in the third century. The maxims appear on the surface to be rules of natural correspondence that could be paraphrased in the following style: "Maxim 181—When in Cold Damage illnesses a floating and smooth pulse appears, it is because Heat has developed in both the exterior and the interior. The illness can be overcome with White Tiger Decoction." As all contemporary foundations texts make clear, however, the significance of the *Treatise on Cold Damage* to contemporary medical practice goes beyond its authoritative cataloguing of pathological correspondences; it has been worked up into a clinical specialty with complex characteristic methods and an extensive secondary literature.

The *Treatise on Cold Damage* is one of the most important classic works of Chinese medicine. It is paired with the *Inner Canon* in many contexts, the assertion often being made nowadays that the latter text is the theoretical classic, whereas the former is the clinical classic. Zhang Ji is, moreover, the earliest major figure in the history of medicine to be accorded an unambiguous historicity in contemporary accounts of the development of Chinese medicine, and his grave in a remote town in Henan Province is a pilgrimage site for doctors who consider themselves members of the Cold Damage school.[82]

Master Zhang is credited by some with having forged from the fragmentary and rather abstractly recorded medicine of his time a complete system of medical practice. According to the major Cold Damage teaching text in current use, the six warps method not only "comprehends the physiological functions and pathological changes of the visceral systems and circulation tracts, qi and Blood," but also includes modes of "analysis, generalization, and inference" through which the various syndromes manifested in the course of development of an exogenous illness can be perceived.[83] In devel-

---

81. Hubei College of Traditional Chinese Medicine, ed., *Shang Han Lun Xuandu* (Shanghai: Shanghai Science and Technology Press, 1979), p. 79.

82. Other figures traditionally accorded originary importance, such as Hua Tuo and the sage-kings Shen Nong and Qinshi Huangdi, are now generally depicted as symbolic of the early period of the people's struggle against disease. In the 1980s and early 1990s several major professional meetings were held in Zhang Ji's birthplace of Nanyang, Henan, allowing doctors from Cold Damage studies departments all over China to pay their respects at the master's grave. Also visiting the grave when I was there in 1991 were many ailing petitioners and their relatives bearing offerings to Zhang Ji and seeking a cure through his divine medical intervention.

83. Hubei College, *Shang Han Lun Xuandu*, p. 2

oping this method, Master Zhang took into account such factors as the strength or weakness of orthopathic qi, the "characteristic features" (*shuxing*) of illness factors, and changes in the "configuration and force of illnesses" (*bingshi*). It is with respect to these considerations that a complete system of syndrome differentiation and treatment determination was developed: "The *Treatise on Cold Damage* is not only a matrix for differentiating syndromes; it is also a standard for determining treatments."[84]

Nevertheless, the same texts that emphasize the wide scope of the six warps method caution that it cannot replace other diagnostic analytics, such as the eight rubrics and visceral systems methods.[85] Since the method concerns itself chiefly with exogenous Heat illnesses, in which temporal course tends to neatly manifest as a movement from outside to inside, it offers no refinement of methods useful in illnesses of other types. In addition, the *Treatise on Cold Damage* focuses on key symptoms for diagnosis rather than on all possible or likely manifestations. Subsequent writers in the Cold Damage school have filled out the canon in this respect with general clinical knowledge that incorporates diagnostic categories of the eight rubrics, visceral systems, and so on. Thus, although six warps analysis can be both subtle and wide-ranging, it is not logically autonomous or exclusive.

The nature of the specific temporal, local, and qualitative conjunctions with which six warps analysis concerns itself can be seen more clearly in the following enumeration taken from a foundations text:

> 1. *Mature yang:* indicates exterior qi. This qi is rooted in the source [*yuan*] yang of the Kidney visceral system, it travels and flows outward to the skin, and it is in charge of the task of protecting the outside. The circulation tract [*jingmai*] goes down the back of the body, ascending to the neck and head and descending to affiliate to the Urinary Bladder. The Urinary Bladder is the visceral system of mature yang, it rules qi transformation [separation of clear from turbid] in the excretion of urine, and it is classified as [relatively] interior among the outer [visceral systems].

---

84. Ibid.

85. A work supplementary to the *Treatise on Cold Damage* is also attributed to Zhang Ji; this is *Essentials of the Golden Casket,* which has stood since the Song dynasty (960–1279) as the "internal medicine" section of the original *Treatise on Cold Damage and Miscellaneous Disorders.* The methods set out in this work rely much less heavily on six warps classification; where there is no clear movement from outside to inside, the warp classes are less useful than the principles of physiology and patterns of pathological influence that can be revealed through visceral systems analysis. This suggests that the six warps method, like that of the four sectors, is concerned with specifying the spatial, temporal, and qualitative conjunctions occurring in illness processes in which heteropathic qi has originated outside the body. It is less useful in the large class of disorders that is nowadays managed by the Chinese medical specialty of internal medicine (*neike*). But actual practitioners of internal medicine routinely deal with exogenous illnesses, and the six warps method has been applied to many conditions that are not clearly of external origin.

2. *Yang brilliance:* indicates interior qi (Middle *Jiao*, Stomach, and Intestine qi mechanisms). [It is] in charge of the transmission and guidance [of substances] derived from digestion. The circulation tract descends from the face through the chest and abdomen to the foot. The Stomach is the visceral system of the yang brilliance warp.

3. *Immature yang:* indicates qi that is half exterior and half interior. Inside it rules the Triple *Jiao,* the Gallbladder is its visceral system, and it has the functions of turning the pivot between qi and fluids and clearing and regulating the watercourse. The circulation tract goes down the sides of the body and is affiliated to the Gallbladder.

4. *Mature yin:* indicates intermediate [*zhong*] qi. [It] receives warming from the yang of the Lower *Jiao* and the Kidney system [and] has the function of transmitting and assimilating food essences and fluids. The circulation tract enters the lower abdomen and is affiliated to the Spleen.

5. *Immature yin:* indicates source qi. On the inside [it] rules the Heart and Kidney systems, which are where important functional substances of the body's life activity are located. The foot immature–yin circulation tract rises through the throat to the base of the tongue.

6. *Attenuated yin:* indicates the qi of yin exhaustion and yang birth. The Liver is the visceral system of attenuated yin; it rules upward and outward dispersion, hosts interior Wind and Fire, and has the function of regulating the qi mechanisms of the visceral systems. The circulation tract is affiliated to the Liver. Meets the *Du* tract at the top of the head.[86]

Even though these brief characterizations of each of the six warp categories are oversimplified (perhaps because they were written for students in a crash course), they condense many of the complex classificatory relationships of the Cold Damage specialty. Each warp class is here used to assemble various types of information useful for understanding pathological manifestations: the relative interiority or superficiality of phenomena associated with that warp, the visceral functions belonging to it (described with special reference to forms of qi transformation), and the paths of the relevant circulation tracts where manifestations of illness might be expected to show. The text goes on to classify and describe the forms of pathology for which six warps analysis is used: Syndromes belonging to the three yang warps usually include unambiguous Heat disorders, and "mature yin rules interior Cold-Damp, immature yin rules interior depletion-Cold, and attenuated yin rules mixed manifestations of Cold and Heat."[87]

These rules of thumb undoubtedly facilitate syndrome differentiation. Where eight rubrics analysis reveals that the illness is characterized by Cold and Damp in the interior, the doctor can turn immediately to the relatively small subset of exogenous illnesses classified as mature yin illnesses and

---

86. Office of the 1977 Physicians, *Zhongyi Jichuxue,* p. 145.
87. Ibid.

concentrate on differentiating among those possibilities. He may not find a situation among the illnesses of the mature yin warp that corresponds exactly to the illness at hand, in which case he can devise more creative means of classifying the symptoms and differentiating a syndrome. But a manageable region of explanations and therapies can be readily delineated from the host of possibilities using simple rules like these.

In addition, the severity of an illness and the length of its course are conventionally seen to move through the six warps in sequence, from the very common "colds" belonging to the mature yang category to the comas and strokes to be found in the attenuated yin category. This understanding is consistent with the characterizations of each warp in terms of relative interiority or superficiality, a technique directly parallel to the time and space sequence of the four sectors.

This characterization of the six warps shows them both as classificatory rubrics, in which things of unlike type but similar in their position in a range of possible effects are placed into relations of commonality and as positions established in differential networks of dynamic relations. This dual sense of the term mirrors the more general relation of yin and yang, which are also both classificatory rubrics and dynamic positions. (Classificatory dynamics of this sort are also discussed in connection with the eight rubrics.) Moreover, like the six warps, the yinyang relation condenses analogous dimensions of quality (hot and cold, bright and dark, etc.), space (inner and outer, up and down), and time (day and night, winter and summer) into conjunctions that can allow a complex specification of a concrete situation through yinyang analysis. The yinyang logic of classification and dynamic relation enables a technique for describing states to be translated into a technique for perceiving processes. The six warps diagnostic may be Chinese medicine's most refined application of this principle.

But the yinyang relation is more than a logical principle. In contemporary Cold Damage discourse the classificatory dynamism of yinyang and the six warps is filled with physiological and pathological content. The foregoing delineation of the affiliations of the six warps is supplemented, for example, with the comment that "the substance of the warps is qi, they include the circulation tracts and the visceral systems, in physiological function they are interconnected, and in pathology they influence each other."[88] The sense of the term *jing* (here, warp classes) can be grasped in light of this explanation; illnesses are classed under six warps rubrics with reference to the physiology of the circulation tracts, which are the interconnected pathways linking the visceral systems in networks of qi. The symptomatic manifestations of

---

88. Ibid. See Beijing College of Traditional Chinese Medicine et al., ed., *Essentials of Chinese Acupuncture* (Beijing: Foreign Languages Press, 1980), pp. 31–35, for a description of nomenclature, interconnections, visceral system affiliations, and function of the circulation tracts.

exogenous illnesses can be affiliated to warp classes on the basis of qualities attributable to disorders in the various tracts or viscera, and their course can be understood partly with reference to the relations of physiological and pathological influence obtaining among the circulation tracts and visceral systems. In other words, in this Cold Damage diagnostic method the warps are mainly useful as classificatory rubrics. But any set of classes in the Chinese sciences can be expected to show patterns of interaction and mutual influence among the categories, and in this case such patterns are explained by the physiology of the circulation tracts, the substance of which is qi. This physiological and pathological content unifying (up to a point) the affiliations of the six warps makes them good to think with and a good way of linking Cold Damage knowledge to the rest of the Chinese medical tradition.

Contradictions between tract and visceral systems physiology and pathology and six warps classification could undoubtedly be found. But few Chinese doctors of the Cold Damage persuasion would find such contradictions very engaging. The six warps method is first and foremost a practical classificatory procedure designed to facilitate treatment determination and formula writing. The cryptic wording and sentence structure of the *Treatise on Cold Damage* can be straightforwardly understood in this light. All the 397 passages collected in the most widely used versions of the text are as terse as the two items translated here, and the compilation of the volume now in use demands careful attention to the relations that must obtain among the passages if any of them are to make internal sense. These relations have been constructed by relying much more on clinical insights than on theories of literary form.

Consider the two passages (maxims 181 and 350) previously cited. Both open with the general class "Cold Damage." In this case Cold Damage refers to illnesses that have already manifested as a mature yang syndrome of the Cold Damage type and are now shifting to become a syndrome of the yang brilliance warp. Thus, floating pulse, characteristic of the mature yang condition, remains and shows that there is heteropathic qi remaining in the body exterior; but the smoothness of the pulse betrays a movement toward the interior, which places the condition in the "half exterior, half interior" location of the yang brilliance warp. Thus, there is "Heat in both exterior and interior" (maxim 181). This classification then makes it possible to affiliate a treatment, White Tiger Decoction, to the syndrome. If, by contrast, the pulse is floating (exterior, mature yang), but there are "attenuated yin" (*jueyin*) symptoms (which range from cold extremities to dizziness and fainting, and betray interior disorder) (maxim 350), the syndrome is one of Heat predominating in the interior; White Tiger Decoction is, however, still appropriate for its treatment.

To read such a collection of short passages as a clinical manual requires that a great deal of supplementary material be brought to bear. Thus, to know that these two syndrome types are both classified as belonging to the yang brilliance warp, one must first realize that (1) a floating pulse indicates illness on the exterior and is typical of mature yang syndromes, (2) yang brilliance is the class in which simultaneous interior and exterior locations are implicated, (3) yang brilliance ordinarily follows mature yang in the developmental course of exogenous illnesses, and (4) the use of a single prescription for several kinds of illness implies substantial classificatory and pathological commonality among them.

Students of medicine today do not always need to make complex judgments at this level, however; their textbooks classify the various passages of the *Treatise on Cold Damage* into six chapters reflecting the warp classes that (quite often only tacitly) organize the clinical groupings taken up in the work. Nevertheless, a reading of these short epigrammatic passages cannot provide even the barest of classificatory pointers unless they are related to each other and given a discursive continuity that is not explicit in the text itself. It is in this space of ascribed continuity and argument in the *Treatise on Cold Damage* that authority, innovation, and elaboration of and accommodation to clinical experience are given their most significant play.

Because investigations in the Cold Damage scholarly line are explorations of a medical method, rather than systematizing descriptions of physiology or natural structure, there is a strong emphasis in technical Cold Damage discourse on variations in the use of drugs and classic prescriptions. In fact, many syndromes are referred to solely by the name of the drug formula that treats them. Differences in drug use are also the most troubled area of contradiction between Cold Damage and Warm Illnesses theories. In addition, in teaching the six warps method, Cold Damage scholars emphasize tables that summarize relevant portions of the *Treatise on Cold Damage* in a form that renders them maximally informative for clinical judgment. Such organizing mnemonics are almost more central to the Cold Damage subdiscipline than to the *Treatise on Cold Damage* itself. Table 4.10 is an example.

This table is a summary of the content (some explicit, some exegetical) of the passages cited. Other tables used in teaching the portions of the *Treatise on Cold Damage* dealing with yang brilliance illnesses summarize the differences between circulation tract syndromes and visceral syndromes and set out the characteristics of several important syndromes to which passages are devoted in the text: Heat Disrupts Chest and Diaphragm syndrome, Restrained Spleen syndrome, and Damp-Heat Jaundice syndrome. The relevant maxims are cited by number in the tables. In an important respect, such tabular presentations are the real content of the *Treatise on Cold Damage,* at least as it was taught in Guangzhou in the 1980s. Whereas the *Inner Canon* is often read for philosophical content and for insight into

Table 4.10   Passages on Yang Brilliance Illnesses

Formative factors	Wrong treatment of mature yang or immature yang illnesses; fluid damage with drying of Stomach; heteropathic qi bogging down and becoming Heat. Yang becoming predominant and collecting in body interior; food backing up; heteropathy entering the interior, transforming into Dryness, and developing a repletion (maxims 184, 186, 190).
Illness mechanisms	Fluid damage with transformation into Dryness; Stomach Heat ablaze (maxim 185).
Characteristic qualities	Interior repletion Heat syndromes.
Major symptoms	Fever, spontaneous sweating, no intolerance of cold; pulse large (maxims 187, 191).
Treatment principles	Tract syndromes: clear. White Tiger Decoction is the representative prescription.
	Visceral syndromes: Drain. Carry Qi Decoction is the representative prescription.

SOURCE: Mimeographed handout to the *Treatise on Cold Damage* classes, Guangzhou College of Traditional Chinese Medicine, Spring 1983.

general patterns of natural and medical experience, the *Treatise on Cold Damage* exists less as a canonical text than as a set of indications to guide and organize medical practice. For such use a table is as good as an epigram.

Of the cases translated in Chapter 3, Case 1 provides the best example of the use of the six warps method. Although the vocabulary of the published case history is that of Warm Illnesses theory, the most interesting feature of Dr. Ye's management of the case is the relationship it reveals between four sectors and six warps analytics.

The closing statement of the case history makes reference to "the skill of my teachers in their mastery of the therapeutic principles of our sage forebears". Given that Dr. Ye, the teacher in question, mainly uses the theoretical vocabulary of Warm Illnesses teachings, this comment draws attention to the Cold Damage foundations of this relatively recent school of thought as well as to certain features of Dr. Ye's approach that do not belong to the Warm Illnesses idiom.

When analyzed according to the six warps method, this case of Spring Warm presents mainly as a yang brilliance visceral system syndrome, specifically a case of Dry repletion of the Stomach. The authority for this diagnosis is passage 250 of the *Treatise on Cold Damage*:

Third day of mature yang illness: Sweating has not flushed it out, [and] there is steaming feverishness (a); this is classed with the Stomach (b). Stomach-regulating Carry Qi Decoction rules it. ([maxim] 250)
    [Annotation:]

(a) "steaming feverishness": This describes a fever like hot qi steaming out from the inside.

(b) "classed with the Stomach": [This] indicates transmission [*chuan*] into the yang brilliance warp [from the mature yang warp].[89]

This passage appears in the chapter of a major Cold Damage textbook covering yang brilliance syndromes and is subclassified as a yang brilliance visceral system syndrome of the Dry repletion type. It is a good example of the kind of spatial, temporal, and qualitative conjunction that six warps analysis can elucidate.

A mature yang illness, which classically involves exterior symptoms of fever, intolerance of cold, headache, and floating pulse, has transmitted inward from the skin and muscles to one of the yang viscera after several days of illness. The usual therapy for mature yang illnesses is sweating to flush heteropathic qi out of the exterior. Zhang Ji describes here a situation in which heteropathic qi was too strong or therapy too timid to allow the illness to be effectively flushed out in its mature yang phase, such that in a few days it has transmitted inward to the visceral system affiliated to the yang brilliance warp, the Stomach. Extreme heat affecting the Stomach can be expected to produce Dry repletion symptoms if we recall that the Stomach likes Damp and that it is a major component of the up-down watercourse system. The eight rubrics analysis of Case 1 shows a consistent picture of interior Heat repletion to support this supposition.

That Dr. Ye drew on this classic Cold Damage analysis cannot be doubted since the first three drugs of his prescription are the three drugs combined by Zhang Ji in Stomach-regulating Carry Qi Decoction. The relationship may be indirect, however, since Barrier Cooling Powder, the prescription he cites, is an eleventh-century elaboration on several prescriptions originally from the *Treatise on Cold Damage*. Dr. Ye, however, has further elaborated Barrier Cooling Powder by adding a large amount of Anemarrhena, one of the three ingredients of the White Tiger Decoction used to treat yang brilliance circulation tract syndromes. He seems to have determined that this case of Spring Warm has both yang brilliance visceral system features and yang brilliance circulation tract features. Consequently, the prescription has elements from both "representative prescriptions" mentioned in Table 4.10. It can be seen from an analysis of the symptoms recorded in the case how he arrived at this conclusion:

Unremitting high fever	Passage 250, "steaming feverish-ness," yang brilliance visceral
Agitation and irritability	Passage 212, "heart-mind agitated," yang brilliance visceral

89. Hubei College, *Shang Han Lun Xuandu,* p. 83.

Dry mouth, excessive thirst	Passages 224, 226, "mouth abnormal" and "agitation-thirst," yang brilliance tract
Red face	Interior Heat
Foul mouth odor	Passage 224, "mouth abnormal," yang brilliance tract
Tongue and lips dry	Passage 173, "dryness on tongue," yang brilliance tract
Occasional delirious speech	Passages 225, 217, 220, "wild" or "delirious speech," yang brilliance visceral
No appetite	Stomach disorder
No bowel movement	Passage 251, "lower abdomen distended and full," yang brilliance visceral
Pulse smooth and rapid	Passage 219, "pulse sliding and rapidly pulsing," yang brilliance visceral (massy fullness subclass)

The progress of the illness in Case 1 toward a cure of both visceral systems and circulation tracts can be traced through the second and third examinations with reference to this classificatory breakdown of symptoms into Cold Damage categories.

The subclasses of visceral and tract syndromes within the yang brilliance warp are far from being mutually exclusive; they share many symptoms, a condition that stands to reason when the intimate relationship between circulation tracts and their associated viscera is considered. But the *Treatise on Cold Damage* proceeds with reference to key orienting symptoms by which an appropriate classification can be accomplished; the marked presence of a few key symptoms and the absence or relative unimportance of others can narrow down the illness to a highly specific syndrome subclass. In this case the mouth symptoms indicated strong tract involvement, and the lack of appetite and constipation indicated visceral disorder. Other marked symptoms, such as high fever and agitation, are found in both subclasses and did not help discriminate between them.

Dr. Ye appears to prefer four sectors analysis in his spatiotemporal location of the illness and characterization of its qualities. He also shows particular concern for regenerating fluids and preventing further damage to them from interior Heat, an emphasis characteristic of the Warm Illnesses school of thought. But patterns of prescription formation and drug use are the central expression of an account of an illness, and in this respect Dr. Ye's treatment harks back to Zhang Ji and the *Treatise on Cold Damage*.

There is no major contradiction in this regard when the case is examined in detail. The prescriptions recommended in Warm Illnesses texts for Spring Warm syndromes tend to nourish fluids at the same time that they clear and drain Heat. Dr. Ye, by contrast, has delayed his major effort to regenerate fluids until his second and third prescriptions, in his first prescription attending fairly strictly to clearing above and draining below.

It could be argued (and some contemporary scholars do argue) that the illness factors responsible for the onset of illness would be quite different for the two schools of thought—Cold qi for Cold Damage theorists and Warm qi for Warm Illnesses theorists—and that this would constitute an internal contradiction in the analysis of the case. But the illness factor does not seem to be a major concern, nor need it be, considering that there is agreement between the two approaches that the condition of concern at the moment is interior Heat. Moreover, the commentary emphasizes that the Warm Illnesses syndrome of Spring Warm often skips the defensive qi level and manifests at the outset as a syndrome of the active qi level; this appears to Dr. Ye to be a case of this kind. But the six warps analysis used in planning the drug treatment in the case is presumably just as applicable regardless of whether the illness has followed the orthodox Cold Damage course and manifested first as a Cold Damage syndrome of the mature yang warp. This situation thus reminds us that causality operates in the present rather than as a sequence of events in which the cause is temporally located as an originating agent or event. The relationship between the manifest illness and its root is one in which symptoms manifest conditions of a less visible domain.

The elaborate controversy in professional Chinese medical discourse concerning the relative merits of Warm Illnesses and Cold Damage explanations and methods concerns itself with problems of the kind that can be found in Case 1. In fact, it is when doctors "get down to cases" that problems are most likely to arise. For example, when during my stay in Guangzhou a teacher from the *Treatise on Cold Damage* teaching department at the college himself fell ill with an acute febrile illness, he was treated partly by his teaching colleagues and partly by Warm Illnesses adherents. (Guangzhou being a southern city, the latter group is more populous in the hospital affiliated to the college of Chinese medicine there.) He told me with some amusement that his bedside was the scene of considerable theoretical wrangling; these struggles were not inconsequential because the various positions entailed quite different herbal prescriptions.

All aspects of pathology can be differently understood in the two schools, from illness factors and systems affected to the typical forms of movement between and among the four sectors and the six warps and the differences between these modes of movement. Much is made of the historical connection of the two specialties, Warm Illnesses theory having been built on a Cold Damage foundation, as it were. Whether this historical relation constitutes an improvement on Zhang Ji's system or merely an addition to it, however contradictory, engages considerable interest among some specialists. But clinicians preferring one or the other of the two modes of practice continue to work side by side with colleagues of the opposite persuasion, and numerous complex syntheses of the kind represented in Case 1 are no doubt achieved.

Concluding Remarks on Analysis

In this chapter I have discussed five methods of analyzing illness symptoms. I have shown that clinical analysis mainly consists of classifying effects under rubrics that are positions in dynamic sequences, the result being a minute specification of the illness in qualitative, temporal, and spatial terms.

The manifest symptoms of an illness are generated by the particular yinyang relationship that is its root. These symptoms can be classified through the various diagnostics such that the qualitative and spatiotemporal patterns of the illness as a whole can be perceived. In keeping with yinyang logic, detailed classification enables a more general dynamic perception of the illness process. That is, because yin and yang are both rubrics and dynamic positions, a disorder once analyzed in yinyang terms is thereby located in a spatiotemporal process that can be predicted and manipulated.

I have emphasized that the specificity of the syndrome is achieved in the analytical phase through the perception of a specific conjunction of qualities and spatial and temporal locations. These are not wholly different aspects of the syndrome or manifestation type, however. Locations and qualities are separated for analytical purposes only; they have no pure existence, and recognition of the necessary interpenetration of the analytic aspects plays a role in diagnosis and therapy. I made the point, for example, that the interior and exterior differentiation in the eight rubrics method is more qualitative than spatial since it makes only a rough dyadic distinction between superficial and deep illnesses. The illness phases of the four sectors and six warps, in addition to being simultaneously temporal and spatial, all have eight rubrics qualitative values affiliated to them. Similarly, the viscera, which I have treated as spatial locations, are strongly colored by eight rubrics qualities.

Thus, for example, the Kidney and Heart are both yin visceral systems (*zang*) by virtue of being more inner than their yang partners, the Bladder and Small Intestine *fu*. But the Kidney is relatively yin to the Heart's yang, and the two engage in an important form of Cold-Hot exchange: Cold Kidney Water cools Heart Fire, and Heart Fire warms the yin chill of Kidney Water. Spatial visceral relationships, then, are at the same time qualitative and temporally locatable, and the syndrome differentiation and treatment determination process must always reunify what it analytically separates in classification. The differentiation of the syndrome is that reunifying move.

Quality and spatial and temporal location can be seen as facets of a unitary illness process; these facets are picked out and compared and classified as a way of specifying the unique pattern that is being manifested by the disorder. Such distinctions, however arbitrary, remain important as perceptible dimensions through the course of the illness. This is because movement along one dimension necessarily alters other aspects of the illness.[90]

The four sectors and six warps methods, for example, can be seen as efforts to delineate the usual affiliations of positions along each dimension, as in the association of mature yang illnesses with Heat symptoms (a quality) involving certain circulation tracts on the exterior (a place) in early stages of illness (a time). Here the class heading, mature yang, is more than a circulation tract site of illness; rather, it is a three-dimensional grouping of effects. The specification it achieves articulately represents the silent unity of the illness itself as a faceted, imaginable, expressible, and nameable conjunction of effects.

It has been emphasized that the analytic methods are neither mutually exclusive nor noncontradictory. Seldom are they all used with equal care and emphasis, but to use only one method is likely to produce errors in diagnosis. Most practitioners try to fit the analysis to the illness condition, although there are complex elements of preference involved, especially in the joint or separate use of four sectors and six warps analytics.[91] The goal of this phase of the *kanbing* process is the specification of the illness to the point that the syndrome can be differentiated from all other possible syndromes. The interaction of the analytic methods to that end are diagrammed as in Figure 4.1.

---

90. The necessary conjunction of movement in one dimension with pathological change in others is mirrored in physiology. Body substances (*jing,* qi, Blood, dispersed fluids) transform into each other as they move through physiological processes and are "generated," "ruled," or "stored" by the visceral systems. Thus, many terms encountered in writing on physiology refer to forms of transformation in their use of the suffix *hua.* Examples are *shenghua* (generation-transformation), *yunhua* (movement-transformation, but translated in connection with Spleen function as transmission and assimilation), and *chuanhua* (transmission-transformation).

91. Advocates of the Warm Illnesses school (i.e., four sectors analysis) are more likely to have mastered the methods of the Cold Damage school (i.e., six warps analysis) than Cold Damage advocates are apt to have mastered four sectors analysis. Those who argue for a Warm Illnesses approach are inclined to see it as an improvement on Cold Damage teachings rather than a replacement of it; but Cold Damage school doctors quite often dismiss Warm Illnesses methods as an unnecessary elaboration of a perfectly good method for differentiating syndromes and determining treatments. Indeed, one of the most important differences between the two schools may be their divergent approaches to formula prescription. The link between a syndrome and its affiliated formula in the Cold Damage method is so close as to be almost obligatory. A Cold Damage practitioner's virtuosity would be gauged more by his brilliant diagnoses, his ability to link an illness up to the correct passages in the *Treatise on Cold Damage,* than by his imaginative tinkering with drugs. The reverse is arguably the case for Warm Illnesses–oriented practitioners.

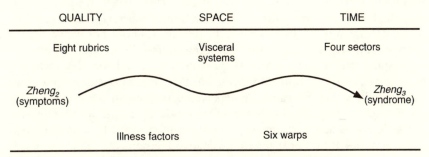

FIGURE 4.1   Interaction of analytic methods in syndrome characterization

This figure differentiates the analytic methods from each other with reference to the dimensions of quality and location. No one path through this field of possible applications of analytic methods can be sketched in here; methodological applications vary with the illness and the doctor. In addition, no one order in which a practitioner "thinks of" these elements can be posited. One leading writer has, however, attempted to outline a protocol for the logical sequence of analytic methods in the clinical encounter in his theoretical foundations textbook. Although his method makes eminent sense, one suspects a certain disciplinary impulse in his efforts to make this sequence of decisions appear to be the natural sequence:

> A general principle for the order of deployment of clinical analytic methods is that the sufferer's chief complaint, or the most painful and acute symptoms or bodily signs, is [taken to be] the main symptom of the given illness. One must first center on the main symptom and differentiate it as either exogenous or internal damage. If it is exogenous, it must be distinguished as either Hot or Cold: Exogenous Cold heteropathies are classed as Cold Damage, and their syndromes should be differentiated by means of a six warps sequence; exogenous Heat heteropathies are classed as Warm Illnesses, and their syndromes should be differentiated according to a four sectors or Triple *Jiao* sequence. . . . If it is internal damage, it should first be differentiated as depletion or repletion: Depletion syndromes differ in terms of qi and Blood, yin and yang, and one should put the visceral systems and circulation tract [diagnostics] into play. If it is a repletion syndrome, one must consider what sort of heteropathic qi is involved and use visceral systems and circulation tract [analytics] accordingly. [92]

This explanation is a good example of the sort of strategy that senior Chinese doctors use in differentiating syndromes and particularly demonstrates the importance of the sufferer's chief complaint in determining what will be perceived and treated. But I have never seen two experienced doctors

92. Liu et al., *Zhongyi Jichu Lilun Wenda,* p. 97.

mobilize precisely the same protocol in their clinic work. Although many may share strategic preferences with the author of this text, few would do it just like this, I suspect. In particular, the neat division of labor between Cold Damage and Warm Illnesses methods seems unlikely to be very popular.

Despite efforts such as this to provide a protocol for diagnosis, the analytic phase of the *kanbing* process must be seen as opening up a range of possibilities that are variously deployed according to the conditions of the moment. These conditions naturally include the habits and the training of the doctor as well as the manifestations of illness with which he is dealing.

In Figure 4.1 the most purely qualitative method, the eight rubrics, is placed at one end and the most purely temporal, the four sectors, at the other. (Note that illness factors are considered to have a spatial element because the factors are themselves classified as outer, inner, and neither inner nor outer.) It also roughly distinguishes them with reference to logical priority: Eight rubrics and visceral systems analysis feed into and are encompassed by the four sector and six warps methods.

Cases 2 , Two Cases of Foetal Death, and 3, Stomachache, being illnesses in which the heteropathy is internal, rely primarily on visceral systems imagery to characterize the illness for them. In Case 3 Dr. Zhong can see a visceral systems problem immediately since the pain is localized in the stomach; he uses illness factors and eight rubrics methods to help him interpret the symptoms and discover an underlying Liver system disorder. Because the illness is not an exogenous febrile illness, neither four sectors nor six warps analysis is relevant. Both patients of Case 2 also require a complex calculation of relations among the visceral systems, including the Triple *Jiao.*

The first case begins with an eight rubrics classification that indicates a clear repletion and is successfully treated with a prescription specific for inducing motion in lower visceral systems. In the second, more complicated case Dr. Deng concentrates on deficiencies in qi and Blood, thought of both in vital substances (visceral systems) terms and in four sectors terms. He does not refer to the eight rubrics in his commentary, nor do illness factors figure very prominently. Case 1, Spring Warm, is the only case that seems to trace a path through most of the analytic resources diagramed in Figure 3.1—its symptoms are readily characterized in eight rubrics terms, and syndromes classed under the general type of Spring Warm are named with reference to them (e.g., Interior Heat syndrome). In addition, the nature of the illness factor is of classificatory interest, and the commentary discusses several possibilities. The affected visceral systems are named and targeted in the prescription, although they may be at issue more as components of the six warps than as part of a separate visceral systems analysis. And a four sectors analysis is built on a six warps foundation, which is entirely appropriate for this exogenous Heat illness.

In tracing the analysis of these illnesses, I have shown that movement through the progressive analytic field diagramed here involves an increasing classificatory specification of the illness. The manifestations of the disorder are being circled around, as it were. Their various facets and aspects are being minutely described through the application of sensitive classificatory differentiations, each set of which is well adapted to only one or a few aspects of the illness. The result is a unique, yet medically legible pattern of affiliations. It is this pattern that is named as the syndrome.

Main entrance to the Guangzhou College of Traditional Chinese Medicine. Photo by Eric Karchmer, 1992.

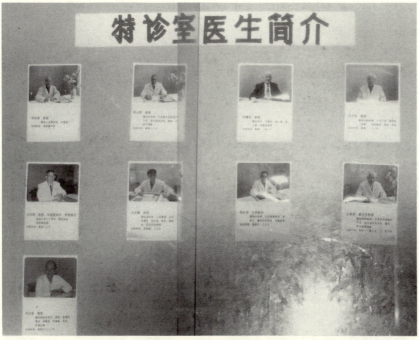

This sign greets patients at the entrance to the hospital of Chinese medicine on the campus of the Guangzhou College. Its title reads: "A Brief Introduction to Doctors of Specialist Clinics." Such signs began to appear in hospitals in China in the 1980s. These displays help patients decide which doctor and clinic to register for or to remember the proper names of the doctors or clinics they have come to find. Photo by Eric Karchmer, 1992.

Patients and their families and companions wait outside outpatient clinics at the Guangzhou College Hospital. The small clinic rooms, doors open, are along the left side of the corridor. Photo by Eric Karchmer, 1992.

Dr. He Sixun feeling a patient's pulse and reading previous entries in the patient's clinic record book. Guangzhou, 1983.

Dr. Cheng Xizhen taking a pulse and listening to the patient's history. Photo by Eric Karchmer, Guangzhou, 1992.

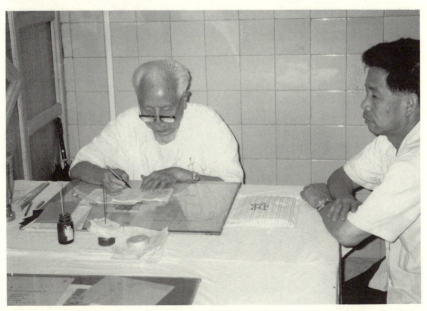

Senior Doctor Liu Shichang writing a prescription in a patient's clinic record book. Photo by Eric Karchmer, Guangzhou, 1992.

Dr. Tao Enxiang talking with a patient and her son in an outpatient clinic of Chinese medicine in a large Beijing hospital, 1990.

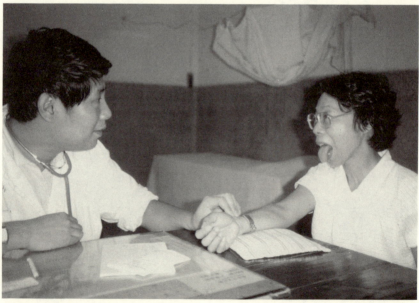

Dr. Qiu Zhuoyi conducting an examination in his cardiology clinic in 1988. Dr. Qiu did cardiology research in the United States for a year and has developed a joint Chinese and Western medical practice in the Guangzhou College Hospital.

Dr. Li Mingzhong (*above*), director of a hospital of Chinese medicine in a Shandong county town, posing with part of his library of medical books. Dr. Li specializes in a form of Chinese medical practice that uses the analytic systems of the *Book of Changes* as a major resource, 1990.

Dr. Guo Hongjie (*right*) posing in front of her small private clinic, where she practices Chinese medicine and provides routine public health and family medicine services. Shandong, 1990.

Herbal medicines growing in a small plot in the courtyard of a village clinic, Shandong, 1991. This garden is the hobby of a member of the staff at the clinic; most herbal drugs are produced in large volumes by specialized farmers.

Plantains drying for use in herbal prescriptions in the same village clinic courtyard. These will be added to the stocks of herbals in the clinic's pharmacy that are bought from bulk suppliers.

In the storeroom of a small herbal medicines factory, Shandong, 1991.

Bulk drugs stored outside the same herbal medicine factory.

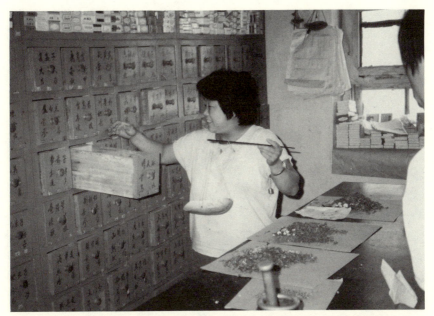

Shang Yufen, the pharmacist at a village clinic in Shandong, dispenses herbal medicines from her well-stocked pharmacy, Shandong, 1988.

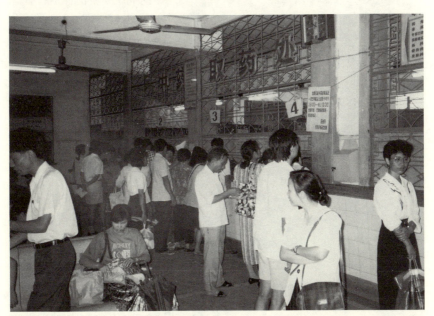

Patients waiting and lining up to collect packages of herbal medicines from the pharmacy windows at the Guangzhou College Hospital. Photo by Eric Karchmer, 1992.

Feng Dazhi (*above*), a former bare-foot doctor now working in the health station of a Shandong village, decocting an herbal prescription for the author's husband. The herbs themselves were brought from Guangzhou; no one dispenses Chinese medicines anymore in this village. The health station concentrates on public health services and Western-style primary care.

Equipment for decocting herbal prescriptions (*left*) in quantity in the Guangzhou College Hospital. Photo by Eric Karchmer, 1992.

5

The Syndrome-Therapy Pivot

Syndrome differentiation and therapy determination [*bianzheng lunzhi*]—also called syndrome differentiation and therapy deployment [*bianzheng shizhi*]. The process of using "theory, methods, formulae, and drugs" clinically, the basic characteristic of the Chinese medical art. That which advances a general analysis of the signs and symptoms manifested by a sufferer by means of the four examinations and eight rubrics, visceral systems, illness factors, illness mechanisms, and other basic theories of Chinese medicine and differentiates [the condition] as some kind of syndrome [*zhenghou*] is called syndrome differentiation [*bianzheng*]; that which works out therapeutic measures on the basis of the syndrome differentiation is called treatment determination [*lunzhi*].[1]

The analytical phase of the *kanbing* process characterizes symptoms such that the specific form and likely future of an illness can be perceived. The diagnostic methods described in Chapter 4 are generally called *bianzheng fangfa,* and they concatenate to a point at which a specific syndrome can be discerned, minutely characterized, and named. In this chapter, then, I will explore in detail the nature of the syndrome ($zheng_3$) and discuss the relationship between syndromes and treatment methods.

This relationship is often asserted to be one of extreme closeness and interdependence. The national foundations textbook *Zhongyixue Jichu* (Foundations of Chinese Medicine), in an explanation that was often provided in essentially the same form by teachers in Guangzhou, clearly states that

> *bianzheng* and *lunzhi* are the two most important links in the concrete clinical utilization of Chinese medicine's theory, methods, formulae, and drugs; they are interconnected as two inseparable parts in the process of diagnosing and treating diseases. *Bianzheng* is to discern [*renshi*] the disease; *lunzhi* is the technique and method of targeting the syndrome and choosing a responsive therapeutic technique and method.

---

1. Editing Committee of the Unabridged Dictionary of Chinese Medicine, *Zhongyi Dacidian, Jichu Lilun Fence* (Beijing: People's Health Press, 1982), s.v. *bianzheng lunzhi.*

Bianzheng is the prerequisite and basis for deciding therapy, and the effectiveness of the therapy is the standard by which to test whether the differentiation of the syndrome has been correct or not. Only if an appropriate treatment method is chosen at the same time that a correct syndrome differentiation is made can the anticipated effectiveness be achieved.[2]

The relationship posited here, the syndrome (*zheng₃*) as the prerequisite to treatment (*zhi*) and the treatment as the test of the syndrome, incorporates the two linked and opposed aspects of the central turning point in the clinical encounter (Figure 3.2, phase C). An examination of this pivot can illuminate the specific relationship between sources and manifestations that is pertinent to Chinese medicine; that is, it can place medicine within a broader Chinese metaphysic and relate it to other forms of indigenous Chinese knowledge. In addition (and this is the aspect of the problem on which I will focus), it is at this turning point in the clinical encounter that the doctor's agency and powers can be most clearly perceived. To this end, let us first consider the connotative range and functions of the term *zheng₃*.

Defining the Syndrome (*Zheng₃*)

Implicit in much contemporary Chinese writing about syndrome differentiation is a contrast between Chinese illness syndromes, *zheng₃*, and the "diseases" of Western medicine (*jibing* or *bing*).[3] Little of what Chinese doctors think about the relationship of these two terms has appeared in print as an explicit comparison, but Liu Changlin's philosophical study of the *Inner Canon* has made some interesting distinctions:

Bianzheng lunzhi is a special method of researching and managing disease in Chinese medicine. The original meaning of the term *zheng₃* was that of signs manifested on the outside. *Bianzheng*, then, probed the internal essence [*benzhi*] of illness changes through analysis of the patient's external signs. The term "syndrome" [*zhenghou*] generally referred to the results of the *bianzheng* process; it was the epitome of the mechanisms of illness factors and illness changes. *Zhenghou*, sometimes called *zheng₃* for short, is not the same concept as symptoms. Symptoms are the various surface phenomena of diseases. . . .

Western medicine takes the body's anatomical physiology, biochemistry, cytology, and histology as its foundation, mainly choosing a reductionist

---

2. Beijing College of Traditional Chinese Medicine, ed., *Zhongyixue Jichu* (Shanghai: Shanghai Science and Technology Press, 1978), p. 97.

3. I generally translate *bing* as illness and *jibing* as disease. The latter compound is confined to relatively modern Chinese usage, an environment in which cosmopolitan science and biomedicine are important, whereas *bing* is, judging from recent archaeological finds, among the most venerable of Chinese words in continual common use.

analytical method to know the human body. Thus, Western medicine's channel for knowing about disease is to find, on the basis of the structural organism's material substances, the concrete morphological place and substantial process that produce the illness, using techniques of physical diagnosis, biopsy, chemical analysis, microscopic examination, and X-ray fluoroscopy. On this basis [Western medicine] then studies the substantial basis [of these locations and processes] and the mechanisms of their pathological changes to advance a means of dealing with the disease.[4]

This discussion, in keeping with recent usage, does not question the "reality" of the notion of disease and indeed incorporates the word for disease into the definition of the syndrome. But the difference between the two terms is lengthily presented as a difference of perspective and practical methods; seen in this way, diseases and syndromes are equally real and equally socially contingent. That is, both syndrome and disease are defined, not as entities existing in nature independently of human activity, but as constructs resulting from specific types of analysis of highly various effects.

A definition of syndrome differentiation from a foundations text incorporates a synthesis of the two terms quite clearly:

Syndrome differentiation in Chinese medicine considers the human body in conditions of pathology, its functional state during some given time period. It recognizes the essence of disease [*jibing*] from the point of view of organic responses, and by analyzing disease through the symptoms and signs that manifest at that time, it further comprehends the internal connections of these clinical manifestations. It thereby infers the principles of the pathological changes and uses a down-to-earth [form of] materialist dialectic thought to propose an abstract concept, thereafter establishing a whole set of concepts of the syndrome differentiation that respond to the internal essence of pathological changes.[5]

At a general level, this synthesis is sensible, dignified (in the sense that Chinese medical knowledge is not devalued), and politically correct. But a sense of contradiction remains in the literature. Liu Changlin's more philosophical description of the microbiologically and anatomically based disease of Western medicine is formed in part by comparison with the Chinese medical syndrome; viewed from the perspective of clinicians in the United States, this description might appear oversimplified. But some such view of disease as reductionist, penetrative, and dependent on technology has in turn influenced the concept of the syndrome as discourse on the unification of Chinese and Western medicine has proceeded. The syndrome, one

---

4. Liu Changlin, *Neijingde Zhexue he Zhongyixuede Fangfa* (Beijing: Science Press, 1982), p. 205.

5. Liu Yanchi, Song Tianbin, Zhang Ruifu, and Dong Liantong, eds., *Zhongyi Jichu Lilun Wenda* (Shanghai: Shanghai Science and Technology Press, 1982), p. 97.

suspects, must stand in contrast to the central Western medical concept of disease (i.e., it must be central and fundamental in its theoretical position even if entirely different in its meaning) so that comparisons can be coherently made.

Struggle over definitions continues. Deng Tietao provides an example of definitional polemic in his *Zhongyi Jichu Lilun* (Fundamental Theory of Chinese Medicine):

> *Bianzheng lunzhi* differs from therapeutic methods that attack symptoms part by part, as in "When you see fever, reduce fever; when you see coughing, arrest coughing; when the head aches, dose the head; when the feet hurt, dose the feet." It also differs from those kinds of therapeutic methods that don't distinguish primary and secondary, don't differentiate stages of illness, and use one prescription or one drug to treat one illness. . . . *Bianzheng lunzhi* can dialectically discern the relationship between the illness [*bing*] and the syndrome, seeing that one kind of illness can include several different syndromes as well as seeing that different illnesses in the course of their developmental process can manifest the same syndrome.[6]

In addition to satirizing what he sees as a rather wooden approach to diagnosis in Western medicine, Dr. Deng betrays here his conviction that syndromes can be subsumed within diseases (although he obviously uses the more general term *bing* deliberately here), while attention to subtle Chinese medical distinctions can improve the ability of doctors to treat disease. He dares to suggest that the attentiveness to time and the holistic insights of Chinese medical methods are objectively superior to the mechanistic reductionism of Western medicine. Others would disagree with him, but this is beside the point here. What is important about the syndrome-disease contrast in writing of this kind is that the author links the difference between the two concepts to wider unique features of Chinese medicine ("holistic, processual, dialectical," etc.). The question of the nature of the syndrome is clearly near the heart of "modernization" (*xiandaihua*) concerns.

How, then, is the syndrome consensually defined, for example, in the sort of teaching text that is produced by national committees? *Foundations of Chinese Medicine* enters the fray as follows: "Syndromes [*zhenghou*] are not the same as symptoms [*zhengzhuang*]; rather, they are all the types of symptomatology generalized and analyzed, the pathological epitome of every facet of the situation—the illness factors, locations, qualitative changes, and the relative strength of heteropathic and orthopathic qi—in a certain phase of a disease."[7] The syndrome results from human activity: It is a generalization and analysis of diverse manifestations into a "pathological epitome" or

---

6. Deng Tietao, ed., *Zhongyi Jichu Lilun* (Guangzhou: Guangdong Science and Technology Press, 1982), p. 5.

7. Beijing College, *Zhongyixue Jichu*, p. 97.

summation. Symptoms, *zheng₂* or *zhengzhuang,* are much more immediate than the syndrome into which they are gathered, they arise from "a certain phase of a *disease.*" Here disease is a category that has meaning but by virtue of its insensitivity to symptomatic vicissitudes has little clinical use. The syndrome is a form of abstraction from the level of concrete symptoms, a product of the doctor's work. Its significance is related to its nuanced accommodation of pathological changes.

One of the great virtues of syndrome differentiation is its inherent temporality. Thus, Deng Tietao explains the relationship between symptoms and syndromes as follows:

> The notions of *zheng₃* and *zheng₂* are not the same. *Zheng₂* are symptoms such as headache, cough, fever, intolerance of cold, insomnia. These are the various superficial phenomena of diseases. The *zheng₃* is the syndrome [*zhenghou*], an epitome [*gaodu gaikuo*] of the illness factors and processes, sites of pathological changes, qualities of heteropathic qi, and relative strength of heteropathic or orthopathic qi *in each phase of the developmental process* of the disease. Thus, [the syndrome] can be deeper, more complete, and more exactly reflective of the root qualities [*benzhi*] of the disease than the symptoms are.[8]

In addition to incorporating the notion of disease in a conventional modernizing way, this clarification demonstrates a certain source-manifestation relationship between "root qualities" and "superficial phenomena": The syndrome, a product of a doctor's analytic work, approaches closer to the source than the symptoms do. This view is not only consistent with Deng Tietao's more or less Maoist epistemological project (he often addresses medical problems in terms of analytic structures drawn from Mao's philosophical essays, in this case "On Practice" and "On Contradiction"),[9] but also has analogues in much more ancient Chinese scientific and philosophical practice. The world is nothing but the myriad things unless these things are understood in relation to the generativity of unseen sources. Ultimate sources may be beyond the ken of mere humans, but throughout the course of Chinese history Daoists, philosophers, officials, and poets have often spoken of their efforts as attempts to get closer to sources.

Statements of this kind also indicate that the syndrome is a moment of a continuing illness process; as the illness worsens or improves, the clinician will have to reconsider the nature of the syndrome. One illness might be a series of syndromes, each entailing new treatment methods and drug formulae.

This process can be perceived in the three case histories included in this

---

8. Deng, *Zhongyi Jichu Lilun,* p. 6; emphasis added.

9. See my "Problems of Knowledge in Contemporary Chinese Medical Discourse," *Social Science and Medicine* 24, no. 12 (1987):1013–1021, for relationships between medical discourse and Maoist epistemology.

book. Although sequences of syndrome names through the course of an illness are seldom listed, it is understood that the syndrome that is differentiated on the first examination is only one (although often the most crucial one) of a sequence. If the illness proceeds toward recovery in a satisfactory manner, subsequent syndromes need not be explicitly differentiated.

In Case 1 the syndrome was Spring Warm repletion in the yang visceral systems, which is characterized by constipation and agitation or irritability. After the first treatment both of these key symptoms were markedly altered, and by the time of the third examination the illness had moved to the defensive qi sector and could no longer be characterized as a repletion of any visceral system. Had it been newly diagnosed (e.g., by a different doctor), it would have been diagnosed as one of the exterior syndromes characteristic of the defensive qi sector.

The second example of a dead foetus failing to descend in Case 2 displays an interesting play of syndrome differentiation and treatment determination. Since the author discusses his management of the case in terms of his decisions on drug formulae, the syndrome must be inferred from the treatment methods. (This mode of inference is taken for granted in sophisticated Chinese medical writing.) He began with a treatment that simultaneously redressed the qi and fluid depletion and attempted to induce downward flow through lubrication (a purgative technique that is more conservative than the "assault downward" technique, which he wanted to avoid). By the time of the fifth examination, he had abandoned the idea that digestive system fluid depletion was the root problem and seems to have seen the illness as a serious whole-body stasis of both qi and Blood; the treatment that eventually worked was a simple and radical formula based on the principle of enlivening Blood and moving qi. This series of different syndrome differentiations implicit in different treatment methods is not simply a function of failures of the doctor's perception or a sign of a therapeutic strategy of mindless trial and error. Doctor Deng would argue, I suspect, that his original diagnosis would have been appropriate to an earlier stage of the illness but that the extended period of time that the heteropathic qi of the dead foetus had been in the patient's body had escalated the seriousness of the illness and produced a more advanced syndrome type. At the same time the repletion had further weakened the patient's defenses; thus, a therapy that differentially attacked the dead foetus while strengthening the mother, its host, needed to be designed.[10]

Case 3 is much simpler but also incorporates a shift in the syndrome observable through alterations in therapy. The original treatment principle di-

---

10. I have discussed this case at length in my "Time and Text," in Charles Leslie and Allan Young, eds., *Paths to Asian Medical Knowledge* (Berkeley and Los Angeles: University of California Press, 1992), pp. 62–73.

rectly attacked the Heat repletion in the Stomach, the illness root being seen as stasis of long duration. After this static condition had begun to alleviate, the gastric cavity was still distended and full, making it possible to detect a Spleen dysfunction, which was treated in the second formula.

These three cases show (what is constantly emphasized in the modern literature on the syndrome) that "in Chinese medicine's clinical work, in diseases of the same type the 'syndromes' can differ, so the therapies can also be different. ... Yet different diseases in the course of their pathological process can manifest the same syndrome; hence we can use the same method to treat them."[11]

Definitions of the syndrome like those cited previously refer to several kinds of intellectual activity that are important in the process of differentiating the syndrome: *Foundations of Chinese Medicine* speaks of synthesizing (*zonghe*) and analyzing (*fenxi*), which result in a summary (*gaikuo*) or epitomization; Dr. Deng explains syndrome differentiation as a process that subjects the signs and symptoms collected through the four methods of examination to analysis, synthesis, summary, and judgment.[12] The relationship between analysis and synthesis in statements like these is one of direct contrast and complementarity. Analysis, as the Chinese term *fenxi* suggests, consists almost invariably of breaking a complex effect such as an illness, a prescription, or a syndrome name into parts; this could also be seen as characterizing facets of a complex effect through classification. Synthesis is usually seen as being pursued simultaneously with analysis, as the relations among components are perceived, and they are summarized into a better-understood unified effect.

The major source of my perception of these two processes and their relationship is class lectures in Guangzhou, in which analysis and synthesis of syndromes and prescriptions were undertaken in sequence as didactic exercises. At the time I noted that analysis took place with primary reference to the classificatory affiliations of components (e.g., the qualities, *xingzhi*, of drugs or symptoms) and that synthesis tended to involve a perception of relationships internal to the effect in question and an epitomization of it in a syndrome or prescription name. In addition, the term I have translated as summarizing or epitomizing, *gaikuo*, or *gaodu gaikuo*, was constantly in use and referred both to an additive summary of effects and a contraction and condensation of them into a short statement or formula. The syndrome is asserted to be such an epitome.

When the syndrome is perceived at least in part as additive (and certainly the long, involved definitions that are provided in modern texts support this

---

11. Jiangsu Province Department of Health, ed., *Zhongyi Jichu* (Suzhou: Jiangsu Science and Technology Press, 1977), p. 4.

12. Beijing College, *Zhongyixue Jichu*, p. 97; Deng, *Zhongyi Jichu Lilun*, p. 6.

perception), it does not seem reductive in the same way that many of the important disease concepts of biomedicine are. Major characteristics of the illness as a whole are encoded in the syndrome name. Consequently, introductions to the meanings and practices of *bianzheng* frequently rely on an unpacking approach to clarify the nature of the syndrome. A 1977 foundations text provides one such example:

> The *zheng₃* of *bianzheng* is an epitomization of the causes, sites, qualities, state of struggle between heteropathic and orthopathic qi, and other aspects of the disease, and it indicates the direction that therapy should take. Take the syndrome "Liver and Gallbladder Damp Heat Accumulating and Congealing," for example: It tells us that the heteropathic qi is Damp Heat, the site of pathological change is in the Liver and Gallbladder system, the quality of pathological changes is Damp Heat accumulating and congealing, and the state of struggle between orthopathic and heteropathic qi is a repletion syndrome with a predominance of heteropathic qi but no weakening of orthopathic qi; all this shows that the treatment method should be to clear Damp Heat and cause it to flow downward from the Liver and Gallbladder.[13]

In the course of such an analysis the concrete symptoms are not mentioned. But they hardly need to be; any clinician should know immediately what symptoms these conditions are likely to produce. This passage also demonstrates well the intimate link between the syndrome and its coordinated treatment method.

Differentiating the Syndrome (*Bianzheng*)

Bianzheng is a process and a methodology; it begins in (and in most usages subsumes) the analytic phase of the clinical encounter (Figure 3.2, phase B) and culminates in the epitomizing *zhengzhi* moment (Figure 3.2, phase C). There are at least two aspects to the differentiation being accomplished. One aspect is the differentiation of the syndrome as summation, all the qualities and locations of the illness being distinguished from all possible (or at least, logically adjacent) qualities and locations—for example, Hot rather than Cold, centered on the Heart system rather than on the Spleen, and relatively early and slight rather than advanced and severe. The other aspect is the differentiation of this syndrome as epitome from all possible (and especially all similar) syndromes. This requirement presents problems that are a major concern at several levels in contemporary Chinese medical discourse and that open the question of the differential identity of any syndrome.

---

13. Office of the 1977 Physicians of Western Medicine Class in Chinese Medicine, ed., *Zhongyi Jichuxue* (Guangzhou: Guangdong College of Traditional Chinese Medicine, 1977), p. 4.

As is evident in the discussion of Liver and Gallbladder Damp Heat Accumulating and Congealing syndrome, there can be a direct relationship between the results of differentiating analysis and the name of the resulting syndrome. But syndrome names come in many forms and are used at several levels of generality. Those that condense a list of relevant analytic terms into a name like the Liver and Gallbladder syndrome are usually specifications or subclasses within higher-level generic syndromes. Such generic syndrome names have several sources. Some are named primarily with reference to a locus classicus (Spring Warm), others describe self-evident injuries or mechanical disorders (Foetus Dead in the Womb), and still others refer to a broad symptom class (Stomachache).

Differential recognition of the syndrome can therefore take place in at least two steps. In the first step it is often relatively simple to place the illness in a generic syndrome category: Spring Warm occurs in the spring and manifests a high fever, and Stomachache and Foetus Dead in the Womb are even easier to settle on diagnostically. Some of these large classes of syndromes are well described and broken down into subclasses in the literature, and they are carefully taught as problems of differentiation. Others, such as Stomachache, are vast and rather vague—in many texts Stomachache is not discussed as a separate class but is subsumed in a variety of other generic syndromes. The identification of a commonly recognized generic syndrome delimits an area of recorded (and probably indexed and anthologized) medical experience. Within this area the appropriate syndrome differentiation can be made.

The second step of differentiation generally involves the elimination of syndromes recorded in the medical archive that are similar to but not quite the same as the illness at hand.[14] How is this finer level of differentiation pursued in practice? One important method is that of distinguishing for each syndrome a small set of key symptoms whose presence or absence should definitively indicate the correct syndrome classification of the illness. Nowadays comparisons between similar syndromes are often presented in tabular form, both in teaching and in texts of the "crib note" type; but such comparisons have a long history, probably deriving originally from the *Treatise on Cold Damage,* where key symptoms as classificatory criteria are

---

14. On my use of the term *archive:* The role in contemporary Chinese medical life of the voluminous written records of Chinese medical observation and practice, theoretical speculation, and investigations and applications of herbals and other therapeutics is obviously a complex subject deserving much more lengthy treatment than I can provide here. I use "the medical archive" as a blanket term for all manner of written materials from the two-thousand-year history of medicine in China. I do not wish, however, to suggest any necessary unity for the field of medicine or its written history. This discussion explores one way in which texts are deployed in the social life of Chinese medicine. In parallel work I hope to emphasize the social and historical situations of a few specific forms of medical textuality (e.g., published case histories).

prominent in Zhang Ji's method. Table 5.1 is an example of a differentiating table compiled from three maxims of the *Treatise on Cold Damage* and used in a class at the Guangzhou College. It enables the differentiation of a syndrome that has been recognized as a mature yang illness (key symptoms: fever, intolerance of cold, headache), first as a syndrome of the class of "slight mature yang" and subsequently as one of the three similar syndromes commonly found in this class according to their key symptoms. Three different drug formulae are classically used for these conditions; hence the correct identification of the syndrome is important.

When this table is read from left to right, a movement from continuous physiological processes to discontinuous discrete features of an illness can be perceived. This is in keeping with the requirements of any kind of classification, but a table of this kind particularly displays the Chinese medical classification process as an analysis (*fenxi*), as a process of carving a unitary movement up into discrete classifiable (and treatable) types. Thus, the illness process is spoken of, and represented here, as a clear continuum accounting for the similarity of these three syndromes and for their appearance together

Table 5.1   Slight Mature Yang Syndromes

Syndrome Type	Illness Process	Primary Symptoms		Treatment Method[a]	Treatise Text
		Common	Differential		
Unflushed Exterior Oppression	Heteropathic qi weakened but ortho-pathic redoubled	Fever	"Malarial" symptoms; daily 2–3° variation in temp.; red face; itching	Light sweating	(23)
		Intolerance of cold			
	Heteropathic qi even weaker	Much heat	Daily re-currence of slight "malarial" temp.	Moderate sweating	(25)
Interior Heat Exterior Oppression	Exterior heteropathic qi unflushed; oppressive interior Heat	Little cold	Agitation, thirst	Moderate sweating; clear interior Heat	(27)

[a]A column listing a different prescription for each of the three illness processes has been deleted to save space.

SOURCE: Mimeographed handout to the *Treatise on Cold Damage* classes, Guangzhou College of Traditional Chinese Medicine, Spring 1983.

in one group of mature yang illnesses (which group itself—"slight mature yang syndromes"—results from a prior classification that has broken up the continuities of the struggle between heteropathic and orthopathic qi on the exterior). One aspect of the dialectical nature of Chinese medicine's classificatory method is made evident in these nested categories, within each of which certain specific continuous processes operate. A clinical ability to move readily back and forth between process and class, commonalities and specificities, flow and fixity, at more than one level is encouraged, even required, in the process of characterizing, specifying, differentiating, and epitomizing illnesses.

The two syndrome types and three subtypes organized in Table 5.1 do not exhaust the clinical possibilities of slight mature yang illnesses. Quite often there is no syndrome available to be drawn from the medical archive that accords in every detail with the illness at hand. But the classical syndromes are well characterized and can be combined to produce a clear picture of a dual or plural condition. Case 1, Spring Warm, is a case of this kind: The Heat is seen to be affecting both the viscera and the circulation tracts (a combination of two syndromes) and to be moving (i.e., caught at a transitional moment) from the active qi sector to the constructive qi sector.

The judgments that doctors must make at the pinnacle of the *bianzheng lunzhi* process are summed up in the metaphor of the illness root. The cliché "In treating illness, trace the root," drawn from *Basic Questions* (*juan* 2, section 5), is frequently cited both in print and oral explanations of Chinese medical methods. The word and the concept of illness root are not, however, self-evident even in Chinese usage. As might be expected, the word *root* (*ben*) appears frequently in the *Inner Canon*, where its meanings vary according to the context. This polysemy becomes a problem only as this medical classic is appropriated in a modern rhetoric of authoritative sources. In this process such items of classical terminology are explored for their potential as technical terms, and efforts are made to fix their meaning and to range entailed clinical procedures around them, with the *Inner Canon* as authority.

The most frequently cited example of the notion of root is, as noted in Chapter 2, the opening lines of section 5 of the *Basic Questions:* "Yin and yang are the Dao of heaven and earth. They are the network of the myriad things, the father and mother of alteration and transformation, the root and beginning of life-giving and death-bringing, the abode of vitality and intelligence. The treatment of illness must trace this root."[15] Since everything phenomenal is rooted in yinyang, the yinyang root of illness must also be sought. This statement is often cited in Maoist-influenced discussions of

---

15. Cheng Shide et al., eds., *Suwen Zhushi Huicui, juan* 2, sec. 5 (Beijing: People's Health Press, 1982), pp. 82–83.

bianzheng lunzhi. The yinyang root is seen as the "essence" or "primary contradiction" of an illness, and the syndrome is tacitly or explicitly seen as the manifestation that expresses the specificity of this contradiction.[16]

Elsewhere in the *Inner Canon* and its secondary literature, the significance of the word *root* cannot be rendered quite so straightforwardly. *Juan* 22, section 74, a long and very technical chapter of the *Divine Pivot*, uses the metaphor of "branches and roots" (*biao ben*) to distinguish the aspect of the illness that should be treated most aggressively. In this usage, root does not appear to have the same degree of stability that would be asserted for the yinyang root of illness. It can refer to a wide range of phenomena and seems to have a strongly heuristic value. In the Maoist discourse that has been adapted to modern medical writing, the use of root to refer to the aspect of a condition that should be therapeutically targeted is seen as "grasping the primary contradiction." This usage is explained in one modern text under that heading as follows:

> Branch and root are a relative concept used to explain the relation between primary and secondary aspects in the contradictions of various illness syndromes. For example, with respect to orthopathic and heteropathic qi, orthopathic qi is the root and heteropathic qi is the branches; with respect to the onset of disease, the illness factor is the root and the symptoms are the branches; with respect to the site of pathological changes, the internal viscera are the root and the body exterior is the branch; and with respect to the sequence of illness onsets, earlier illnesses are the roots and later illnesses are the branches.
>
> The onset, development, and changes of diseases, especially of complicated diseases, generally incorporate many contradictions. Among them are the primary and secondary contradictions; the two aspects of a [single] contradiction also [each] have a main and a secondary aspect. Moreover, in the course of development of disease, sometimes a secondary contradiction can elevate itself to become the primary contradiction; or a primary contradiction can recede and become the secondary contradiction; or if an old contradiction is resolved, new contradictions can arise; and so on. In general, disease is complex and rapidly shifting, illness syndromes often have differences of primary and secondary, slight and severe, so in therapy we must have distinctions between prior and latter, urgent and less urgent.[17]

---

16. Cf. Mao Zedong, "On Contradiction," in *Selected Readings from the Works of Mao Tsetung* (Beijing: Foreign Languages Press, 1971), pp. 85–133. There is also a tacit comparison with the concept of disease in Western medicine here; I suspect that some of the modern emphasis on seeking illness roots is an attempt to locate within the Chinese medical tradition a notion of illness sources that is as discriminant and causally powerful as the "economical" and reductive models perceived in the Western sciences. Mao Zedong proposed his notion of primary and secondary contradictions and "essences" (*benzhi,* or basic substantial character) in a project of developing an indigenous Chinese socialist science. Since the writing of his early philosophical essays in the 1930s, scientism has, if anything, become more hegemonic in Chinese intellectual discourse.

17. Office of the 1977 Physicians, *Zhongyi Jichuxue,* p. 168.

This passage takes the root-branch dyad as a mode of analysis within the syndrome once it has been differentiated. The root is no longer a whole yinyang contradiction but rather a specific aspect of it that is salient in the context of a concrete therapeutic project. The identification of root and branch aspects depends on a combination of type and stage of illness and the point of view taken by the analyst; thus, the root and branch of an illness can conceivably change during the course of therapy. This flexibility is held to be important partly because the analysis of the syndrome presents a major practical problem; the materialization of treatment methods in formulae and drugs in the latter phases of the *kanbing* process requires a number of subtle quantifications in which decisions regarding the "primary and secondary contradictions" must be made. This passage suggests that the metaphor of the root allows ever finer differentiations; just as yin and yang can always subdivide into yin-in-yang and yang-in-yin, presumably the branch-root distinction can be continually refined in a process of subdividing the illness into primary and secondary aspects.

Whether the root is seen in a given situation as the syndrome itself, as its primary internal contradiction, or as a temporary focus of intervention, a strong reference is being made to the correctness of syndrome differentiation procedure. The metaphor of root and branch is highly evaluative and incorporates the possibility that wrong (or too superficial, branch) differentiations might be made. Wrong judgments can, of course, become evident in medical practice in tragic ways, and wrong therapies can be more disastrous than the presenting illness.

Although *bianzheng* is a diagnostic process that could be seen as strictly technical—that is, the separation of one syndrome from among many in a system of cut-and-dried differences—the imperative to trace the root transforms it into a process in which the doctor must aggressively and imaginatively seek out the source of the illness. This requires that primacy be accorded to some elements to establish a hierarchy of forces among all features of the illness. Since ideally the *bianzheng* process should always involve a simultaneous classification and dynamic analysis, it is not surprising that the syndrome should often be seen as the root. In diagnosis the syndrome is more than a summation of analyzed symptoms, more than a mere label or name; it is a central generative condition. It is not only a descriptive class but also an array of forces that can worsen or improve the illness condition.

Insofar as a case of Spring Warm syndrome is felt by the doctor to have a palpable and consequential reality, then he undoubtedly views it as much like other cases of Spring Warm he has seen. But since Spring Warm cannot be studied in a laboratory, the likeness between illnesses classified as the same syndrome is perhaps not as absolute as the likeness between all cases of, for example, Type A influenza. The reality of the Chinese medical illness is not separable from the sufferer and his or her specific conditions and dispositions. Illness manifestations can be redundant—there might be many cases of Spring Warm in a given locale and season—but these redundancies are not caused by the action of a complex illness agent on structurally identical bodies. The syndrome names a redundant pattern in the phenomena that manifest as human illness. Because diseases have differing courses, a "patient" cannot be a "case" of a syndrome. Ideally, the syndrome is not more than the situation afflicting the sick person at a specified moment. As such it is at once a "social" reality (articulately faceted and named with reference to categories and methods from the medical archive) and a "natural" reality (a real and undesirable condition of the world).

Because the syndrome is a name, and usually a name that has been used many times before, the differentiation of a syndrome can delimit a relevant area of the medical literature for consultation. Especially when the dynamics of a condition are complex or equivocal, and fail to suggest a direct intervention, the doctor should be able to draw on the experience of his medical forebears. Even a tentative or overgeneral syndrome identification will help him draw useful material from the medical archive.

To assert that the root aspect of the illness must be selected out for especially aggressive treatment is to suggest that the choice of a treatment method, a named formula, and a group of drug qualities that can address the differentiated syndrome may be far from simple and self-evident. The *lunzhi* side of the *bianzheng lunzhi* couple is not merely the selection of a *zhi* to match the $zheng_3$ from a well-organized and indexed, fixed, and eternal catalogue of successful treatments. Judgment, scholarly resourcefulness, and intellectual dexterity are always required.

Tracing the root, then, locates the judgment and actions of the doctor in a position superior to the methods of *bianzheng lunzhi* that can be described, recorded, or advocated. Guidelines, hints, and rules of thumb are provided in both canonical works and modern texts, but materials of this kind can never fully accommodate the concrete situations with which doctors are faced. Nor are they expected to. Modern discussions of tracing the root always include paragraphs on the necessity of accounting for variations of time, place, and person in determining treatment. The mechanical techniques that can be explained in texts must be transcended as doctors trace the roots of actual illnesses; medical judgment in its highest development must respond to the concrete specificity of the illness at hand.

This project of tracing the root in diagnosis and treatment is not a quest for one cause of the illness so that all other factors can be discarded as side effects or epiphenomena. Causation in Chinese medicine operates on many fronts at once, presenting many complications to analysis. Therefore, the syndrome must epitomize, rather than reduce, and tracing the root involves active choices as a complete, organized, and hierarchically coherent image of the situation is constructed. Root as source, whether it focuses on the syndrome or on one side of its "specific contradiction," privileges one or a few aspects of the illness such that treatment can be quantitatively tailored to the illness with the greatest possible effectiveness. But "secondary contradictions" are not left to resolve themselves; therapeutic responses to them are carefully woven into the drug formula in proportion to the importance accorded them in the root and branch model that has been constructed.

Determining Treatment Methods (*Lunzhi*)

The syndrome is the highest epitomizing point of the *bianzheng* process. It encapsulates (and in its name often makes reference to) the various aspects and components of the illness that have been revealed through analysis and is the most complete unified summary of the illness. Showing the root and source of illness manifestations, it is a high point of generalization and abstraction in *kanbing*. It is matched on the *lunzhi* side by equally epitomizing and abstracted treatment principles and treatment methods. These are introduced in *Foundations of Chinese Medicine* as follows:

> Therapeutic principles [*zhize*], or methods [*faze*] of treating disease, have been formulated under the guidance of a holistic concept and the basic spirit of *bianzheng lunzhi;* they are the principles [*guilu*] of therapy that form the common guiding ideas for clinical treatment, for the establishment of methods [*fa*], for the organization of prescriptions, and for the use of drugs. Therapeutic methods and concrete treatment techniques [*fangfa*] are not the same. Therapeutic methods are used as the general principles [*zongze*] that guide treatment techniques, and any concrete treatment technique is in general determined [*guiding*] from a therapeutic method and belongs to a certain therapeutic method. For example, speaking about any kind of illness syndrome from the point of view of the relationship between heteropathy and orthopathy, one cannot depart from the heteropathy-orthopathy struggle and the changes of their [relative] increase and decrease, domination and weakness; therefore, the general therapeutic principles must be to support orthopathic qi and expel heteropathic qi. Thus, methods [*fa*] selected under the guidance of these general principles, such as increasing qi, moistening yin, and nourishing Blood, are all concrete techniques of supporting orthopathic qi; and sweating, inducing vomiting, downward attack, and other such methods are all concrete techniques of expelling heteropathy.[18]

As is evident by now, syndromes and treatment methods are intimately linked. Many examples cited herein have shown how certain treatment methods are affiliated to certain syndromes and conditions in standard ways. In Case 1, for example, because the illness was a syndrome in the active qi sector and a yang brilliance condition, clearing Heat and draining repletion

---

18. Beijing College, *Zhongyixue Jichu,* p. 137.

were the treatment methods to be employed. Basic and more advanced textbooks constantly affirm these natural affiliations. An exemplary decompo-
sition of the illness of headache into the various syndromes that might produce it in the context of a root-branch discussion and the listing of the
treatment method appropriate to each syndrome is a good (if simplistic) example of conventional *zhengzhi* pairings:

> Headache can be induced by many kinds of factors, such as exogenous [heter-
> opathy], Blood depletion, Phlegm Dampness, Blood stasis, [or] Liver yang
> attacking upward. Thus, in treating it, one cannot simply choose pain-
> stopping methods that address the symptoms alone. Rather, one must go
> through a complete general analysis to find the reasons for the illness in order
> to differentiate whether therapy is best advanced by using methods of flushing
> the exterior, nourishing Blood, drying Dampness and transforming Phlegm,
> enlivening Blood and transforming stasis, or steadying the Liver system and
> returning yang to latency. Only then can a satisfactory result be achieved.[19]

In practice, however, there is nothing automatic about linkages of this
kind. Treatments must be selected and critically put into play in response to
the unique features of the concrete illness situation. The management of
the second instance of a dead foetus failing to descend (Case 2) is a good
example; ordinarily one would "attack downward" (*gongxia*) the repletion
blockage of the abdomen with attacking and draining drugs, but Dr. Deng
hesitated to use such radical therapy lest he injure the mother's orthopathic
qi, which was already depleted. When his tentative "lubricating" approaches
failed, he chose to enliven Blood and move qi, thereby simultaneously
bolstering orthopathic qi and encouraging downward movement of the
blockage.

Beyond standard correspondences, textbooks include only a few guidelines for effecting a link between the syndrome and its treatment. These
focus on situations in which traditional affiliations are not likely to work. A
discussion such as the following—of straight (*zhengzhi*) and "reversed"
(*fanzhi*) methods—is usually included in treatment methods sections of
texts:

> The *Basic Questions, juan* 22, section 74, takes up two kinds of treatment
> principle: "That which opposes is straight therapy, that which follows is re-
> versed therapy," but in principle both are concrete uses of the therapeutic
> method ["]In treating illness, trace the root.["] So-called straight therapy
> [*zhengzhi*] is that which by means of analyzing the clinical syndrome (i.e., the
> presenting manifestations of an illness) differentiates the essential qualities of
> Hot or Cold, repletion or depletion in the pathological changes; then it differ-

---

19. Ibid., p. 138.

entially selects from various treatment techniques—"When there's Heat, Cool
it," "When there's Cold, Heat it," "When there's depletion, replenish it,"
"When there's repletion, drain it"—to resolve it. Because it belongs to a kind
of normal treatment technique that cures by working in opposition to [the
direction of change in] the condition, therefore it is said that "that which
opposes is straight therapy," and it is also called "opposing therapy." Because
clinically in a great number of diseases the symptomatic manifestations correspond to the characteristic qualities (e.g., in Cold illness we see cold manifestations, in Hot illnesses we see hot manifestations, in depletion illnesses we see
depletion manifestations, in repletion illnesses we see repletion manifestations),[20] straight therapeutic techniques are clinically the most frequently used
kind.

But there are some diseases, especially those that are complex or serious, in
which the manifest syndrome and the quality of the pathological changes are
not consistent, so that they manifest certain bogus images. In treating these,
one cannot simply treat Cold when cold appears, or treat Heat when heat
appears; rather, one must penetrate the bogus images, differentiating the genuine from the fake, and treat [the illness's] root quality. For example, in exogenous Heat illnesses, at times when interior Heat strongly dominates, it is
possible to have the Cold image of chilly extremities because dominant yang is
cross-cutting [*ge*] yin; this Cold image is inauthentic because Heat domina-
tion is still [the illness's] essential character, and therefore it is still necessary
to use Cooling drugs to treat it. Thus, this approach is called "with Cold
factors, Cold techniques used" [*han yin han yong*]. . . . The abovementioned
"with Cold factors, Cold techniques used" [principle] . . . is a treatment technique that differs from the usual methods in that it treats by going along with
the [direction of the] disease syndrome; therefore, it is said that "that which
follows is reversed therapy," or it is called "following therapy." But the condition that it follows is the bogus manifestation; because of this, so-called reversed therapy in reality is still a form of straight therapy, still under the guidance of the therapeutic principle of tracing the root and the method of
treating by centering on the intrinsic root quality of the disease.[21]

In this approach a root-branch distinction is made, genuine and bogus
symptoms are distinguished, and both straight and reversed methods boil
down to treating the root. The necessity of distinguishing between bogus
and genuine expressions of an underlying pathological process reinforces
the point that the syndrome-therapy relationship is far from being an auto-

---

20. This apparently tautological remark plays on the fact that both symptoms and syndromes
are subject to classifications in which the terms *Cold* and *Hot, depletion* and *repletion* function. The
distinction is not between Cold and cold, but between source (syndrome) and manifestation
(symptom). As is shown in the following paragraph, there is no tautology involved when one
speaks of contingent similarities between the source and manifestation levels of the illness.

21. Beijing College, *Zhongyixue Jichu*, p. 138.

matic correspondence. The syndrome root must be correctly understood, and deeper sources must be distinguished from shallower manifestations. If bogus symptoms are taken too seriously, the therapy built on a wrong perception of the illness will only make matters worse.

A further (and parallel) application of root-branch thinking has to do with distinguishing very urgent conditions from less urgent ones so that treatment priorities can be set.[22] Under certain conditions it might be necessary, according to this view, to distinguish the secondary but more life-threatening symptoms from those reflecting the root or primary contradiction, treating these branches first and undertaking treatment of the root condition only after the patient's condition has stabilized. An example of such a situation is given in a 1977 foundations textbook: "When a chronic Liver patient develops an acute and severe syndrome of swelling, distention, and fullness of the lower abdomen, short and difficult breathing, and constipation and enuresis, in treating it, one should first resolve the branch syndrome of abdominal fluid by causing excreta to flow, thus reducing abdominal fluid, then treat the root illness of the Liver."[23] The nature of the chronic Liver complaint is not specified here, but it is probably a form of depletion and would require a treatment method of the assist-orthopathic-Qi type after the abdominal swelling (a repletion) was treated with methods of the expel-heteropathic-Qi class.

More fundamental than these methodological guidelines for complex clinical situations, however, is the necessity of regulating the yin and yang relationship. This principle of Chinese medical therapy is so basic and obvious that some textbooks do not even bother to describe it among the treatment principles, although there is no shortage of references in classic texts to regulating yin and yang. One suspects that only rapid modernization has made it necessary to once again be explicit and "theoretical" about such things. The regulation of yinyang and its associated problems pervade the *bianzheng lunzhi* process, however, and most therapeutic principles could be described quite exactly in yinyang terms.

The many methods of regulating yin and yang can be seen as commonsensical when the nature of the yinyang relationship is understood. These principles and methods are well described in a few paragraphs near the end of *Foundations of Chinese Medicine*. The passage closes with a long quotation from *Basic Questions* (*juan* 2, section 5) detailing various connections between disordered yinyang states and specific treatment methods, conclud-

22. Cf. ibid., p. 139; Office of the 1977 Physicians, *Zhongyi Jichuxue*, pp. 168–169; Deng, *Zhongyi Jichu Lilun*, pp. 156–157; Liu Yanchi et al., *Zhongyi Jichu Lilun Wenda*, pp. 167–168; Zhao Fen, ed., *Zhongyi Jichu Lilun Xiangjie* (Fuzhou: Fujian Science and Technology Press, 1981), pp. 399–401.

23. Office of the 1977 Physicians, *Zhongyi Jichuxue*, p. 168.

ing as follows: "Examine the illness's yinyang to differentiate where it is tough and where yielding. In yang illnesses treat the yin; in yin illnesses treat the yang. Stabilize the qi and Blood, and each will take care of its own domain [*ge shou qi xiang*]."[24]

The yinyang logic of the connection between the syndrome and its treatment is evident in this pithy statement. Since yin and yang, yang qi and yin Blood, are opposed and interdependent aspects of any concrete situation, action that affects one aspect necessarily affects its opposite aspect. Insofar as the syndrome presents a pattern of specific yinyang relations, the treatment must be matched to respond to it with specifically opposed operations.[25]

But this is not a relation of essentially different opposite substances mechanically overcoming each other. It is a delicately constituted relationship of complex dynamic phenomena in which it is also necessary to "seek the yang within the yin" and "the yin within the yang," combining drugs with yin and yang effectiveness in proportions such that the two aspects can help as well as oppose each other as illness and therapeutic results unfold in time. The subtlety of this form of intervention is indicated in a text edited by Deng Tietao in which he discusses various corollaries of the principle of regulating yin and yang:

> Because yin and yang are dependent on each other, when treating a syndrome of uneven weakness of yin or yang, we still often choose methods of "seeking out the yang in the yin" or "seeking out the yin in the yang." In other words, when you replenish yin it is appropriate to add some yang-replenishing drugs; when you replenish yang it is appropriate to add some yin-replenishing drugs, thereby making "yang reach its apex with the support of yin so that generation and transformation are inexhaustible [and making] yin reach its apex with yang on the rise so that [the body's] wellsprings flow forth without stint."[26]

The proper regulation of the yinyang relation requires a firm grasp of the difference between their characteristic forms of activity: Yang generates and transforms; yin "flows forth" (i.e., manifests yang active impulses in "structed" material forms). Each has its "domain," and in medicine their proper relationship requires that each be effective in respect of its type of physiological responsibility. Thus, for example, the phrase *yin even, yang*

---

24. Beijing College, *Zhongyixue Jichu,* p. 140.

25. Also note that the *zhengzhi* relationship discussed in connection with syndrome differentiation, in which the syndrome determines the treatment and the treatment tests the differentiation of the syndrome, is a form of yin and yang relation emphasizing their interdependence. Here I focus on the way in which the syndrome determines the form that treatment will take, but recall that if the treatment must be modified, the syndrome stands to be altered as a result.

26. Deng, *Zhongyi Jichu Lilun,* p. 159.

hidden (*yin ping yang mi*) from the *Inner Canon*[27] is constantly cited when yinyang aspects of therapeutic management are at issue. The phrase is used to describe the proper relation of yin and yang in conditions of good health: Yin phenomena, the structive results of active yang processes, should exhibit no marked excesses or deficiencies, and yang activity should be evident only in this very evenness of manifestation.[28] Sometimes in modern medical writing the healthful yinyang relationship is described as homeostasis or equilibrium;[29] but such descriptions are invariably accompanied by this classic phrase asserting the qualitative difference between their two forms of activity. Hence homeostasis and equilibrium are not a quantitative equality of yin and yang any more than yin and yang aspects of phenomena are material quantities of substance. Rather, each must avoid excess and deficiency of its own form of activity within its own domain of responsibility if illness is not to erupt.

This insight does not resolve all the problems inherent in the management of the yinyang relationship. Although a form of equilibrium is often advocated, the qualitative differences between yin and yang as abstracted forces means that complex decisions must be made in the course of therapy. In certain physiological contexts or illness moments yang should be dominant and in others yin should be. This is the normal "waxing and waning" of yin and yang, and doctors must find ways of working in tandem with those shifts that are natural both to physiology and pathology. Given the complexity of the yinyang processes in which intervention is desired, there is no predetermined end point that can guide treatment, no one stable yin-

---

27. Cheng et al., *Suwen Zhushi Huicui, juan* 1, sec. 3, p. 47. It is interesting to note that in most modern editions of the *Basic Questions* the character *mi* (meaning secret or hidden) is used instead of the (possibly more problematic) homophone that appears in the edition cited here. The latter *mi* refers as much to density or closeness, as in weaving or planting, as it does to secrecy. The context of the phrase supports an interpretation of "yang dense and invisible" or "yang forming a dense barrier on the outside." Such a reading would support John Hay's argument that much of Chinese medical physiology involves dense centers and dispersed peripheries ("The Human Body as a Microcosmic Source of Macrocosmic Values in Calligraphy," in Susan Bush and Christian Murck, eds., *Theories of the Arts in China* [Princeton: Princeton University Press, 1983]). If yin flows forth evenly, it does so because its active yang source is suitably dense. The simple modern reading as "hidden," of course, contradicts this model. I have leaned toward a translation of "hidden" for this discussion of contemporary discourse because modern use of the phrase is much broader than its original context warrants; in addition, most recent annotators seem to find the *mi* character meaning secret unproblematic.

28. It is particularly useful here to recall Porkert's long discussion in which he distinguishes yin and yang along "structive" and "active" lines. It is only by assuming this very dynamic process in which "matter" is continually being generated that phrases such as *yin ping yang mi*—often cited and never explained, in my experience—can be understood. See Manfred Porkert, *The Theoretical Foundations of Traditional Chinese Medicine* (Cambridge, Mass.: MIT Press, 1974).

29. See, for example, Deng Tietao et al., *Zhongyi Jichu Lilun*, p. 158.

yang relationship. In practice doctors must develop an ability to perceive excess and deficiency and to play along with the inherent generative and checking relationships of physiology in their attempts to limit excess and fill in deficiencies. Once the marked excesses and deficiencies of illness states are eliminated, yin and yang are assumed to be working together wholesomely once again.

Yin even, yang hidden is thus a description of a state in which the yinyang dynamic is simply invisible. In this context illness is a state in which an unevenness in the yinyang relation pathologically reveals yin and yang in their relations of struggle, interdependence, and mutual transformation. In this phrase the word for "even," *ping,* indicates an absence of highs and lows in any whole (in the *Treatise on Cold Damage* the term *pingren* refers to healthy people), a smooth and undifferentiated manifest surface within which yang hides. It could also be argued that seeing yang as hidden entails that yin be equally invisible since the two define each other and absence of one leaves no reference point with which to discern the presence of the other.

Health is no more easy to define in Chinese medical discourse than it is in our own, but marked deviations from usual bodily experience and practice are evident to both doctor and patient. It is these that are analyzed in their yin and yang aspects and treated with coordinated formulae of drugs having yin and yang qualities. The treatment methods (*zhifa*) are a key link in this coordination of drugs with illness conditions, and it is significant that they tend to be entirely organized under the matched rubrics of "assisting orthopathic qi" and "expelling heteropathic qi."[30] Pathological excess and deficiency—repletion and depletion—are defined (these days) in terms of orthopathic and heteropathic qi: Repletion is a state in which heteropathic qi is excessive, and depletion is the state of orthopathic qi being deficient. The various treatment methods that "assist orthopathy" or "expel heteropathy" are therefore direct responses to states of excess and deficiency revealed through yinyang-oriented syndrome differentiation. In other words, treatment cannot go beyond these various responses to excess and deficiency, and each treatment amounts to a specific mode of "bolstering" (*bu*) or leveling off by draining (*xie*).

A centering process that acts by drawing in deviations and filling up gaps in a continuing flow of "physiological activity" (*shengli huodong*) appears here as the pattern of medical action.[31] The course of medical intervention is

---

30. Cf. Beijing College, *Zhongyixue Jichu;* Office of the 1977 Physicians, *Zhongyi Jichuxue,* p. 169; Deng et al., *Zhongyi Jichu Lilun,* p. 157; Jiangsu Province Department of Health, *Zhongyi Jichu,* p. 42.

31. James Hevia, "Guest Ritual and Interdomainal Relations in the Late Qing" (Ph.d. diss., University of Chicago, 1986); and Angela Zito, in several forthcoming papers, demonstrate that a centering process was quite self-consciously employed in Qing imperial ritual.

not determined with reference to any predetermined goal; rather, the physician must maintain a sense of the location of the center at each stage, evening out the excesses and deficiencies that constitute deviations from this shifting middle path. Chinese medical action is thus intrinsically temporal and activist; intervention is required in every pathological yinyang situation as the illness develops, and the state of play must often be reevaluated in the expectation that new excesses and deficiencies will develop. Treatment seldom departs far from concrete illnesses, which are not helpfully thought of as if they were tokens of a type. For Chinese medicine, contingency is not what threatens a course of treatment but rather what shapes it.

Treatment determination, then, is limited by the syndrome differentiation process while not being completely determined by it. The syndrome, which connects the phenomena that have been channeled through the *kanbing* process to past medical experience via a conventional (if often long) name, both defines a region of the archive within which therapeutic options will be found and opens that region to flexible medical judgment. This form of judgment is often described as *linghuo*, a compound of words for "magic" and "alive," a term that can be only weakly translated in most contexts as "flexible," "adept," "sensitive," "efficacious," or "virtuoso." The following homily is an example:

> In treating illness, one must both control the principles and pay attention to flexibility [*linghuo*]. The therapeutic principles recorded above and the therapeutic techniques that are related in the three sections below are the principles we ought to grasp first in clinical treatment of illness, but in their concrete deployment we must approach them flexibly [*linghuo*]. Because diseases are extremely complex and constantly changing, and also because the factors that influence diseases are very many, clinically we must perform a concrete analysis of a concrete situation, attain [an understanding of] changes through knowledge of the ordinary, and deal with them adeptly [*linghuo*].[32]

This sort of statement could be dismissed as simply a caveat that theory can never account for all clinical situations, telling us nothing very deep about modes of Chinese medical action. But when the frequency of the concept of flexible virtuosity in the Chinese medical literature is considered, and the constant denial that tables of correspondence and formal protocols (which are in any case few) can capture the essence of medical decision-making is taken seriously, a marked image of doctor as virtuoso begins to emerge.

This image is reinforced by published case histories. Consider the diagnosis and treatment determination of Case 3, for example: The syndrome

---

32. Jiangsu Province Department of Health, *Zhongyi Jichu*, pp. 43–44.

was differentiated as "qi slowed and Blood static, stagnation of long duration transformed into Heat, giving signs of collateral circulation tract damage." The conventional and logical treatment of this condition would be "to enliven Blood and transform stasis" (*huoxue huayu*), which procedure was indeed employed. But two important differences of emphasis were introduced. In the process of enlivening Blood, the physician focused on the Blood-qi relationship and aggressively treated qi movement; and although the symptoms primarily implicated the Spleen-Stomach complex, Dr. Zhong also targeted the Liver in the design of the prescriptions. In these two respects, then, Dr. Zhong displayed his mastery of the overarching principles of *bianzheng lunzhi* as he located and operated on the roots of the illness: He located qi movement as the root problem in disorders of Blood flow and found the visceral system root in loss of regulation in the Liver.

This case exhibits the treatment methods as modes of action that are far from automatic. The linked methods of enlivening Blood and transforming stasis are not deviated from, but the more concrete techniques employed involve choosing among options that range throughout the physiological network of dynamic relations and require subtle differences of emphasis on yin or yang (in this case Blood or qi) aspects of the condition. Tracing the root, then, appears as a mode of action that begins after the differentiation of the syndrome has delimited a copious logical and historical space, any narrowing of which can result only from reliance on the experienced judgment of the doctor.

The Archive, the Past, the Doctor as Agent

I have demonstrated how the syndrome differentiation process draws in large part from the medical archive, the vast body of clinical, theoretical, and exegetical works (categories that can in no sense be seen as exclusive of each other) recording the "experience of the Chinese laboring masses in their two-thousand-year struggle against disease." I have shown how syndrome identification is advanced by the analytic methods of the eight rubrics, illness factors, visceral systems, four sectors, and six warps. In general the characteristics of the illness that become visible in the analytic phase of *kanbing* lead through linguistic articulations and simple mnemonics and rules of thumb to a named syndrome that can open up a relevant area of the archive for use.

I have argued that the use of the medical archive in the determination of treatment is not an enslavement to the dead hand of tradition. Given the analytic power of *bianzheng* methods, the straightforward (but not ironclad) correspondences between them, and the specifics of treatment in the field of formulary and the materia medica, it could be argued that the "medical tradition" hardly needs to be referred to at all. The practices of the clinical encounter conceivably could be operated as a sort of technology that is more or less unthinkingly applied as a diagnostic and therapeutic system. The *bianzheng lunzhi* methods are explicit, subtly and complexly differentiated, and effective; they can be summarized in tables and lists of rules, and the action appropriate to each disorder can be memorized. Why, then, should Chinese doctors derive not only their inspiration but also their mundane conceptual tools from an archive that stretches over two thousand years of recorded history and keep insisting that this is what they are doing in everything they write? Why is it necessary to emphasize the study of the classics and the attainment of an "excellent grasp of the therapeutic principles of our sage forebears"?

The past of biomedicine is for us, after all, of academic interest, a hobby for antiquarian physicians or a weapon for social critics. Where science derives its truth from correspondence to a nature that is both ahistorical and governed by laws inaccessible to direct experience, and where medical practice relates its efficacy primarily to a scientific foundation, the knowledge of an earlier generation can quickly become quaint or repellent "beliefs" that are of no relevance to contemporary therapeutics.

To understand why the Chinese medical past is neither quaint nor repellent to leading Chinese doctors, and why no uncritical romance with the new has developed for them in spite of a firm commitment to "scientific modernization" in the field, we need to examine the uses of the past on Chinese philosophical terrain. This is a ground that has no history of seeing "nature" as separate from "man" or an epistemological tradition concerned with truth over efficacy, the eternal and universal over the changing and contingent. Lacking a deeply ingrained fact-value distinction—this being a recent, hard-won, and often challenged achievement of Western philosophy—Chinese medicine nevertheless has ways of dealing with questions of relative value. Put another way, Chinese medical work is pervaded with questions of value precisely because no one can escape to the supposed neutrality of "just the facts."

The Chinese medical past is important in present practice partly because medical discourse is consequential discourse. It is not idle speculations or descriptive rhapsodies emitting from philosophers in mountain retreats; rather, it is concrete action with the simple goal of relieving suffering. In any such consequential discourse, the differentiation of correct from incorrect must have a high priority. It could be argued that this concern has increased since the large-scale institutionalization of Chinese medicine in the 1950s; in such institutions senior doctors now cooperate or compete in the management of illnesses and are in a position to inspect and criticize each other's work. But even such an early classic as the *Treatise on Cold Damage* devotes considerable attention to the recognition of incorrect treatments and their rectification. Medical discourse is not "simply" verbal, philosophical, symbolic, or ideological. The unity of knowledge and practice asserted by Mao Zedong in "On Practice" (as well as by some of his philosophic forebears, such as Wang Yangming and Karl Marx) is nowhere more clear than in the daily practice of Chinese medical institutions of all kinds. Medicine in contemporary China is a central exemplar of correctly informed action.[33] And in Chinese medicine correct action is (we are constantly told) informed by experience.

This notion of experience (*jingyan*) is at the center of Chinese medical decisionmaking, and it stands as the major reference point for distinguishing good actions from inept or incorrect ones.[34] The relatively young scientific research movement that is now expanding in the colleges of traditional medicine may propose "objective, external" standards, but these are very limited in their applicability compared to the idea with which I opened this book: "We take experience to be our guide."

Experience is important at two temporal levels. The first is the level of the archive, in which the "experience of the Chinese laboring masses in their two-thousand-year struggle against disease" is recorded. The second is the level of the individual doctor and his life in medicine, which results in his "heart-mind attainment" (*xinde,* usually translated as knowledge or understanding), his personal authority, and his own special position in relation to

---

33. I do not wish to imply that Chinese medicine is widely held to be symbolically central in China, although it may be; but it is at least clear that a certain type of senior Chinese doctor (and a few senior cadres involved in Chinese medical administration) make this point implicitly in their writing and teaching on Chinese medical theory and "the dialectics of nature." See, for example, Li Jinyong et al., eds., *Zhongyixue Bianzhengfa Jianlun* (Taiyuan: Shanxi People's Press, 1983); Liu Ruchen et al., eds., *Zhongyixue Bianzhengfa Gailun* (Guangzhou: Guangdong Science and Technology Press, 1983); Wang Zhong, "*Zhongyixue Bianzhengfa Yanjiu,*" in Dialectics of Nature Research and Teaching Section, *Ziliao Huibian* (Guangzhou: Guangzhou College of Traditional Chinese Medicine, 1983), vol. 3, pp. 48–114.

The strategy of these leaders has been to simultaneously insist that medicine, with its "spontaneous materialism and naive dialectics," is entirely consistent with Marxism-Leninism and to emphasize that medicine is a "great treasurehouse" (Mao's phrase) of the precious accumulated experience of China's laboring masses. The rhetorical force in socialist China of centering these two features of Chinese medical action is (ideally, at least) to make the field ideologically unassailable; microbiologists might wish they had such weapons with which to justify their work in the service of the people.

34. In this connection it is worth noting that in most contemporary contexts within the world of Chinese medicine where error is mentioned, the identification and correction of errors is retrospective. This is in keeping with the point made in Chapter 4 and 5 that the correctness of analyses and therapies is only ultimately knowable from their results. It is in addition an important rationale in the present-day rhetoric of Chinese medicine for continuing to study the past to avoid its errors as well as elevate its essential contributions. See Xu Fulin, *Gujin Jiu Wu* (Changsha: Hubei Science and Technology Press, 1985), which is a compilation of bungled cases with didactic discussions.

the past and present of medicine.[35] Practices of teaching and study link these two levels in a filial continuity.

That experience functions as a major locus of evaluative reference rooted in *kanbing* is clear in a variety of contexts. Contemporary Chinese medical journals, for example, publish a great many case reports in which one or two cases are described, their interest being not that the illness is unusual (the most common rationale for publishing a single case in American medical journals) but that the treatment of a relatively ordinary illness was both unconventional and successful. Such widespread publication of not quite routine case reports reflects a continuing process of practical evaluation of therapeutic strategies by working doctors. Although there has been controlled clinical research on traditional Chinese therapeutics in the modern People's Republic, these scientific approaches to the evaluation of experience are much less common than evaluation by experience, that is, in normal clinical work.

Doctors experiment all along the treatment side of the *bianzheng lunzhi* process, substituting and modifying treatment methods, formulae, and drugs. When these explorations achieve good results, this success can be a contribution to medical experience and to the medical archive through a written report and discussion of the case. That such a process of sharing clinical experience of treatment success should continue on such a large scale in a modern China that is pervaded with the ideologies of modernization and science testifies to the importance of experience in the social, practical, and intellectual life of Chinese medicine.

As can be seen in Cases 1 through 3, doctors selectively draw procedures from the archival record of previously effective actions and put them to use in their own practice, constantly evaluating such procedures as they observe the progress of their patients toward recovery. If one method shows no marked effectiveness, another is tried. This process is particularly evident in Case 2; Dr. Deng's commentary to the case explores in detail his mode of

---

35. A recently published series of biographies and autobiographies of senior Chinese doctors, Zhou Fengwu et al., eds., *Ming Laozhongyi zhi Lu,* 3 vols. (Jinan: Shandong Science and Technology Press, 1981–1985), is interesting in this respect. Deng Tietao's autobiographical essay in vol. 2 asserts that "the great treasurehouse of Chinese medicine has three main components: The first is its vast body of ancient records; the second is the precious learning and rich experience of Chinese medicine, especially that stored in the brains of old Chinese doctors; and the third is the carefully harbored and time-tested drug formulae of the masses" ("Wanli Yuntian Wanli Lu," p. 4). This is not an unconventional list. In the early 1980s I saw little evidence of research on discovering and testing the "drug formulae of the masses" within the profession of Chinese medicine, but a large compilation of a wide range of folk healing techniques has recently appeared. See Liu Daoqing et al., eds., *Zhongguo Minjian Liaofa* (Hebei: Farmers' Press of the Central Plains, 1987). Numerous dictionaries of "secret prescriptions" began to appear in the late 1980s and early 1990s.

consulting the archive and modifying its formulae for ways of causing the stubborn foetus to descend.

The *bianzheng* process analytically characterizes the illness such that a syndrome can be differentiated. This process is also the opening of a certain space in the archive within which experience can be most usefully and responsibly drawn on. These simultaneous processes of constraining action and enabling it, like *bianzheng lunzhi* itself, cannot be separated. The *bianzheng lunzhi* pivot of the *kanbing* process is not unique in displaying such a dual aspect, however. It could be argued that every moment in *kanbing* is equally constrained and equally open as, on the syndrome-differentiating side, complex classificatory judgments are made and, on the treatment-determining side, formulae and drugs are selected and modified to respond to specific features of the illness. Practice operating through time continually produces new situations in which the possibilities for action by trained and conscientious people are limited (in a yin depletion illness, it would be foolish to drain fluids; no such option presents itself), while they are also richly enabled (the very category of yin depletion incorporates tools of varying fineness, from very broad yinyang logics to long lists of formulae and drugs).

This enabling aspect will become more clear in the discussions of Chinese medical formulary and materia medica. It derives from the linked and complementary relationships that hold between the various classificatory methods on the two "sides" of the *bianzheng lunzhi* pivot. Although these methods do not form a single system of either knowledge or methods, as they are used in clinical work they can be coordinated to supplement each other and to describe and manipulate the many aspects of illness.

No amount of mere book learning can produce a doctor who knows how to correctly deploy the analytic methods, how to forge the most effective relationship between syndrome and treatment principle, or how to design formulae that are most elegantly responsive to the specificities of the illness process under the concrete conditions of clinical work. The whole practical world of Chinese medicine reproduces the conviction among its adepts that only experience can teach such skills, personal experience that is enriched through study of past medical work and the guidance of clinically seasoned teachers. Practice (of seeing patients, of studying, of teaching and being taught) accumulated as experience is the ground on which the past can serve the present.

The archive as a record of practice is often conceived of nowadays as the "laboratory" in which the "essential" effective elements of Chinese medicine have been tested and distinguished from "the dross" (which can be safely discarded, at least from a clinical point of view). In these discursive concerns with experience, practice, and the evaluation and deployment of techniques and insights from the medical archive, the hoary absolutes within which Western science developed—Nature, Truth, and Law—are markedly absent.[36] Instead the social values of effectiveness, responsiveness, and service and the personal values of virtuosity and connoisseurship—goodness in several senses of the word—dominate Chinese medical texts. This discourse of goodness and humanity is historical because such values cannot be aimed at in theory; they can be implemented only by accepting teaching from the past. Actions can be evaluated only with reference to results, that is, through reading historical narratives. The *bianzheng lunzhi* pivot, then, is the privileged moment in the *kanbing* process where a connection to the past of medicine is forged; at that point the doctor adeptly brings personal and collective experience to bear on a present condition of pathological change.

---

36. See Joseph Needham's classic discussion of the concept of law in the indigenous Chinese sciences, "Human Law and the Laws of Nature," in *The Grand Titration* (London: Cambridge University Press, 1969), pp. 299–331. I am frequently asked by sympathetic readers of my work on Chinese medicine how doctors recognize error. The foregoing discussion is an attempt to address this very legitimate question. But the question itself is indicative of the degree to which problems of evaluation are constantly referred to an epistemological base in our culture. For biomedicine, scientific knowledge (ultimately of natural law) seems to provide the solid ground on which medical judgments should, we think, be made. Where no such value-free basis is posited, it is difficult for us to see how a judgment can be made. In fact, of course, we make such "unfounded" judgments constantly, and so do highly responsible doctors.

6

Remanifesting the Syndrome and Qualifying the Therapy: Formulary and Materia Medica

Formula [*fangji*]: called *fang* for short. Designates a medical formula [i.e., a prescription]. The *Bibliography of the Sui Dynasty* says, "Medical formulae are the art that eliminates illness and defends life." *Ji* refers to regulating the volumes or dosages of drugs in prescriptions [*tiaoji*]. The *Bibliographical Record in the History of the Former Han Dynasty* says, "In regulating the one hundred drugs, harmonizing them is what matters." Formulae are the manifestation of treatment methods; they are prescriptions composed of various drugs coordinated in accord with principles of combination and generalized clinical experience.[1]

The herbal drugs of the Chinese materia medica are seldom prescribed in isolation. They are almost always combined into formulae consisting of from four to twenty or more drugs in quantities specified by weight. Examples of formulae are incorporated in Cases 1 through 3. The principles of composition, preparation, and modification of such formulae are covered in the subdiscipline of formulary (*fangjixue*) and taught as a separate course in contemporary colleges of Chinese medicine.

Remanifesting: Formulary and the Production of Prescriptions (*Fang*)

The design and writing of formulae are an important part of the clinical encounter, as was seen in the description of *kanbing* activities in Chapter 3. In routine Chinese medical practice, every illness is taken to have its corre-

---

1. Editing Committee of the Unabridged Dictionary of Chinese Medicine, *Zhongyi Dacidian, Jichu Lilun Fence* (Beijing: People's Health Press, 1982), pp. 72–73. The two bibliographies referred to in the definition are Ban Gu, *Han Shu Yiwen Zhi,* 1st century A.D. (Shanghai: Commercial Press, 1955); and Zhang Sun Wuji et al., *Sui Shu Jingji Zhi,* 7th century (Shanghai: Commercial Press, 1957).

sponding *fang:* The moment a patient sits down, a prescription form is prepared with his registration number attached to it, and no patient leaves the doctor without a formula that has been produced in response to his complaint. This small but eloquent detail from the clinic embodies, then, an important assumption of Chinese medical work—that the patient, not the doctor, determines that she is ill. The reality of the illness state is not at issue. Theoretically, at least, there are no "malingerers" simply by virtue of the fact that all illnesses are treatable as reported with a formula that both strikes at the syndrome root and deals with the miscellaneous symptoms.

The herbal prescription is at once a specific response to the illness and its most articulate expression. Doctors are able to read illness states out of prescriptions alone, and discourse at the higher professional levels often takes the form of comparisons, exegeses, and partial analyses of herbal formulae, leaving unmentioned the obvious accompanying symptoms, diagnostic categories, and so on. (The commentary on Case 2 is a good example of this reading of formulae, its intelligibility being dependent on the familiarity of readers with the prescriptions discussed.) Much of the medical archive, in addition, takes the form of *fanglun,* "discourse on formulae," and in the contemporary literature no published case history, however short, omits the *fang,* complete with quantities of drug used.

Theoretically, formulae could be generated through the application of a few basic principles, treating Hot with Cold and Cold with Hot, draining repletions and replenishing depletions, and so on. An eight rubrics analysis of the symptoms would in many common illnesses provide a rationally adequate framework for the application of such principles, and drug qualities are specified in such a way that they could be readily deployed as instruments for Warming and Cooling, replenishing and draining (e.g., with Sweet and Bitter "flavors," respectively; the flavors, characters, efficacies, and usage of drugs will be discussed in detail in the latter part of this chapter). This is not, however, how formulae are composed in normal modern medical practice. Rather, formulae are asserted to be intimately related to treatment principles, and hence to syndromes and the whole *bianzheng lunzhi* process, as follows:

> Formulae are a component of "theory, methods, formulae, and drugs," [*li, fa, fang, yao,* Chinese medicine's basic arsenal], and it is only on the foundation of syndrome differentiation and the establishment of a [treatment] method that formulae can be utilized appropriately. Thus, it is desirable to first clarify the relationship between formulae and treatment methods before we can more completely and exactly compose prescriptions or deploy drugs.
>
> The term *treatment method* refers to the major methods of therapy. They are constituted from the process of grasping causes and considering treatments, which is done according to clinical symptoms and syndrome differentiation and is based on exact components. Once the treatment method has

been determined, it becomes the main principle that guides clinical use of the formula and the production of new prescriptions. For example, in treating Wind-Heat Exterior syndrome, one would first settle on the treatment method of flushing the exterior with Pungent and Cool, and only after that could an exterior-flushing Pungent and Cool formula be selected to use in the treatment. Thus, in the treatment of disease, the "formula" [*fang*] may remain uncertain [i.e., it can vary], but the "method" [*fa*] must be firmly settled. For this reason, in the clinical process of differentiating syndromes and deploying treatments, formulae are subsumed within methods, and treatment methods are the basis of formulary. Hence our forebears summarized the relationship of the two as follows: "Formulae are established from methods; use the methods to control the formulae."

Formulae are the concrete expression of treatment methods. If one had only a treatment method and no drug formula, the treatment method could not be manifested, and the whole *bianzheng shizhi* process could not be completed. Take, for example, the case of treating Wind-Heat Exterior syndrome discussed above: Its treatment method of flushing the exterior with Pungent and Cool simply must pass through the effectiveness of a Pungent-Cool exterior-flushing formula if it is to become manifest.

Generally speaking, the relationship of treatment methods and formulae is extremely close. One cannot have a method without a formula, and no formula is possible without a method. Only after the method has been fixed can a formula be composed through the coordination of drug qualities. Thus, "theory, methods, formulae, and drugs" have come to epitomize the complete system of Chinese medicine.[2]

This passage, which opens the national textbook *Fangjixue* (Formulary), unequivocally links formulae and formulary into an overarching *bianzheng lunzhi* process such that the *fang* must be seen as a specific response to the syndrome that has been characterized and differentiated in previous phases of the clinical encounter. In addition, the passage reminds us that formulae are much more numerous than treatment methods and that order can be brought to the *fanglun* archive by using "the methods to control the formulae."

There are, of course, vast numbers of *fang* to choose from in the medical archive.[3] Although many medical treatises employ the form made classical in the *Treatise on Cold Damage*—that of unifying $zheng_3$ and *zhi* by providing a

2. Guangzhou College of Traditional Chinese Medicine, ed., *Fangjixue* (Shanghai: Shanghai Science and Technology Press, 1979), p. 1.

3. Even if only resources published in recent years are consulted, the number of named and cataloged formulae in the Chinese medical literature is very impressive. Editing Committee of the Unabridged Dictionary of Chinese Medicine, *Zhongyi Dacidian, Fangjixue Fence* (Beijing: People's Health Press, 1983), includes about 6,000 *fang;* and a specialized dictionary of formulary boasts 12,500 entries, almost all of which are *fang* names with specifications (Jiang Keming and Bao Minghui, eds., *Jianming Fangji Cidian* [Shanghai: Shanghai Science and Technology Press, 1989]). The national text Guangzhou College, *Fangjixue,* has selected about 200 (not including

formula for every syndrome—not every recorded syndrome has a single corresponding "classical" formula that must be used in its treatment. Moreover, it would be impractical for doctors to memorize all the previously effective syndrome-formula pairs recorded in the literature. A classification scheme must be employed to organize frequently used formulae such that the range of choices can be restricted to manageable areas of practical relevance.

Various approaches to classification have been used in the course of the development of formulary as an identified area of medical knowledge, but the most common one in contemporary use takes treatment principles as its rubrics. The rationale for this procedure is explained in *Formulary*, emphasizing the practicality of such an ordering in the context of clinical work:

> In general, the typing of formulae in historical times was done according to illnesses, according to syndromes, according to illness factors, according to the various medical subdisciplines, according to visceral systems, according to treatment methods, or according to all these combined into one schema. These classifications, both the complex and the simple, all have their rationale. But typing according to treatment method has been the most common; it is consistent with clinical practice and manifests the relationship between formulae and treatment methods. This text [is organized] on this principle, unifying the "great methods" [*dafa*] that are widely used in modern clinical practice.[4]

A 1973 clinical handbook of formulary makes a further distinction between formulae that are broadly useful and those that are more specialized:

> Formulary also makes a difference between broadly useful prescriptions and prescriptions for specialized use. For broadly useful prescriptions such as Bolster Spleen Increase Qi Decoction (which replenishes qi), Four Things Decoction (which replenishes Blood), Six Flavor Foxglove Pills (which replenish yin), or Cassia Aconite Eight Flavor Pills (which replenish yang), their range of uses is quite extensive. Prescriptions for specialized use are used only for certain symptoms; Rhubarb Tree-Peony Decoction, for example, according to its use classification clears Heat and flushes toxins, but it is mostly used for appendicitis. And Ten Tephrosias Pills according to their use classification cool Blood, but they are mainly used to stop bleeding.[5]

---

variants) to explain in detail. A handbook edited by the Beijing College of Traditional Chinese Medicine et al. for a wide range of practitioners (*Shiyong Zhongyixue*, 2 vols. [Beijing: Beijing Press, 1975]) includes 362 *fang;* and a clinical handbook devoted to formulary (Shanghai College of Traditional Chinese Medicine, ed., *Zhongyi Fangji Linchuang Shouce* [Shanghai: Shanghai Peoples Press, 1973]), covers 380. Recently, many compilations of "secret formulae" have added thousands of *fang* to those that are readily available in modern reference works.

4. Guangzhou College, *Fangjixue*, p. 4.
5. Shanghai College, *Zhongyi Fangji Linchuang Shouce*, pp. 6–7.

The use of the treatment methods (*zhifa*) as classificatory guidelines for the selection and use of formulae provides a powerful way of linking the various conceptual resources of *bianzheng lunzhi* to the use of drugs in concrete interventions. As has been discussed at some length, the relationship between a syndrome and its treatment methods is both logical and subject to the judgment of the doctor. In addition to the conventional linkages between syndromes and treatments to be found in the medical archive, principles such as the balancing of yin and yang play a large role in a *zhengzhi* process that affords a certain space for discretionary medical action. Once an appropriate set of treatment principles has been settled on, they can refer attention simultaneously forward to the drug qualities available to be assembled in a prescription (e.g., Cool, Pungent) and backward to the characteristics of the syndrome (e.g., Hot, repletion) and to the modes of analysis that led to its characterization. The eight rubrics, with their strong yinyang logic, are the chief thread that runs through and links these sequential aspects of *kanbing*.

Formulary cites a Qing period scholar, Cheng Guopeng, on the link between treatment methods (the "eight great methods") and the eight rubrics: "When we discuss an illness situation, the eight terms of Cold and Hot, depletion and repletion, exterior and interior, and yin and yang can encompass [*tong*] it, and when we discuss formulae for treating illness, the eight methods of inducing perspiration, harmonizing, draining, reducing, inducing vomiting, clearing, warming, and bolstering exhaust them."[6] Treatment methods relate to but are not solely explainable in terms of eight rubrics concepts. As the eight classic methods listed by Cheng indicate, there is a strong reference to concrete body processes such as sweating, vomiting, and excreting as well as to somewhat less visible modes of physiological activity (harmonizing Hot and Cold elements, reducing and clearing out local excesses, replenishing depletions, etc.) that nevertheless have a certain immediacy in terms of bodily experience. Treatment methods, by virtue of being more concrete, are more restricted in their applicability than the abstract eight rubrics are.

Quite often the relationships between symptoms and treatment strategies are obvious. The method of flushing the exterior, for example, is usually used where heteropathic qi is engaged in struggle with strong orthopathic qi on the body exterior, producing fever, intolerance of cold, headache, and other superficial or upper body symptoms. Flushing the exterior is subsumed within the great method of bringing out sweat. To induce sweating is to act on the body exterior in response to exterior symptoms, and it produces an outward movement of fluids that can carry the invading heteropathic qi with it. Consequently, the eight rubrics analysis of an illness

---

6. Cheng Guopeng, *Yixue Xinwu*, 1792; cited in Guangzhou College, *Fangjixue*, p. 1.

showing these symptoms, as an exterior repletion of Hot or Cold, leads quite naturally to a treatment principle of inducing sweating to flush the exterior.

Not all treatment methods are so self-evident or so readily accommodated with reference to this simplest and most powerful of the analytic methods. But the number of treatment methods in use in any one time or place is not likely to be large, and their efficacies and conditions of applicability can be easily learned.

As classificatory rubrics for formulae, then, the treatment methods are extremely effective. *Formulary* uses eighteen main methods as chapter headings, subdividing these into sections according to certain features of the component drugs or according to certain aspects of a formula's efficacy. Chapter 1, for example, "Exterior Flushing Formulae," is subdivided into (1) Pungent and Warm exterior flushing (7 *fang*), (2) Pungent and Cool exterior flushing (5 *fang*), and (3) exterior flushing through assisting orthopathic qi (3 *fang*) sections. Organized in this way, the textbook covers 197 main formulae and 122 variants. Students are encouraged in the editors' note to become familiar with 140 to 150 of the commonly used *fang*, and in the intensive class I attended in Guangzhou 100 formulae were covered.

This apparent diversity may be radically reduced in a doctor's clinical years after he has graduated from medical college. Neophyte practitioners usually work under a senior Chinese doctor, and many of these use variants of only a few formulae. One doctor whom I observed in the clinic for a period of some weeks used a "replenishing Liver" formula for almost all his patients, modifying it quite freely in response to their specific symptoms. His rationale was that most illnesses were cured by encouraging better movement of physiological qi, and he saw the Liver system as the visceral root of qi movement. This doctor's (more or less self-selected) clientele, moreover, included a great many hepatitis patients (common in South China), and he was always concerned to prevent the development of hepatitis in patients weakened by other illnesses. Always replenishing Liver qi was not necessarily, then, an inappropriate or overly rigid limitation of method.

The mere selection of the proper formula from among a great many possibilities does not constitute a satisfactory response to any illness; illnesses are more individual than the standard formulae imply. All the specifying power of the descriptive and analytic methods described thus far must be brought to bear if the correct formula is to be selected and appropriately customized:

> In general, the combining principles of formulae are a component of Chinese medical syndrome differentiation and therapy deployment; they are a concrete utilization of the "theory, methods, formulae, and drugs" of Chinese medicine. Only after there has been a clear and exact clinical syndrome differentiation, only after clear distinctions have been made between the slight and the

severe, the slow and the fast of the illness condition and the primary and secondary aspects of the syndrome, only after a therapeutic principle has been decided on and ruling and assisting drugs have been selected, can a formula be composed and effectively put into use.[7]

Because modifications to formulae are not only allowed but are routinely required, a problem arises. The extent to which specificities should be dealt with by modification within the formula as opposed to sophisticated choice from among the range of possible formulae is a problem concerning which there is little theoretical guidance. That this is a problem is clear from the following Qing period directive:

> If you intend to use an ancient prescription, you must first consider whether the syndrome from which the patient suffers tallies in every respect with that set out at the head of the old prescription and also whether the drugs used in the prescription are without exception compatible with the manifest syndrome. If they are, use it; if they aren't, modify it. If modification is impossible, choose another prescription.[8]

Named formulae drawn from the archive are often referred to in explaining treatment strategies and are usually used at least as a framework, but they are very seldom applied without modification or elaboration. To understand the extent to which internal modifications enable a therapy that is an adept response to a concrete illness, the principles of arranging the proper relations in formulae must be considered.

The most commonly cited principle of this kind employs the language of rulership. Before modern times formulae were said to have been composed of drugs having relations of the "monarch-minister" (*jun-chen*) type, with the addition of two other categories called "assistant" (*zuo*) and "emissary" (*shi*). Modern textbooks explain that these terms are no longer in use because they have a "feudal coloring";[9] there is, however, no unanimity regarding the terms or even the number of categories with which they should be replaced. The most comprehensive modern scheme uses the four roles of ruling (*zhu*), supporting (*fu* or *fuzhu*), assisting (*zuo*), and sending (*shi*) drugs. These roles are characterized as follows in *Formulary:*

> *Ruling* drugs: drugs that counter the illness factors or the main syndrome and play the main role in therapy.
> *Supporting* drugs: drugs that help the main drug to strengthen therapy.
> *Assisting* drugs: [The term] has three meanings. (1) Drugs that treat accompanying or secondary syndromes. (2) Drugs used where the main drug has toxic qualities or is particularly harsh and must be moderated in the clinical arrangement of relations in the formula; in other words, "used in

---

7. Shanghai College, *Zhongyi Fangji Linchuang Shouce*, p. 3.
8. Xu Dachun *Yixue Yuanliu Lun*, c. 1757; cited in Guangzhou College, *Fangjixue*, p. 5.
9. Ibid.

arranging relations in the formula in response to the main drug's one-sided-ness." And (3) [drugs that] play a role the opposite of assisting, used when it is necessary to adopt a following therapy because the illness configuration resists the drugs [of a more conventional opposing therapy], . . . as, for example, in the phenomenon of adding a small quantity of Cold or Cool drugs into a Warm or Hot formula [or vice versa] to reduce a mutual antipathy of Cold and Hot into which drugs cannot advance.

Sending drugs: drugs that follow circulation tracts or drugs that regulate the qualities of other drugs.[10]

The social metaphor incorporated in the preceding formulation is quite explicitly intended to clarify (and render more memorable) the proper general form of relations among individuals in a purposeful grouping. Thus, when textbooks argue for the use of complex formulae over individual drugs, the maxim "Drugs possess the unique strengths of their individuality; formulae possess the wonderful powers of an ensemble" is cited;[11] and the monarch-minister principles are described as "dividing the labor" of the various drugs while "intimately linking them together."[12] The famous Yuan period doctor Li Dongyuan (1180-1251) is also quoted as follows: "The volume of the monarch drug is the greatest, the volume of the minister drugs is secondary to it, and the volume of the assistants is smaller still. One can't make the ministers exceed the monarch. Monarch and minister have their proper order—the one gives off and the other takes in [*xiang you xuan she*]—and it is thus that they ward off heteropathic qi and drive out illness."[13]

Despite a concern with feudal colorings, then, clinicians still seem to rely on a hierarchical ordering of drug relations such that each element both takes care of its own domain (*ge shou qi xiang*)—that is, has its own area of responsibility—and is caught up in relations of a specific type to other elements. Li Dongyuan's discussion of the relative volumes of drugs playing different roles,[14] when considered together with the qualitative relations of supporting, assisting, and sending, reveals that the secondary roles serve to specify and manifest the broad powers of the ruling drug(s).

The language of these drug formula–combining principles suggests a view of Chinese medical therapy as symbolic or allegorical, perhaps deriving its longevity chiefly from its ability to reflect and articulate a social order. This is not an inappropriate conclusion, providing we acknowledge that all language is pervaded by metaphor, that languages and metaphors have histories, and that all medicine is therefore thoroughly cultural and historical. A medicine that is symbolic is not necessarily ineffective thereby, and various

---

10. Ibid.

11. Ibid., p. 4.

12. Ibid., p. 5.

13. Ibid.

14. Unfortunately, the quantitative discriminations mentioned by Li do not always work that way in practice. In other words, the most voluminous drug is not always the ruling item in the *fang*.

medical techniques that are very effective at relieving suffering are not as a result less symbolic.

Symbolic analysis has subtle dangers, however. If we assume that symbols stand in the same relationship to what they express as does a (suspect) mental construct to a real structure, a symbolic interpretation of Chinese medicine can only mislead us. A drug formula is as real as and a good deal more concrete than "the hierarchical social structure" it is supposed to symbolize. One suspects that Western analysts see monarch-minister relations as symbolic of the social mainly because these analysts have little confidence in the medical efficacy of Chinese prescriptions. They may acknowledge that some herbal drugs have physiological powers while failing to see any utilitarian reason for the effort that has been expended over the centuries in refining the relative quantities of drugs in formulae. This leads them to see the chief charm of formulary as metaphorical since it could not possibly be instrumental. Such an analysis hints that the Chinese doctors for whom formulary is a central component of their skill are deceiving themselves about something that we (as outside observers) can see quite clearly is illusory.

With regard to this particular social metaphor, it is more useful, I think, to indulge our sociological impulses by comparing the contexts in which the Chinese use a language of rulership: How do the relationships of drugs in formulae compare with the relationship of a lord to his servants, a father to his extended family, a teacher to his students, or a classic author to his followers? Similar languages are used to explore all these forms of relating in rich literatures extending over long periods of time. What is a highly technical development in medicine may be elsewhere more poetic or more politically contingent. From the point of view of Chinese scholars, these arenas of language use complement and enrich one another, but one need not be dismissed as less "real" than the others.

The relational principles used in formulary can be better understood through the analysis of a specific prescription. The first one used in Case 1, a modification of Barrier Cooling Powder (a formula drawn from an eleventh-century work), can be analyzed in terms of ruling, supporting, assisting, and sending relations.[15] This formula for the treatment of Spring Warm repletion in the yang visceral systems was published as follows:

---

15. Barrier Cooling Powder is found in the formulary of the Imperial Medical Office *Tai Ping Huimin Heji Jufang,* published after 1078 (Editing Committee, *Zhongyi Dacidian, Fangjixue Fence,* s.v. *liang ge san*). The discussion of the four roles in the first *fang* of Case 1 that follows is not necessarily the only possible such reading of it. I have the impression that, although these hierarchical relational principles may play a large role in *fang* composition for many doctors, they are more coherent in writing formulae than in reading them. That is to say, when doctors specify the quantities of drugs to be used in their daily writing of formulae, they may have the proper proportions of ruling, supporting, assisting, and sending drugs very much in mind. But the many after-the-fact interpretations of formulae that I heard did not emphasize these four roles; rather, they emphasized the specific efficacies and qualities of each drug.

1. Weeping forsythia (capsule)	9 g
2. Black-roasted jasmine seed	9 g
3. Mild skullcap (root)	6 g
4. Wind-weed asphodel (rhizome)	12 g
5. Fresh rhubarb	6 g
6. Mirabilite	4.5 g
7. Tricosanthes fruit	9 g
8. Citron (roasted fruit)	4.5 g
9. Four o'clock (root)	6 g
10. Fresh licorice root	2.4 g
11. Dried dendrobium (stem)	9 g

The commentary on the case notes that Barrier Cooling Powder has the function of clearing above while draining below. The verb "to clear" (*qing*) in the terminology of treatment principles usually means to drive a superficial heteropathy from the relatively exterior and upper parts of the body, usually through sweating. In this case, "draining below" refers to simultaneously bolstering fluids in the lower parts of the body and encouraging excretion. One would expect that the ruling drug should have efficacies that, once specified by subsidiary drug functions, can accommodate both these purposes.

Judging by the relative volumes prescribed, wind-weed asphodel is the ruling drug;[16] the materia medica literature specifies its efficacies as "clears Heat and puts down Fire, nourishes yin with moisture and moistens Dryness."[17] In other words, asphodel is good for clearing above, and its "moistening" qualities here function to induce downward flow. If we recall that supporting drugs generally replicate and supplement the powers of the ruling drug, assisting drugs either treat secondary symptoms or moderate harshness in the ruling drug, and sending drugs either moderate the other drugs in the formula or target specific locations, we can understand the relative significance of the various drugs in the formula through an examination of their qualities and efficacies:[18]

1. Weeping forsythia (capsule), 9 g: Bitter and Chilling; enters Heart and Gallbladder tracts; clears Heat and flushes out Heat toxin, reduces swellings and eliminates pus. Usually used to treat colds due to

---

16. Although the ruling drug is not always the most voluminous, in this case many of the drugs simultaneously address Heat repletions in both the upper and lower parts of the body, and asphodel is used in the maximum amount recommended by standard sources. Its supporting drugs in this prescription are used in recommended minimum volumes.

17. Editing Committee of the Unabridged Dictionary of Chinese Medicine, *Zhongyi Dacidian, Zhongyao Fence* (Beijing: People's Health Press, 1982).

18. This analysis uses conventional drug qualities listed in the standard reference works cited elsewhere in this chapter both for characterizing items from the materia medica and determining their relative roles in the formula.

Wind and Heat excesses, swollen and sore throat, mental agitation, and thirst in Heat illnesses. *Supporting* drug (because of clearing-and-flushing-Heat-in-Upper-*Jiao* functions and because strongly indicated for this kind of Spring Warm syndrome).

2. Black-roasted jasmine seed, 9 g: Bitter and Chilling; enters Heart, Liver, and Stomach tracts; drains Fire and eliminates agitation, clears Heat and causes Dampness to flow, cools Blood and dispels stasis. Usually used to treat mental agitation and insomnia in Heat illnesses. *Supporting* drug (because of Fire-draining, agitation-eliminating, and Heat-clearing functions and because specific for agitation and insomnia).

3. Mild skullcap (root), 6 g: Bitter and Chilling; enters Heart, Lung, Gallbladder, and Large Intestine tracts; clears Heat and dries Dampness, drains Fire and flushes out Heat toxin, pacifies foetuses. Usually used to treat fevers of Warm illnesses, agitation and thirst, cough resulting from Lung Heat, and other conditions. *Supporting* drug (because of Heat-clearing and flushing functions and because of ability to treat fevers, agitation, and thirst). Also an *assisting* drug (because of draining function).

4. Wind-weed asphodel (rhizome), 12 g: Bitter and Chilling; enters Lung, Stomach, and Kidney tracts; clears Heat and puts down Fire, nourishes yin with moisture and moistens Dryness. Usually used to treat high fevers of Heat illnesses, agitation and thirst, cough resulting from Lung Heat, constipation, and other conditions. *Ruling* drug (because of high volume and because of wide range of functions, including clearing above and draining below through moistening, ability to treat fevers, agitation and thirst, and constipation).

5. Fresh rhubarb, 6 g: Bitter and Cold; enters Stomach, Large Intestine, and Liver tracts; drains Heat toxin, mobilizes static accumulations, moves static Blood. Usually used to treat constipation resulting from repletion Heat, delirium and mania, and other conditions. *Assisting* drug (because of strong draining function, treatment of repletion Heat-induced constipation).

6. Mirabilite, 4.5 g: Bitter, Salty, and Chilling; enters Stomach and Large Intestine tracts; drains Heat, induces bowel movement, softens hardenings. Usually used to treat static accumulations resulting from repletion Heat, abdominal swellings, constipation, and other conditions. *Assisting* drug (because of strong draining function, treatment of repletion Heat-induced constipation).

7. Tricosanthes fruit, 9 g: Sweet, Bitter, and Chilling; enters Lung, Stomach, and Large Intestine tracts; clears Lungs, transforms Phlegm, relaxes chest area and dispels congelations, moistens bowels. Usually used to treat coughing and shortness of breath resulting from

Phlegm and Heat and other clogging conditions of the chest and Lung visceral system as well as constipation. *Supporting* drug (because of function of clearing Heat-induced conditions in the Upper *Jiao*). And an *assisting* drug (because of secondary capacity to treat constipation).

8. Citron (roasted fruit), 4.5 g: Bitter and slightly Cold; enters Lung, Liver, and Spleen tracts; mobilizes qi and relaxes middle, transforms Phlegm, aids food digestion. Usually used to treat stopped-up qi, accumulated [undigested] food, Mucus and catarrh disorders, swelling of sides and chest region, and other conditions. *Assisting* drug (because of capacity to contribute to draining of Lower *Jiao* by mobilizing digestive functions in the Middle *Jiao*).

9. Four o'clock (root), 6 g: Sweet, Bitter, Cooling, slightly toxic; drives out Wind, clears Heat and flushes out toxins, causes urine to flow, drains Lower *Jiao,* enlivens Blood and reduces swellings. Usually used to treat joint aches and pains resulting from Wind and Damp, tonsillitis, and sometimes constipation. *Assisting* drug (because of draining functions; probably added to treat throat symptoms not mentioned in case history).

10. Fresh licorice root, 2.4 g: Neutral and Sweet; enters Spleen and Lung tracts; harmonizes Middle *Jiao,* slows acute conditions, stops aching, drives out Phlegm and stops coughing, flushes out toxins, regulates the relations of other drugs. Usually used to treat stomach conditions and very frequently used to regulate and moderate drug efficacies in formulae. *Sending* drug (because of its use in this formula to moderate the harshness of the rhubarb and sodium sulphate).

11. Dried dendrobium (stem), 9 g: Sweet, Clear (flavor), slightly Chilling; enters Stomach, Lung, and Kidney tracts; nourishes yin with moisture, nourishes Stomach, clears Heat and generates fluids. Usually used to treat Heat illnesses with fluid damage, rising depletion fire, mouth dry with excessive thirst, spontaneous sweating, and other conditions. *Supporting* drug (because of clearing Heat and because it supplements the capacity of the ruling drug to generate fluids).

This analytical breakdown produces a clear picture of a formula that is divided into primary and secondary (clearing Heat from upper areas and draining it from lower, respectively) functions. The ruling drug, asphodel, has capacities to accomplish both tasks, although, as is fitting, its "clearing above" capacities are more marked. It is supported by forsythia, gardenia, tricosanthes, dendrobium, skullcap, and four o'clock in the former function of clearing Heat; and it is assisted by rhubarb, sodium sulphate, citron, skullcap, tricosanthes, four o'clock, and dendrobium to drain the Lower *Jiao*. Fresh licorice root is used as a sender to moderate the harsh draining qualities of the two primary assisting drugs, rhubarb and sodium sulphate. The replenishment of fluids is another secondary function that is well represented in the formula by the assisting drugs of dendrobium and tricosanthes; these two supplement asphodel's marked capacity to nourish fluids.

The formula is modified from Barrier Cooling Powder, and an examination of Dr. Ye's alterations to the textbook formula provides interesting insights into his understanding of the case. *Formulary* lists the ingredients of Barrier Cooling Powder as follows: rhubarb, 600 g; mirabilite, 600 g; licorice root, 600 g; jasmine seed, 300 g; mint leaves, 300 g; skullcap, 300 g; and forsythia, 1200 g. In this formula forsythia appears to be the ruling drug; the textbook commentary suggests that jasmine seed and skullcap support it in clearing Heat and putting down Fire in the Upper *Jiao,* while mint and bamboo leaves (with which the decoction is prepared) clear Heat in both the Upper and Middle *Jiao*. Sodium sulphate (in mirabilite) and rhubarb are used as assistants to drain the Middle and Lower *Jiao,* and honey (also added in decocting) and licorice root act as senders to moderate the harsh action of these two important purgative drugs.

This division of functions within the formula is quite similar to that of Dr. Ye's modified version, even though he adds five additional drugs and deletes one. The most marked difference between the formulae is Dr. Ye's demotion of forsythia to the role of supporter and its replacement in the ruling position with asphodel. There is only one relevant difference between these two drugs: Both clear Heat and put down Fire, but asphodel also replenishes fluids, a function that Dr. Ye clearly thought needed to be more strongly emphasized in this case. It is characteristic of approaches deriving from the Warm Illnesses tradition to protect fluids from damage resulting from Heat. Perhaps this global bias on the part of Warm Illnesses–oriented doctors explains his silence in his statement of the treatment principle on the need to replenish fluids.

In addition, among the drugs added by Dr. Ye are several that treat throat symptoms and Phlegm (tricosanthes, citron, four o'clock); I think it can be assumed that, although not mentioned in the description of the case, Dr. Ye found Phlegm and sore throat (common accompaniments to Spring Warm) and added a further dimension of assistance to the formula to deal with these symptoms. This further specification below the level of the treatment principles (which do not mention transforming Mucus or smoothing the throat in Case 1) is taken for granted in formulary. The ideal formula should respond to all the symptomatic manifestations of the illness process. There will almost always be a few that are not fully dealt with by the rather sweeping generalizations embodied in treatment principles. Although these might eventually resolve themselves as the root of the disorder is treated directly, the ideal approach is to relieve as much of the manifest illness as is practicable without generating a formula that is internally antagonistic.

Dr. Ye's modified Barrier Cooling Powder, then, has one ruling drug, aspects of which respond to all the facets of the syndrome. Supporting drugs strengthen its efficacy, especially against Upper *Jiao* Heat and Dryness. Its various assistant drugs perform three functions that are secondary to the primary functions of clearing Upper *Jiao* Heat: They are draining the Lower *Jiao*, replenishing fluids, and ameliorating the Lung symptoms of sore throat and Mucus. And one sending drug serves to moderate the onesidedness of two important assisting drugs. In general this hierarchy is one in which the ruling drug has the widest powers and is used in the greatest volume but requires the support and assistance of other drugs to pick out some of its efficacies as primary functions and to specify and direct others as secondary functions.

This mode of "dividing labor" and forging "intimate links" within the formula is not strongly determined by intrinsic qualities of the drugs themselves. That is to say, many of the drugs in this formula can play the role of ruling drug in another formula designed to treat another syndrome; and asphodel or forsythia can play the role of supporter, assistant, or even sender when it is used in other formulae. The highly focused efficacies of these drugs are a function of their positions relative to one another. Once the appropriateness of this formula has been evaluated clinically—that is, through giving a dose or two and observing the results—the positioning of drugs will be changed, some will be dropped and others added, and the whole hierarchy will be reevaluated with reference to the clear goals of therapy.[19]

The complex links among the analytic methods that have allowed a syndrome to be differentiated, the treatment methods that have been chosen to respond to that syndrome, and the formula that embodies these methods and responds to individual symptoms are clear in a careful reading of this case. Some "short forms" of the clinical encounter, in which direct links between, for example, symptoms and drugs, are explicitly made in practice will be discussed. Regardless of whatever shortcuts might be taken, a strong relationship is always likely between the formula and some form of treatment method or strategy. As was pointed out, "One cannot have a method

---

19. A term that is frequently used for formula writing, *chufang*, is of interest here; I have translated it as "positioning formulae". The even more common expression, *zhifang*, which means to formulate or arrange drugs in their proper relationships, is a term that might be seen to continue the social metaphor of monarch-minister relations in formulary. The verb *zhi* is often found in premodern political discourse to refer to the administrative placement of people and the regulation of social relations.

without a formula, and no formula is possible without a method."[20] This relationship is one in which the treatment method encompasses but does not fully determine the formula. Not only the choice but also many details of the final form of the prescription will be left to the doctor as he "customizes" his response to the concrete situation.

The relationship between technical operations and the discretionary space within which doctors produce their "designer drugs" is well summarized by a paragraph introducing formulary in a widely used handbook of Chinese medicine:

> After drugs have been subjected to certain principles of combining them in composing a formula, they can realize each other through mutual assistance, thereby elevating effectiveness, or they can realize each other through mutual opposition, thereby regulating [inappropriate] dominance and bias, controlling toxicity, and moderating or reducing undesirable responses. More important, in combining [drugs], one can thoroughly plumb complex illness manifestations, [understand the specific] strength and weakness of the illness heteropathy and the orthopathic qi, and grasp the main contradiction. Starting off from a holistic viewpoint and in accord with the basic theory of Chinese medicine, [one can] correctly manage heteropathy and orthopathy and the dialectical relationship between local and general. Moreover, one can concretely deal with the concrete situation according to whether the illness condition is [changing] slowly or rapidly, [respond to] loss of regulation in yinyang and qi and Blood, and [distinguish] the major and minor aspects of root and branches, etc. For example, it is possible to choose [the complex therapies of] jointly replenishing qi and Blood, harmonizing and flushing [both] exterior and interior aspects, applying both Cold and Hot, replenishing and draining at the same time, letting opening and closing help each other, replenishing qi to halt [yang] collapse, etc. At the same time one can organize [prescriptions] according to [variations in] the place, the time, and the person [affected]. Proceed from the concrete illness condition, understand, and utilize adeptly [*linghuo*].[21]

Adeptness can be evaluated; inept or clumsy interventions can be denounced. The importance of maintaining refined judgment in medical work is emphasized at the outset of *Formulary:* "any one effective and reliable formula must have strong countering force, must be rigorously organized, must have a clear and exact significance, must stress its main elements, must attain multiplicity without miscellaneousness as well as the economy of sticking to the essentials."[22] This passage makes clear that there are many wrong ways of designing formulae, that there are notions of elegance involved in the writing and reading of them, and that part of good formula design is to

20. Guangzhou College, *Fangjixue*, p. 1.
21. Beijing College, *Shiyong Zhongyixue*, p. 462.
22. Guangzhou College, *Fangjixue*, p. 5.

work from and clearly express a strategy of combating the illness. This is the essence of *lunzhi*, and, like military strategy, it is ultimately attributable to the adeptness of the doctor, whose flexibility and responsiveness can be acquired only through experience and practice.

Even in today's scientistic environment (or perhaps especially) there is a poetics of formula selection and design. The principles of elegance, economy, clarity, and rigorous organization are part of a lively aesthetic sensibility on the part of working Chinese doctors.[23] A well-designed formula should respond in every particular to the complexity of the syndrome presented, should demonstrate a deep appreciation of the ancient insights embedded in the classical formulae used, and should articulate the uniqueness of the illness condition clearly and exactly with its complex quantification and careful selection of drugs (including local variants and special modes of preparation). A good formula can be read "back" to the illness in such detail that experienced clinicians feel they can almost see the patient before them and hear his account of the symptoms.

If the great interest of my teachers in Guangzhou in the evaluation of drug formulae is an index, then much of the intellectual life of Chinese medicine revolves around the reading and writing of prescriptions. They can be read only by "insiders," they embody history in a way that materializes it in the present, and they can serve the people in the most immediate way. In addition, the process of honing one's clinical judgment in the aesthetic and practical evaluation of a wide range of formulae ramifies into social differentiations; scholarly factions, relative clinical brilliance or ineptitude, and even political commitments (e.g., to "tradition" or "dialectics") can be discerned. Skilled readers may position themselves (and their teachers and students) as they read within a complex field of technical possibilities that is fully revealed to them only in the literature of cases and prescriptions. Perhaps most telling, in the contemporary profession of Chinese medicine a relatively small number of "medical workers" concern themselves with "theoretical foundations," "medical history," or "the dialectics of nature." All, however, are interested in formulary.

Qualifying: Materia Medica (*Bencao*)

Qualitative abilities of drugs: The qualitative abilities of drugs are their characters [e.g., Hot or Cold] and flavors combined with their functions (i.e., the pharmacological role of drugs). Every type of drug has a certain qualitative

---

23. See Wang Xudong *Zhongyi Meishuxue* (Nanjing: Dongnan University Press, 1989), for a study of Chinese medicine from the point of view of the science of aesthetics. In it he takes up the aesthetic standards and principles of Chinese medicine's various subspecialties, including "aesthetics in the design of prescriptions and the use of drugs" (pp. 211–224).

ability. In sum, the main qualitative abilities of drugs are qi (character), flavor, ascension/descension, floating/sinking, and tract affinity. Using characters and flavors to describe the functions of drugs is a special characteristic of the utilization of the Chinese materia medica.[24]

The analysis of modified Barrier Cooling Powder earlier in this chapter described how individual drugs have qualities and efficacies that make it possible to structure a formula in response to a complexly characterized syndrome. These qualities are described, classified, and studied in a subdiscipline that is nowadays called *zhongyaoxue,* "pharmacognosy" or "Chinese materia medica." In contemporary colleges of Chinese medicine, students of materia medica are often separated early from students anticipating clinical practice; but every doctor is expected to master the characteristics and uses of several hundred drugs (about 450 were taught in the two-semester course I attended) in the course of his introductory education. In addition, drug properties are often the subject of professional publications, and a great deal of chemical and clinical research in herbal pharmacology has been done in China since early in the twentieth century.[25]

Zhongyaoxue is a modern term. The term *bencao* has been used to refer to medicinal drugs much longer. The earliest complete work on herbal drugs, *Shen Nong Bencao Jing* (The Divine Husbandman's Materia Medica), immortalizes the term in its title. This book dates from the second century A.D.[26]

Bencao is composed of the word for "root" (*ben,* often used abstractly as source, basis, or center) and the word for "grass" or "plant" (*cao*). Both words were and are quite widely used and generic; one translation of the compound might therefore be "main plants." But the term is rich in ambiguities and has considerable metaphorical force. For example, in modern Chinese *cao* connotes something common, to be found everywhere; grass has been used as a symbol of the people and their down-to-earth heroism in movies and monuments in the PRC. And *ben* has special meaning for Chinese medicine as an organizing principle of therapeutic work—"in treating illness, trace the root"—which in recent decades has done battle with biomedical notions of organic causes of illness. In keeping with this discursive emphasis on roots, a pharmacognosy instructor in Guangzhou argued in a class I attended that the term *bencao* could also be read as "taking herbals to be the root and basis of treating illnesses" (*yi caolei wei zhibing de jiben*).

---

24. Beijing College, *Shiyong Zhongyixue,* p. 193.

25. Much of the chemical research is summarized in volume 3 of Jiangsu New Medical College, ed., *Zhongyao Dacidian* (Shanghai: Shanghai People's Press, 1977).

26. Nowadays the term *bencao* tends to refer to classic works of pharmacy. Cf. Ou Ming et al., eds., *Han Ying Zhongyi Cidian* (Guangzhou: Guangdong Science and Technology Press, 1986), s.v. *bencao.*

Modes of drug use are strongly determined by the *bianzheng lunzhi* process that has differentiated a syndrome and begun its remanifestation in the design of a formula. The qualities and efficacies of drugs are specified in terms that forge direct links to symptoms, syndrome features, treatment principles, and the combining principles of formulary. These links are clear in the way the didactic and reference literature on drugs is organized. A passage on wind-weed asphodel in *Zhongyaoxue* (Chinese Pharmacognosy) is an example, translated here along with its framing categories:

Chapter 1: Exterior Flushing Drugs . . .
Section 2: Heat-clearing Drugs . . .
Subsection 1: Drugs that both clear Heat and drain Fire . . .
Type 1: Repletion-Heat drugs that clear the qi level . . .

Zhimu [Wind-weed asphodel]
(from the *Divine Husbandman's Materia Medica*)

Rhizome of *zhimu, wind-weed asphodel* Bunge., a perennial, member of the Lily family. Produced in Hebei (that from Li county is the best), Shanxi, and Dongbei [Manchuria], among other places. Can be gathered in the spring and autumn. Discard the part above the ground and the fibrous part of the root. Wash and sun-dry the root, soften in water, pare away the skin, and slice. Salt roast to use.

Character and flavor, tract affinities: Bitter, Sweet, Cold. Enters Lung, Stomach, and Kidney tracts.

Efficacies: clears Heat and drains Fire, replenishes yin moisture and moistens Dryness.

Usage:

1. Used in Warm illnesses when heteropathy is in the active qi sector, for the active qi Heat-repletion syndromes of high fever and wasting thirst, it has the function of draining Fire and eliminating agitation. It is often combined with gypsum and bamboo leaves, which have approximately the same efficacies.

2. Used to treat cough due to Lung Heat or dry cough of yin depletion, has the capacity to clear and drain Lung Fire, replenish yin moisture, and moisten Dryness. Often used together with fritillary bulb to strengthen its function of clearing the Lung and moistening Dryness, as in Two Mothers Powder of the *Medical Formulae Collected and Explained*.

3. Used for roaring Fires of yin depletion, when high fever steams forth from the bones and there is spontaneous sweating [because] it has the function of moistening yin and putting down Fire. Often needs to be used together with Amur cork-tree bark.

4. Not only can it clear and drain Lung and Stomach Fire; it can also moisten and nourish Lung and Kidney yin. Thus, it is appropriate to use in cases of Yin depletion thirst when the symptoms are dry mouth with thirst, much catarrh, and excessive urination; combined with yam, Schisandra fruit, etc., its efficacy can be strengthened, as in Jade Fluid Decoction.

Quantities used 6-12 grams.

Factors to consider in drug use: use of this drug contraindicated if stools are runny.

Reference materials:

1. *The Divine Husbandman's Materia Medica:* "Rules [yin depletion] thirst in cases of Heat, expelling the heteropathic qi; when there is edematous swelling of body and limbs, causes water to flow downward; bolsters inadequacies, supplements qi."

   Da Ming's Materia Medica: "Treats Heat-induced fatigue of the whole body, penetrates the Small Intestine, reduces Phlegm, stops coughing, moistens Heart and Lung systems, replenishes depletions, calms the Heart, and stops palpitations."

   Systematic Materia Medica: "Calms foetuses, stops agitation in pregnant women, wards off and expels poisons contracted in irrigation work." It also says, "Asphodel's Bitter, Pungent, Cold, and Cool qualities descend to moisten Kidney Dryness and increase yin, and they ascend to clear Lung Metal and drain Fire; hence it is a two-tract drug of the active qi sector."

2. Contains many types of steroid saponins (after water treatment yielding sarsasaponin and a mucus material). Decocted in formulae, it has the function of controlling dysentery, typhoid, and paratyphoid bacilli, intestinal bacteria, cholera vibrio, proteus bacilli, pseudomonas pyocyanae, staphylococci, alpha and beta hemolytic streptococci, pneumonic diplococci, whooping cough bacilli, and common fungi that induce skin pathologies. Animal experiments have demonstrated [that Anemarrhena] has Heat-clearing, Mucus-expelling, and diuretic functions. Moderate quantities of Anemarrhena extract can numb respiratory centers, reduce blood pressure, and numb the heart; larger amounts can stimulate respiration and stop cardiac palpitations.[27]

As can be inferred from the preceding material, drugs are differentiated from each other for medical use along four main dimensions: "character and flavor" (*xingwei*), "tract affinities" (*guijing*), "efficacies" (*gongxiao*), and "usage" (*yingyong* or *zhuzhi*). There are five categories of drug character (*xing*): Cold, Cool, Warm, Hot and Neutral (*ping*). And the "flavors" (*wei*) number six: Sweet, Pungent, Sour, Bitter, Salty, and Clear (*dan*). These are qualities of the drugs themselves, derived, it is argued, from a long period of observation and trial-and-error experimentation in use both as food and medications. Drug flavors are no more self-evidently experiential than drug

---

27. Chengdu College of Traditional Chinese Medicine et al., eds., *Zhongyaoxue* (Shanghai: Shanghai Science and Technology Press, 1978), p. 57. Works cited in the quotation are Wang Ang, comp., *Yifang Jijie* (Collected Explanations of Medical Prescriptions), 1682; Anonymous, *Shen Nong Bencao* (The Divine Husbandman's Materia Medica), 1st–2nd centuries A.D.; Da Ming (or Ri Huazi), *Daming Bencao* (Daming's Materia Medica), 6th century A.D.; and Li Shizhen, *Bencao Gangmu* (The Systematic Materia Medica), 1590.

character is a clear temperature differential.[28] Rather, they are two traditional means of classifying therapeutic properties that can emerge only in use and over time. Because they classify properties, rather than the drugs themselves, these conventional labels concatenate to characterize each drug in a manner that is both complex and logically powerful. A few words serve to describe each drug's specific value, and these same words link the drug into the broader correspondences of the whole clinical encounter.

The Hot-Cold character of a drug has obvious usefulness in combating Cold or Hot symptoms or forms of heteropathic qi. "Treat Hot with Cold and Treat Cold with Hot" are time-honored and straightforward approaches to treatment consistent with the struggle dimension of yinyang relations. The uses of drug flavors are less self-evident, however.

The five flavors are explained as follows in *Chinese Pharmacognosy:*

The five flavors are the five types of Pungent, Sweet, Sour, Bitter, and Salty. Some drugs have a Clear or an Astringent flavor, so in reality the types are not confined to five; but they are customarily still called the five flavors. The five flavors are also an expression of the roles of drugs, different flavors having different functions. As for their yinyang classifications, Pungent, Sweet, and Clear belong to yang, and Sour, Bitter, and Salty belong to yin. Their functions can be generalized as follows on the basis of historical experience of the use of drug flavors.

Pungent has the functions of spreading and disseminating, moving qi, moving Blood, or nourishing with moisture. In general all drugs used for syndromes of the outer aspect (e.g., mahuang and field mint), drugs that treat qi and Blood stasis (e.g., costus for moving qi and safflower for enlivening Blood and breaking up stagnation), and even certain moistening and replenishing drugs (e.g., dodderseed) are of Pungent flavor.

Sweet has the functions of replenishing and supplementing, moderating the Middle *Jiao*, and slowing acuteness. In general all drugs used to treat depletion syndromes with moistening, replenishing, and strengthening (e.g., *dangshen* and foxglove root) as well as drugs that alleviate acute pain and moderate the character of other drugs (e.g., malt sugar and licorice root) are of sweet flavor.

Sour has the functions of contracting and constricting. In general drugs that are of the sour flavor are used in treating depletion perspiration and diarrhea syndromes; examples are medicinal cornel fruit and Schisandra fruit for reducing and controlling semen loss and restraining perspiration and Chinese sumac for contracting the intestines to stop diarrhea.

---

28. Porkert (*The Theoretical Foundations of Chinese Medicine* [Cambridge, Mass.: MIT Press, 1974], p. 113) translates *wei* as "sapor" to discourage confusion of the technical concept with the tastes of food. Drug character, the "four ch'i," is discussed by Nathan Sivin, *Traditional Medicine in Contemporary China* (Ann Arbor: Center for Chinese Studies, University of Michigan, 1987), pp. 181–184, who also points out that modern explanations of the Five Flavors have often made little distinction between the technical term used in pharmacognosy and the flavors of food (which are themselves culture specific in ways not unrelated to drug classifications).

Astringent functions [are] similar to those of sour drugs. [In general drugs that are of astringent flavor are] mostly used to treat syndromes of depletion perspiration, diarrhea, frequent urination, nocturnal emissions, hemorrhage, etc. For example, dragon bones and oyster shells can be used to control semen loss, and halloysite can contract the intestines to stop diarrhea.

Bitter has the functions of draining and drying. "Draining" has a very broad meaning; it can refer both to draining through and out, as in the use of rhubarb to treat Heat-binding constipation, and to downward flow in the interior, as when almond pit is used to treat cough arising from Lung qi counterflowing upward. It also can refer to clearing and draining, as when jasmine is used to treat Heat Excess Agitating the Heart and other such syndromes. Its reference even extends to drying, so it is used in Damp syndromes. Damp syndromes include Cold-Damp and Damp-Heat, which are different, and Bitter drugs of Warm character such as cangshu are useful for the former; Bitter drugs of Cold character such as golden thread root are useful for the latter. In addition, the experience of our forebears holds that Bitter drugs also have the function of strengthening yin, as in the use of Amur cork-tree bark and asphodel for flaccid paralysis resulting from depletion Kidney yin deficiency and simultaneous excesses of Liver and Kidney Fire; here draining has the meaning of draining Fire to save or strengthen yin.

Salty has the functions of softening hardness, dispersing lumps, and draining downward. [In general drugs that are of a salty flavor are] mostly used to treat scrofula, lumpy mucus, abdominal lumps, and Heat-binding constipation—for example, the use of cockle shells to soften and disperse stubborn lumps and the use of magnesium sulphate crystals to drain downward and produce a bowel movement.

Clear has the functions of condensing Dampness and causing urine to flow. [In general drugs that are of a clear flavor are] mostly used to treat syndromes with edematous swelling and urine retention, as with the diuretics *zhuling* and China root.[29]

This discussion of the Five Flavors is summarized in Table 6.1. Both Table 6.1 and the preceding quote make clear that classification by flavor directly correlates drugs to the vocabulary and reasoning of therapeutics. Clinicians are not concerned about whether a substance classified as Bitter actually tastes bitter when eaten, but they must bear in mind that Bitter drugs drain and dry.

The circulation tract affinities of drugs are prominently used in few formulae, and many drugs have no particular ability to seek out one or another visceral system or circulation tract. These are a form of drug quality that refers (perhaps even more narrowly than character and flavor classifications) to the accumulated experience of medical specialists in using these drugs to treat disorders afflicting specific visceral systems. Tract affinities are also logically entailed in other drug qualities. There is likely to be little contra-

---

29. Chengdu College et al., *Zhongyaoxue*, p. 7.

Table 6.1 Characteristics of the Five Flavors

Flavor	Functions	Syndromes Treated	Yinyang Character
Pungent	Spreads and disseminates; moves qi; moves Blood; moistens	Syndromes of the outer aspect; stasis of qi and Blood; syndromes requiring moistening and replenishing	Yang
Sweet	Replenishes and supplements; moderates Middle *Jiao;* slows acuteness	Depletion syndromes; pain	Yang
Sour	Contracts and constricts	Depletion perspiration; diarrhea; semen loss	Yin
Bitter	Drains and dries, strengthens yin	Heat constipation; cough; Heat agitation of Heart; Damp syndromes; yin deficiency syndromes	Yin
Salty	Softens hardness; disperses lumps; drains downward	Scrofula; lumpy mucus; abdominal lumps; Heat constipation	Yin
Clear	Condenses Damp; causes urine to flow	Edematous swelling; urine retention	Yang
Astringent	Similar to Sour drugs	Depletion perspiration; diarrhea; frequent urination; nocturnal emissions; hemorrhages	Yin

diction between drug qualities and efficacies used against specific symptoms (e.g., cooling drugs against Hot symptoms) and the circulation tracts thought to be affected by the illness.

The first formula used in Case 1, for example, coordinates the tract affinities of its component drugs in a way that is consistent with its clear above and drain below treatment principle. The Heat-clearing drugs mainly seek tracts that are affiliated to visceral systems in the Upper *Jiao;* clearing is an activity that refers to the expulsion of Heat from the upper part of the body. And the draining drugs mainly seek Stomach and Intestine tracts, draining in this case meaning to cause excreta to flow. Tract affinities in this formula (mainly Lung, Stomach, Gallbladder, and Intestine systems) appear to be entirely subsumed within the efficacies ascribed to the drugs.

Case 3, however, contains a formula that can be read more clearly if the tract affinities of its component drugs are kept in mind. Dr. Zhong points out in his short commentary that he emphasizes moving qi to cause Blood to flow, but he also employs a visceral systems strategy that coordinates the tract affinities of the drugs he prescribes. A majority of drugs in the formula seek out the Liver visceral system, causing the restored function of the Liver to more effectively disseminate qi throughout the body. Thus, although Dr. Zhong phrases his strategy in terms of Blood and qi movement, and even though the symptoms themselves are strongly associated with the Spleen-Stomach system, he has designed an intervention that focuses on the Liver system.

I have already argued that character, flavor, and (in part) tract affinities are informative classifications of drug qualities chiefly because they can be translated into the language of drug efficacies, which is the same as that of therapeutics. In other words, the drug efficacies are a crucial mode of linking drug use into all other *bianzheng lunzhi* methodology. Given the complexity of the formulae and of the combining principles by which they are designed, this is not a simple reflex relationship. In many cases differing or conflicting drug efficacies must be carefully calculated against each other in the service of a highly nuanced therapeutic strategy. The importance of knowing and properly utilizing drug powers in the composition of formulae can be readily seen in the first formula of Case 1; Table 6.2, a shortened and rearranged version of the analysis advanced of this formula, makes the point clearly. In this table I have deleted the characters, flavors, and tract affinities to highlight the efficacies (*gongxiao*) of each drug; but the organization of the formula, and the way in which it both completely instantiates the treatment method and responds to the secondary Lung system symptoms of mucus and cough, is still clear. This clarity is possible because the same vocabulary is used for drug efficacies as for treatment methods.

In materia medica practice, the category of usage (*yingyong*) or "main illnesses treated" (*zhuzhi*) is less important than an understanding of the clinical applications of whole formulae. In most sources that describe the characteristics of individual drugs, the usage category consists of a list of the main syndromes treated with the drug in question. I suspect that in practice this kind of information is no more than a guide to syndromes treatable by formulae that can have the drug in question as a ruling or supporting drug. Thus, it is redundant of similar information incorporated within formulary but less straightforwardly applicable to clinical situations. That usage is specified for individual drugs, however, in a sense asserts that the practical histories of drugs are a part of their specific character. From the point of view of most academic practitioners, it would be unrefined to use single drugs against any illness no matter how simple, but the relationship between specific drugs and specific syndromes is nevertheless recorded and remembered. Character and flavor can be phrased and may be experienced as "natural" properties of a drug, whereas efficacy, tract affinity, and usage

Table 6.2   Analysis of Efficacies (*Gongxiao*) in Spring Warm Formula

Original Formula No.	Drug Name	Efficacies	Position
4.	Wind-weed asphodel	Clears Heat and puts down Fire; nourishes yin with moisture and moistens Dryness	Ruling
1.	Weeping forsythia	Clears Heat and flushes out Heat toxin	Supporting
2.	Black-roasted jasmine seed	Drains fire and eliminates agitation; clears Heat and causes Dampness to flow	Supporting
11.	Dried dendrobium	Nourishes yin with moisture; nourishes Stomach; clears Heat and generates Fluids	Supporting
3.	Mild skullcap	Clears Heat and dries Dampness; drains Fire and flushes out [Heat] toxin	Supporting Assisting
7.	Tricosanthes	Clears Lungs; transforms Phlegm; relaxes chest area and dispels congelations; moistens bowels	Supporting Assisting
5.	Fresh rhubarb	Drains Heat toxin; mobilizes static accumulations	Assisting
6.	Mirabilite	Drains Heat; induces bowel movement; softens hardness	Assisting
8.	Citron	Mobilizes qi and relaxes middle; transforms Phlegm; aids food digestion	Assisting
9.	Four o'clock	Drives out Wind; clears Heat and flushes out toxins, drains Lower *Jiao*	Assisting
10.	Fresh licorice root	Harmonizes middle; slows acute conditions; stops aching; drives out Phlegm and stops coughing; flushes out toxins; regulates the relations of other drugs	Sending

refer more directly to the qualities of drugs that have been compiled through centuries of medical work.

I have suggested at various points that classification proceeds by identifying the qualities of things to serve as guides in the process of classifying them. I have also indicated that such classifications are not static essentialist taxonomies but rather are dynamic networks of effective interaction among items of the various classes. Materia medica is an example of this classificatory process.

Cold and Hot gradations and flavors are qualities that enable a preliminary narrowing of a physician's options in deploying drug powers. Effective relationships between these qualities and physiological responses to the ingestion of drugs bearing them can quickly become natural and intuitive to the clinician. Those features, such as tract affinities, efficacies, and common usages, that are more technical (in that they result from accumulated medical experience rather than from what is felt to be simple observation) allow for more advanced or customized applications. At least two tiers of classification, then, can be discerned. Character and flavor are qualities that restrict the use of certain drugs to a certain wide range of illnesses. In the process of treating these illnesses, clinicians require greater specification, target certain tracts, and need more finely divided efficacies to respond to more nuanced characterizations of the illness.

The category of usage in modern sources does not organize drugs according to the syndromes they are most often used to treat. In theory a full classification based on usage is possible, of course, but this level of complexity and one-to-one correspondence would defeat the purpose of classification, eliminating the simplicity of working with classes rather than individuals.

Once the full range of the materia medica has been organized into a classificatory framework, drugs can be combined into effective relationships in formulae, and their powers can be brought to bear on physiological processes. The relationships into which individual drugs enter are of two kinds, both of which have been described elsewhere. They are combined into the hierarchical structure of formulae and linked thereby to the whole *bianzheng lunzhi* process; this is accomplished chiefly by means of the relationship between efficacies and treatment methods that informs and organizes all activities in the *lunzhi* phase of the *kanbing* process. And, they are directed against the specific pathological processes of illness; in this process the characters and flavors of drugs are important since, for example, Cold and Cool drugs can be directed against Hot and Warm symptoms and flavors such as Bitter can be directed against various forms of blockage and against Damp.

The general pattern of medical classification is readily visible in these forms of drug use. Qualities enable classification, and classification enables the formation and manipulation of effective relationships among things. Drugs are not inert and discrete objects that can be conveniently placed in taxonomic slots, however. Just as illness symptoms are medically perceived in correlated and textured spatial, temporal, and qualitative dimensions, so drugs are perceived and produced in a similarly dimensional way. Materia medica literature of all kinds makes continual reference to the preferred locales where the highest quality variant of each drug is most commonly found or produced as well as to the botanic features of many varieties. Many *bencao* compilations are profusely illustrated to aid doctors or herbalists in collecting and in differentiating variants from one another for clinical purposes. Moreover, the time of year at which a plant should be collected, the part of the plant that is effective, and the preparation required before it can be stored for use are specified. The qualities of drugs that constitute their medical powers and that are describable and classifiable in ways that link them to medical processes are firmly anchored in certain parts of a plant growing in certain parts of the world at certain times of the year. In addition, these qualities are liberated for medical effectiveness only after processing; they are, in other words, resituated in medical sequences, produced as drug from a plant (or animal or mineral) that in its raw state is only potentially efficacious. Until and unless so produced and situated, herbal drugs have no free, natural, or abstract medical qualities.

When we look at drug deployment in the framework of the whole *kanbing* process, we see that what has been arrived at by the time the drugs have been assembled, cooked, and consumed are the material relationships among several classes of phenomena. It seems that the whole point of medical intervention has been to bring remote things, elements drawn from "other regions" of the myriad things, to bear on illness manifestations. The complex strategies of medical practice amount to a materialization of the actual relationships that obtain between the normal world of a sufferer and the world of more exotic plants, animals, and minerals, the juxtaposition of efficacies and processes that have previously been widely scattered. The distance between a person who is ill in a highly specific way and the particular items among the myriad things that can act on her disorder is closed when she eats or drinks a drug preparation. This reminds us that the polarity of inside and outside, so evident in Chinese medical imagery, although it may become even more acute in illness, can be reduced. All the myriad things are informed by the same principles of action and manifestation. Knowledge and practical mastery consist of playing on these principles to lead illness states toward good outcomes.

7

Classification, Specificity, History, and Action: An Overview of the Clinical Encounter

THE *KANBING* PROCESS DESCRIBED in Chapters 4, 5, and 6 and schematized in Figure 3.2 is a mode of intervention in illness in which analytic and synthetic methods selected from the "treasurehouse" of the medical archive are deployed to characterize a syndrome and design a therapy. The logics of this clinical encounter and the nuances of its proper practice have been explored in connection with the separate phases of a generalized process. Much of this process is not strictly observable in clinics, but its elements can be elicited by allowing Chinese doctors to instruct us both in person and through their published contributions to the extensive discourse of "traditional Chinese medicine." Very diverse practices—pulse-taking and tongue examination, eight rubrics classification, visceral systems spatialization, six warps and four sectors temporalization, the "positioning" of drugs in formulae, the preparation and assembly of a few herbals from a vast materia medica—have here been combined to produce a more or less smooth logical curve. It is now possible to add abstracting insult to generalizing injury by interpreting the hierarchical form of the clinical encounter (as summarized in Figure 3.2) as a series of movements—in and out of "medicine," from speech to silence and back again, from a specificity of suffering to a specificity of "natural" power.[1] It will then be possible to consider the way in which the full and normative form of the clinical encounter allows or even encourages certain variants or shorter forms of dealing with illness. In

---

1. Although I take full responsibility for Figure 3.2 as my own visualization of a practical form immanent in the clinical encounter, it may comfort some readers to know that several Chinese doctors with whom I worked in Guangzhou examined and accepted it as correct. I see it as a form that has thus far escaped explication in the Chinese medical literature mainly because it is quite thoroughly taken for granted.

addition, the yinyang relationship and its clinical regulation will be reconsidered as a form of action in the light of what has been learned about the process of looking at illness in Chinese medicine.

Illness In, Drugs Out

It is significant that the clinical encounter in Chinese medicine is referred to by a term meaning looking at illness (*kanbing*). Although the word for illness, *bing*, can be used in any phase of clinical work, this analysis of *kanbing* shows that the character of the illness changes from a mundane, complex, and quite variously expressed kind of suffering (when it enters the clinic in the form of a "sufferer" [*huanzhe*]) to a highly refined event, a syndrome that can be laid alongside numerous previous syndromes similar to it. It is then remanifested in a correlated form, a drug efficacy for every aspect of the complaint, materialized in several piles of dusty stems, leaves, shells, root slices, and powders and wrapped up in brown paper to be boiled at home. The techniques by means of which this transformation from the mundane to the medical and the remanifestation of the medical in the herbal are accomplished are of little interest to most of the beneficiaries of medicine's "rich experience." And many modern Chinese patients and students of traditional medicine find little in this technical knowledge that accords with their everyday experience or common sense.[2] Yet this basic movement inward toward medical experience (history and the skills and recollections of the doctor) and outward to a more fully informed efficacy may strike them as not only sensible but also necessary.

There is a certain cultural logic to a medicine that mediates in this way between individual (ailing) human beings and the myriad things of the world (some of which are themselves products of human bodies),[3] bringing the myriad things to bear on the human in a rigorously articulated and situationally sensitive form. If we can judge from Chinese patent medicine advertising and conversations in urban Chinese drugstores, the exotic origins, special processing, and long histories of formulae and drugs are as important to health-conscious consumers as they are to the scholarly compilers of pharmacy textbooks (of which the textbook article on wind-weed asphodel in Chapter 6 is an example).

One of the most frequently used tropes in the literature on the materia

---

2. In Guangzhou I had the opportunity to ask many students of traditional medicine about the difficulties they encountered while studying. Most of them said that they found the philosophical foundations of Chinese medicine very foreign and strange ("too abstract" was a frequent complaint), and all insisted that the classical language of the ancient medical works was difficult to understand correctly.

3. Nathan Sivin, "Man as a Medicine," in Shigeru Nakayama and Nathan Sivin, eds., *Chinese Science* (Cambridge, Mass.: MIT Press, 1973), pp. 203–272.

medica is that of gathering, especially from mountains and wild and far places. Qualities of rarity, multiplicity, and dispersion are embodied in prescriptions, gathered together in a bundle to correspond exactly (a reversed image) to the illness, the person, and the historically informed syndrome. This process of bringing the myriad things to bear on human suffering in a positive medical intervention goes beyond the "merely" symbolic, beyond the "correlative thinking" so usefully explored by Joseph Needham,[4] to what might be called "incorporative action." Because Chinese medical classification always implies a dynamic, the discernment and manipulation of differences and resemblances in the *bianzheng lunzhi* process are more than symbolic correlations of (really) unrelated things. They are, rather, intervention in the natural transformations of the world, using actions of a certain quality (Heat, Bitterness) to intervene in activities similar or opposite in kind.

This is no mere juxtaposition of objects classified as opposites; objects are, after all, merely the products of qi transformation, which is the fundamental activity of the world. Patterns of qi transformation can be described not only in physiological terms but also in the language of drug character, flavors, and efficacies. Such a language approaches the dynamic processes that continually produce the visible world; ultimately the myriad things are less interesting in themselves than as temporary embodiments of world-generative activity. Thus, a drug prescription treats kinds of activity that are in this situation pathological (excessive or inadequate) with opposite kinds of activity that can be wholesome in the situation by virtue, not of their essence, but of their opposition. The functional efficacies of the materia medica are literally incorporated in the person of the sufferer, cooling her Heat, replenishing his depletions.

Without the mediation of medical skill, honed in the clinic and in the study of medical history and "theory," the signs of suffering in the opening phase of the clinical encounter could not (doctors argue) rationally be brought together with the far-flung and long-studied efficacies of the things of the world, the *wanwu* of the materia medica. Medicine with its vast records of healing experience knows how to enfold the sufferer in a wholesome history, one that is more richly collective than the narrow personal history that has produced an illness.

Speech and Silence

Figure 3.2 implies a hierarchical relationship between mundane manifestations (signs, drugs) and their written forms (symptoms, prescriptions) and between these written forms and the (in clinic practice often unspoken

---

4. Joseph Needham, *Science and Civilization in China,* vol. 2 (Cambridge: Cambridge University Press, 1956), pp. 279–303.

and unrecorded) *bianzheng lunzhi* pivot. Both the "ascent" to the $zheng_3$ and the "descent" from the *zhi* pass through a level of written manifestation: the list of symptoms in the case record booklet and the written formula, respectively. Put another way, the movement from the signs of illness (i.e., the patient's complaints elicited in the "asking" examination) to a carefully analyzed syndrome via a stage of writing symptoms in a case record booklet is a movement from greater to lesser verbosity. The *bianzheng* side of the clinical encounter develops from multivocal and nontechnical speech to relative silence or taciturnity. (See Figure 7.1, a modification of Figure 3.2.) This could also be phrased as a movement from concrete to abstract and back again, a form of logic (and even history) that has been theorized in Maoist-influenced Chinese medical writing using the language of the essay "On Practice."[5] But the movement that can be discerned between verbosity and taciturnity in discourse and clinical work seems to have escaped written discussion by Chinese medical commentators.

There is, of course, tremendous variation among Chinese doctors in their degrees of "verbosity."[6] Possibly a modern pressure to further systematize and institutionalize Chinese medical knowledge and a widespread interest in educational reform have led to a much greater explicitness about elements of knowledge and practice that could once have remained implicit.[7] Nevertheless, certain widespread practices (or absences) impress one as pertinent to a speech-silence relationship that has at times been explicit in Chinese philosophy and literary and linguistic theory. If "the Dao that can be told is not the eternal Dao, the name that can be spoken is not the eternal name," as Laozi asserted, then systematic silences might result less from laziness or secretiveness than from culture-specific assumptions about language and its limited capacities.

A consideration of the usual form of the case record booklet (see Chapter 3) leads us to ask why, in a medical discipline as philosophically articulate as Chinese medicine, the central diagnostic and therapeutic terms (those for the syndrome and the treatment principle) should so often go unre-

---

5. See, for example, Huang Jitang et al., eds., *Zhongyixue Daolun* (Guangzhou: Guangdong Higher Education Press, 1988), pp. 58–60; and Huang Jitang, "*Zhongyixue Shi,*" in Dialectics of Nature Research and Teaching Section, ed., *Ziliao Huibian* (Guangzhou: Guangzhou College of Traditional Chinese Medicine, 1982), vol. 2, pp. 1–19.

6. I explored some of the implications of variations in verbal practice among senior Chinese doctors in "Speech, Text, and Silence" (Paper presented at the Fifth International Conference on the History of Science in China, San Diego, California, August 5–10, 1988).

7. One kind of evidence for this shift is the growing number of handbooks and manuals that make many features of practical activity in the clinic that were previously drummed into apprentices by teachers absolutely explicit in print; the four methods of examination are an important area where discourse continues to grow both in volume and didactic detail. See, for example, Deng Tietao, *Shiyong Zhongyi Zhenduanxue* (Shanghai: Shanghai Science and Technology Press, 1988).

MEDICAL DISCOURSE   CLINICAL PRACTICE

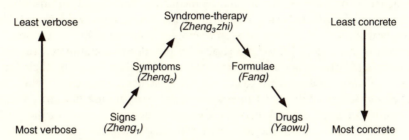

FIGURE 7.1   Verbosity and concreteness in the clinical encounter

corded.[8] I do not think this is an "artifact" of a previous era in which medical specialists worked independently of each other and harbored "trade secrets" (a suspect model in any case). It may, however, reflect a less rigid inside-outside distinction: Only "insiders" (*neihangren*) can read syndromes and therapeutic principles from the symptoms and prescriptions recorded in clinic booklets, but they can do it with a high degree of agreement. That they can do it, however, arises from their shared training and experience, from a shifting synthesis of materials, methods, and insights that cannot itself be conveyed in writing but rather must be acquired (even embodied) in the course of a medical life. A certain silence, then, where the central concepts of a therapeutic event are concerned seems to me to be a practical-symbolic assertion of the shared understanding that medical mastery and medical learning cannot be transmitted directly from person to person in words, that the arena of true medical virtuosity, the *zhengzhi* pivot, cannot be exhausted in mere reading and writing.

If insight, synthesis, and virtuosity cannot be comprehensively written or

---

8. This was the case in the clinics of the affiliated hospital of the Guangzhou College of Traditional Chinese Medicine. In addition, published case histories often fail to record the treatment principle and sometimes even omit a syndrome name for the condition. In cases that incorporate a discussion of the illness by the doctor or one of his assistants (e.g., hospital charts, published cases), the syndrome is sometimes obvious from the "illness mechanism" described, even if no separate category for $zheng_3$ is maintained. But clinic booklets never include more than a hint at such a discussion.

I have encountered one interesting exception to this tendency toward taciturnity about underlying principles in clinic work: A senior Chinese doctor working in the health station maintained by a well-to-do neighborhood of a Shandong county town keeps elaborate case histories for his clinic patients, recording and discussing all the aspects of the *bianzheng lunzhi* process I have discussed and more. These records are not secret (he stores them all on clips hanging from two rows of nails in his office), but they are not really used by anyone but him. They function as his notes to himself, and he consults them with care every time he sees a returning patient.

read, and if their embodiment in working doctors is constantly asserted in practice to be a core value of Chinese medicine, how should we understand the place of medicine's vast written history in contemporary discourse? The medical archive should not be seen as either a coercive influence on present action or a dry and lifeless storehouse of pointlessly accumulated records. Doctors use the weapons that have been used against illness by their fore-bears, always adapting them to current circumstances. And doctors study the lives and works of the great physicians of the past, aiming beyond the case records, biographies, and theoretical works to develop a sense of the living personal experience and the cultivated virtuosity of which such texts are only by-products. The very personal tone in which the great doctors of the past are spoken of, even by "hardheaded" scientifically minded modernizers, argues that the Chinese medical archive is approached as a social relation. The great healers of the past are taken as teachers, and their powers in the lives of currently practicing doctors are not necessarily either greater or smaller than those of other teaching relationships.

That reading is acknowledged as a social relation is consistent with the form in which classic medical works are now known to student doctors: The "original text" of *Basic Questions* or the *Treatise on Cold Damage* is followed on the printed page by footnotes explaining obscure or contested terms, translations into modern Chinese, contemporary and historical exegeses, and sometimes supplementary clinical explanations. Like a senior Chinese doctor, the original is terse, cryptic, and demanding of interpretation; like apprentices, scholars of subsequent generations organize, explain, and elab-orate the essential significance of the canons.

Doctors have a filial duty to learn from their seniors and to embody the heritage of medicine. But filiality is not passive; beyond the agency implicit in self-cultivation is the responsibility to continue the medical lineage, to teach coming generations in a way that lives up to the demands of one's own teachers. There are a yin and a yang to the filiality of teaching: Seniors embody; juniors express. Juniors become seniors and pivot to cultivate a new generation of students. Many senior Chinese doctors organize their clinic work such that their assistants do most of the talking (interviewing about symptoms, explaining about prescriptions); patients are said to be most impressed if a doctor can diagnose the dynamic of their illness simply by looking at them and reading their pulse. One widespread (if now out of fashion) style of teaching required apprentices to "stand behind the teacher's chair and attend on the examination"[9] for years, learning mainly by emulating their mentor's clinical habits and copying out long sections of

9. Deng Tietao, "*Wanli Yuntian Wanli Lu,*" in Zhou Fengwu et al., eds., *Ming Laozhongyi zhi Lu,* vol. 2 (Jinan: Shandong Science and Technology Press, 1984), p. 3.

assigned readings from the classics.[10] The way in which a teacher (often silently) embodies medical virtuosity is a kind of active yang principle that requires its yin in the speech and humble service of students. Only through a long labor of emulation and practice can juniors become seniors, themselves embodying medical skill in ways that can be ever responsive to the new situations presented by clinical work. Silence is maintained, then, not about secrets or some mystical ineffable, but about the complex work of sustaining social relations, of embodying a heritage, and of rising to the challenges of history in the service of the living.

Specificity

One important aspect of the relationship between sources and manifestations in medical practice (setting it apart from more mechanistic dyads, such as cause and effect, which derive much of their interest from a search for nomothetic principles) is the specificity that is sought and generated all along the *kanbing* path. No aspect of Chinese medical experience invites expression as fixed and abstracted predictive relationships, or "laws of nature." Even the most general level, that of syndrome differentiation and

---

10. This apprenticeship model of pedagogy is far from dead. A few anecdotes can demonstrate. Senior doctors at the affiliated hospital of the Guangzhou College often practice with younger colleagues who have themselves had years of clinical experience; these younger doctors are expected to do the initial interviewing and examination of patients as well as keep all the notes on each clinical encounter. One senior doctor I observed often asked his junior colleague (whom I knew as a stimulating and experienced teacher in the classroom) to feel a patient's pulse again and note fine distinctions that he believed only he had been able to perceive. The complexity of these discriminations was lost on me since this senior doctor almost always found the same simple pulse image no matter what the complaint. This particular junior doctor practiced quite differently and achieved much more various results whenever his senior was called away early from the clinic.

One elderly doctor whose practice I was observing instructed me to make two copies of his recent journal articles by hand. He had cast our relationship in a pedagogical frame and felt this exercise would be good for me. Naturally he saw no value in the photocopying services I offered him by way of alternative.

A faculty member of middle years whom I knew well was rapidly becoming an influential theorist in a department pursuing research on one of Chinese medicine's classic books. He had studied as a graduate student with an aging luminary whom I asked to interview. At the interview the senior doctor arrived with his student, my friend, in tow; the teacher had asked him to keep notes of our conversation and provide each of us with a handwritten copy. My friend took this request as an honor and was grateful for the opportunity to hear his mentor's most recent thinking.

The centrality of teaching to the standing of senior Chinese doctors (not to mention other kinds of scholars) is suggested by the widespread practice of purging intellectuals by denying them students. Many "old Rightists" were deprived of opportunities to teach from the mid-1950s to the late 1970s, and this kind of isolation is often reported with special bitterness in narratives that catalog political sufferings.

treatment determination, compares the illness at hand to a syndrome or combination of syndromes drawn from the archive only to delimit an area within which a specific perception is developed and a specific intervention deployed. The general principles that can mediate this comparison, insofar as they are ever stated, are described as guides to action, never as intellectual ends in themselves.

Therefore, an illness can be seen only to a limited extent as a single instance of a syndrome class to which many illnesses, past and future, belong. In other words, a "case" of a *zheng*$_3$ is more than a token of a type. This is not to say that syndrome differentiation is not really a form of classification. Rather, it is to assert that the forms of classification so fundamental to Chinese medical methods are highly contingent and sensitive to the uniqueness and texture of effects in a time and space that are not themselves generalized or abstract.

In the foregoing reading of the practical logics of *kanbing* there have been a number of examples illustrating the importance of locating effects in contingent space and time (and of discerning space and time locations of disorder from an observation of effects). The analytic methods of the four sectors and six warps are an eloquent model of interpenetrating continua of space, time, and substance or quality: Any position on each of these dimensions entails consequences for corresponding positions on the other two. This approach to understanding and participating in natural transformation has been noted in the early sources of Chinese medicine by Shigehisa Kuriyama as follows:

> For us the chasm separating topological similarity and functional identity is not easily crossed. It does not seem enough to say that one point [of the radial pulse] is a few millimeters north of another in order to explain the radical polarity in diagnostic significance. . . . The real difficulty lies in the idea, explicit here, that *places have dynamic propensities. K'an, li, chen, tui*, and *k'un* are hexagrams from the *I ching* (Book of Changes); water, fire, wood, metal, and earth are of course the five agents [phases]. All of these express directions of transformation; all of these remind us (for in the Chinese context this is not a matter of debate) that positions in space are not just abstract points in an isotropic coordinate system but rather gradients of change. Each site in the universe and, by correspondence, each site on the body is engaged in a specific network of responsiveness by virtue of nothing other than its position. Place, not form, determines function.[11]

"Place" here must be understood as inseparable from location in time and an array of qualities. To locate an illness between the active and defensive qi sectors (see Case 1) is to indicate its position in an exogenous-illness

---

11. Shigehisa Kuriyama, "Pulse Diagnosis in the Greek and Chinese Traditions," in Yosio Kawakita, ed., *History of Diagnostics* (Osaka: Taniguchi Foundation, 1987), pp. 55–56.

developmental sequence as well as to say much about its clinical character. Of course, only the refined sensibility of the experienced doctor can fully apprehend the texture of time and historicity of space in a way that is medically useful. In a characterization reminiscent of points I have already made, Kuriyama explains:

> In stating what is the case, [statements such as "North is *k'an*, the site of water"] neither call for nor permit critical examination, rejection, or assent. Rather, they define directions of learning: they invite us to develop our sensibility in such a way as to discern the realities described. For the untrained individual the *k'an* proclivities of the north may seem as unreal or at least as meaningless as "chicory bouquet" and "baroque timbre" are for those unversed in wine-tasting or music; but for the cultivated palate, to take just one example, the chicory bouquet is a fact of immediate experience. To accept the statement "North is *k'an*, the site of water," thus, means nothing more nor less than engaging oneself in a process of self-transformation. The dynamic character of places is a fact that one must learn to sense.[12]

This insight about medical perception and Kuriyama's extended exploration of the philosophical status of correspondence statements in early Chinese medicine make the emphasis in contemporary discourse on virtuosity and experience more coherent. Understanding the entailments of spatial or temporal position requires that time be spent in self-cultivation. In addition, the temporal and contingent nature of the syndrome is clarified. The frequently reiterated definition of the syndrome as a moment in an illness process suggests that its specific character derives from its temporal (and, once it has been analytically characterized, spatial) position in a specific chain of illness events.

Abstract temporal and spatial coordinates, and syndrome classes that completely exhaust the significance of individual illnesses, can no doubt be found in the discourse of contemporary Chinese medicine if they are vigorously sought out. This would not change the fact that very little of medical life, even today, accords logical importance to them.[13] Chinese medical clinicians are interested in differentiations at all levels, using the commonalities that determine and arise from class membership only as guides to achieving a finer differentiation. This makes all theoretical comparison with the very differently organized diagnostic and therapeutic world of biomedicine very difficult indeed.

---

12. Ibid., p. 57.
13. One marked exception is scientific research on the methods and materials of Chinese medicine. Researchers in units such as the Spleen-Stomach theory research unit at the Guangzhou College recognize that replicability and comparability of findings are fundamental to scientific research. But they also acknowledge the considerable difficulty of selecting a series of research subjects who can be said with scientific rigor (the Western variety) to be suffering from the "same" syndrome.

Clearly, many statements in Chinese medical discourse are significant outside a pseudo-scientific discourse on objective truth. The "Heat" of agitation symptoms lodged in the "Heart" is not a quality that anyone (until recently) might have been tempted to quantify in a rigorously replicable way. Rather, it is a vocabulary of contingent location that places the illness (and its sufferer in her role as "sick person") in a richly qualitative landscape of eventful time and historically generated place. This multidimensional landscape is subjective, meaningful as both a complex perception and an array of options open to a practitioner whose arsenal of interventions is indexed by the same vocabulary that describes the situation to be treated. To apply truth criteria to such a discourse is to miss the point entirely.

Specificity is not confined to the domain of the manifest. I have argued that the clinical encounter moves from manifest illness signs to manifest drugs through at least two levels of classificatory processing (Figure 3.2, phases A and B). The uniqueness of the illness is not lost through comparison with the general principles of medical theory and practice, however. Rather, it is situated relative to certain realms of recorded (but still concrete) experience that can most powerfully bring the therapeutic successes of the past to bear. Arguably it is less theory by means of which clinical phenomena are elucidated than it is history—previous specificities recorded, accumulated, and organized for use.

In the discussion of *bianzheng* analysis in Chapter 4, I demonstrated that a number of different stances are taken toward the illness and that syndromes are almost always characterized in the terms of more than one analytic method. These methods, however harmoniously they may be used together, are theoretically discontinuous. Doctors use the analytic methods to describe the various facets of an illness, speaking in technical classificatory idioms, each of which is appropriate for certain dimensions of the problem. No one class can exhaust the reality of the illness; other aspects of this reality are always available for classification and characterization in the terms of other schemes.

The specific substances or phenomena that are classified escape any complete encompassment by the classes themselves. The relationship of a syndrome, for example, to the various classes that have been applied to its analysis is not a part-whole relationship; a syndrome is not a species of a genus. It is in no way analogous to objects in essentialist Western taxonomies. It is, however, a good example of a Chinese object, a contingent conjuncture of diverse natural processes, evanescent, not because it is mystical or immaterial, but because change is inevitable. Classification provides access to processes of change, characterizes them, and helps doctors alter their direction with other products of the same sorts of change. That the specificity of the syndrome always exceeds the capacity of a classification to "explain" it reminds us that the essence of medical experience is treated as beyond the reach of language and texts. The specificity of an illness is never completely touched by medicine; medical perception moves around the illness's surface and infers its roots, doctoring it with weapons that have successfully doctored illnesses in the past. But medical perception does not define or name the illness's essence. The illness in Case 1 is not a "case of Spring Warm disease." It is a specific spatiotemporal and qualitative conjunction of excesses and deficiencies that may be influenced toward a desirable outcome by treatments that have worked for qualitatively similar conjunctions in past medical experience.

Short Forms of the Clinical Encounter

Classification has emerged from these considerations as a method that guides action rather than as a taxonomic description of the fixed natural essences of things. As method, classification can be highly variable. The *kanbing* process depicted in Figure 3.2 incorporates strongly parallel relationships on the basis of which certain alternative procedures can be justified.

The form of the clinical encounter that has been discussed so far is the mode of medically managing illness taught in classes, described and analyzed in textbooks and professional treatises, and assumed in a great deal of theoretical discourse. But some practitioners shorten or simplify this normative form, relying on the many classificatory correspondences they can perceive at levels "lower" than the *zhengzhi* apex.

The general form of the clinical encounter invites "shortcuts" at three levels. A direct movement between signs of illness and herbal treatments is logically possible and frequently employed outside the scope of contemporary academic medicine. A movement direct from symptoms produced by the four methods of examination to the prescription is also easy, being already a component of the "full form" of the clinical encounter. And a shortcut at the level of the analytic methods that directly generates a formula via a shared classificatory language is possible. (These short forms are summarized in Figure 7.2.)

Shortcut One: Signs to Drugs

A considerable amount of therapeutic activity goes on outside the purview of "Chinese medicine" as it has been institutionalized in the PRC, and most Chinese materia medica are readily available without prescription outside medical institutions as raw drugs or as patent medicines. Items from the materia medica corpus are consequently often used independently of the refined procedures of the medically adept. There are many drugs that are

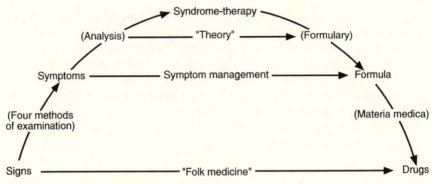

FIGURE 7.2   Short forms of the clinical encounter

popularly known to have Warming or Cooling, replenishing or draining properties, and drug merchants will advise their customers on drug efficacies without going through a formal *kanbing* procedure.

This "popular" route from illness signs to the acquisition and ingestion of drugs cannot be assumed to be straightforward or simple, but it clearly involves a different collection of perceptions and formulations than those that are at work in professional medicine. In addition, nonmedical people use a great many therapies that seldom appear in clinics of traditional medicine, where doctors rely heavily on the conceptual and material technologies I describe here. A recent guide to "folk" therapeutics summarizes its 176 types as including acupuncture, massage, qi energetics (mostly breathing exercises), cupping, fumigating, hot compresses, spine-pinching, and drug preparation.[14] The few sections of this work that involve the use of drugs do not duplicate or parallel the information obtainable from Chinese pharmacy textbooks and reference works.

It should be borne in mind, however, that these latter, more professional sources are widely available and always list for each drug clinical conditions in which it is useful. Although the target illnesses are expressed in a vocabulary that is somewhat specialized, having connotations that are idiosyncratic to medical insiders, most of them are not more mysterious to nonmedical readers than the terms *constipation* or *nausea* would be to English-speaking laypeople. Even though the technically sophisticated reference works of Chinese medicine are intended for use mainly by experienced clinicians, nothing prevents them from being used to guide the wide and various application of single drugs to particular discomforts.

---

14. Liu Daoqing et al., eds., *Zhongguo Minjian Liaofa* (Henan: Farmers' Press of the Central Plains, 1987).

Shortcut Two: Symptoms to Formulae

This movement has already been seen as present even in the complete form of the clinical encounter, becoming important in the practice of formulary when the *fang* that has been generated from the treatment methods is further specified for treating symptoms of secondary importance. It appears, however, that there must be clinicians who work mainly at this level, if only because contemporary discursive emphasis on holism and the centrality of a complete *bianzheng lunzhi* sequence is so earnest and insistent. If no one took shortcuts, there would be no need to protest them so much.

No doctor whom I observed at work at the College of Traditional Chinese Medicine in Guangzhou could be accused of mechanically applying a mere list of drugs to a list of symptoms ("When the head aches, dose the head; when the feet hurt, dose the feet"). Some practitioners I have observed, however, rely on just one or a few formulae for every condition, modifying them in response to the symptoms by substituting drugs effective for those symptoms. This technique obviates the need to carefully requantify every formula to respond to the complex specificity of every syndrome encountered.[15]

One of these doctors was a young woman who had succeeded her locally well-known father in rural Shandong as a practitioner of traditional gynecology; she used his favorite formulae, which were idiosyncratic enough to stimulate criticism from her hospital director when my visit (unfortunately for her) occasioned his presence in her clinic. Another was the senior Chinese doctor mentioned in Chapter 6 who apparently saw most ailments as arising from basically similar conditions, Liver system yin depletion. He almost always replenished Liver yin with the same formula, which he kept under the glass on his desk for the convenience of his assistants, modifying it in response to symptomatic variation. When I pressed him for the syndrome name and the therapeutic principle for each patient (myself earnestly struggling to complete the usual categories in my notes), he had difficulty supplying them and even more difficulty disguising his boredom with the question. I asked several teachers whom I respected for advice on how to ask my questions more appropriately to elicit the *bianzheng lunzhi* categories that we all felt must be present. When I continued to fail in visit after visit to

---

15. My observation of clinic practice in a variety of settings suggests that it is when they design prescriptions that doctors tend to concentrate the most. Even the most talkative senior Chinese doctors focus inward as they meticulously unfold the prescription on the form before them. The shortcutting doctors discussed in this section are often an exception. The one I mention here who kept a copy of his favorite formula under the glass on his table would hastily instruct an assistant about substitutions before moving on to the next patient. (This senior doctor did, however, concentrate intensely on pulse reading.)

this doctor's clinic, my advisers concluded that his practice must simply be "sloppy" (*bu renzhen*).

But practitioners who take such shortcuts should not in my opinion be seen as charlatans. Their standard practice could be justified as appropriate to their (often self-selected) clientele, the local environment, and a certain vision of physiology that is well within the purview of Chinese medical theory. But they do deviate from the textbook rigor I have explored herein, and contemporary academics implicitly criticize such sloppy practice as they build an increasingly highly trained (in the institutional sense) profession. The predictable polemics are involved in this profession-building; an over-literal or incomplete style of practice is likely to be dismissed not only as vulgar but also as dangerous.

Shortcut Three: Analytic Terms to Formulary Terms

I have shown that there are strong terminological ties linking the various elements of the *bianzheng lunzhi* process, one very clear example being the terms of the eight rubrics, which ramify directly into the naming of syndromes, the determination of treatment principles, and the choice of drugs according to their character and efficacies. Similarly, visceral systems locations suggest the use of drugs with appropriate tract affinities, as do four sectors and six warps analyses. Considering the logical power and situational flexibility of the "theory" that links the analytic methods to the principles of formulary and the characteristics of drugs, one wonders why the epitomizing stage of the *zhengzhi* pivot is argued for at all.

In this connection it is worth recalling that the *Treatise on Cold Damage* (the "clinical canon") in its original form hardly speaks of syndromes or treatment principles as such. It is nowadays organized into six sections, distinguishing syndromes of each of the six warps, and many of its dedicated scholars think of it in terms of a *bianzheng lunzhi* system. But it could just as well be seen as a table of correspondences: "Cold damage: pulse floating and slippery, Heat in both exterior and interior. White Tiger Decoction rules it." In maxims of this sort classificatory analysis restates characteristics of the illness in a form that can be correlated to the ensemble of drug efficacies in a formula; the correspondence is clear, and (it would seem) no further protocol should be needed.

Possibly some scholar-doctors of the *Treatise on Cold Damage* tradition routinely make a very high-level shortcut through six warps theory and a memorized treatise without benefit of a vocabulary of syndrome names and treatment principles, feeling that *bianzheng lunzhi* is the sort of ideology they can do without. In addition, one often gets the impression in observing clinical work that the correspondences provided by the eight rubrics are quite adequate for generating the necessary qualities that must be incorporated in most formulae; no syndrome name seems to be necessary for figuring out how to Cool Heat or drain repletion. I think it can be safely assumed that for many straightforward illnesses, doctors need not mentally rehearse a "complete" *bianzheng lunzhi* sequence; where the best intervention is clear and simple, the habits of teachers and personal rules of thumb can produce therapies that are as effective as those of any elaborately rationalized textbook case. In addition, one aspect of the highly valued quality of adeptness shared by senior Chinese doctors is an ability to see what must be done in a flash, for example, after feeling the pulse. Some of these may see no point in rationalizing from their efficacious insight a "system" of categories and correspondences.

The ease with which straightforward therapy can be done on the basis of richly redundant correspondences between the analytic methods and the drug qualities built into formulae requires that the necessity of the *zhengzhi* pivot be reconsidered. Put another way, we must ask in what sense it can be said to be hierarchically superior (in terms of logical coherence, abstractness, explanatory power) to the analytic methods and their parallel forms on the *lunzhi* side of Figure 3.2. I pointed out in Chapter 5 that the syndrome is spoken of as an epitome or a synthesis of all the materials collected, classified, and analyzed in the first half of the clinical encounter. Its name, however, often seems to have a mainly additive quality, as in the excerpt quoted in Chapter 5:

> Take the syndrome "Liver and Gallbladder Damp Heat Accumulating and Congealing," for example: It tells us that the heteropathic qi is Damp Heat, the site of pathological change is in the Liver and Gallbladder systems, the quality of pathological changes is Damp Heat accumulating and congealing, and the state of struggle between orthopathic and heteropathic qi is a repletion syndrome with a predominance of heteropathic qi but no weakening of orthopathic qi; all this shows that the treatment method should be to clear Damp Heat and cause it to flow downward from the Liver and Gallbladder systems.[16]

This explanation unpacks the syndrome name into the classificatory findings of the eight rubrics, illness factors, and visceral systems analytic methods and asserts that a treatment method follows naturally from this understanding. What is not made explicit in this textbook example of a name isolated from its full clinical genesis, however, is the extent to which this is an elegant simplification of a complex illness situation. The subtle judgments that have differentially weighted a variety of clinical manifestations such that the condition can be seen to be *on balance* a repletion, *preponderantly* Damp, and *primarily* located in the Liver-Gallbladder system, rather

---

16. Office of the 1977 Physicians of Western Medicine Class in Chinese Medicine, ed. *Zhongyi Jichuxue* (Guangzhou: Guangdong College of Traditional Chinese Medicine, 1977), p. 4.

than in the Kidney system (which is "upstream" in Five Phases terms) or in the ("downstream") Heart system, have been elided in the final syndrome. Moreover, the specific relationship among characteristics of place (affected visceral systems), quality (Damp Heat), and time (a slowing of physiological processes) is economically stated in this syndrome name. Some combination of quantification and collection seems to be involved here; the quantification involved in judging the relative importance of classificatory qualities allows them, when assembled, to crystallize an image of the illness, a complex unity the discernible facets of which can guide the subtle decisions about quantity that must be made in the writing of a drug formula. Without such a synthesis, I suspect that designing drug formulae, particularly determining the relative volumes of the drugs included in them, would be much more difficult—both more mechanical and more fraught with internal contradictions and hence arbitrariness.[17] Thus, for doctors who acknowledge the specificity of every illness and respond seriously to the charge to mould every prescription to "the place, the time, the person," a syndrome and a treatment principle to match provide a culminating image beyond the details of the analytic methods and the characteristics of drugs. It is from such an image that flexible and efficacious (*linghuo*) action can flow.

Medical action must be more than responsive, however; it must be responsible. No completely free play of drug combinations or thoroughly abstract aesthetics is encouraged or even dreamed of (as far as I can tell) in the formal or informal discourse of Chinese medicine. This overview of the clinical encounter has allowed two types of constraint on therapy to become evident, one being logical and the other historical.

The logical constraint flows (as one might suspect) from parallels in language use. For practitioners who work toward a syndrome and then from a treatment principle, the parallels at lower levels between, for example, a terminology of pathological qualities and a terminology of drug qualities (Cold and Heat being used for both) function less as a determination of therapy than as a check on consistency. In other words, the eight rubrics classification of an illness's relative Heat does not lead directly to the incorporation of Cold or Cool drugs into the prescription. Rather, the higher-order therapeutic method demands Cooling, and as the formula emerges, its amounts of Cold and Cool drugs can be checked against the numbers and types of symptoms manifesting Heat. The requirement that repletions be

---

17. Certain contemporary ideologies notwithstanding, the therapeutic principle does not clearly determine the ideal formula, although as seen in Chapter 6, under contemporary classification schemes, it helps locate a restricted number of candidates. See Nathan Sivin's discussion of the history of modes of classifying prescriptions, *Traditional Medicine in Contemporary China* (Ann Arbor: Center for Chinese Studies, University of Michigan, 1987), pp. 185–194, where the lack of systematicity in relating drug formulae to other phases in the clinical encounter is clear.

drained and depletions be replenished works in the same way, of course. I have often seen doctors, after they have written a preliminary list of drugs for the formula but before they have calculated their volumes, reread the list of symptoms in the clinic booklet or even feel the pulse again briefly to check the adequacy of this "first draft" before going on to refine the array of drugs and quantify the formula.

Historical constraints on therapeutic interventions may seem less "necessary" than logical limits to readers who are not inside the contemporary practice of Chinese medicine, but the frequent citations of the clinical work of "our sage forebears" in discussions of published cases argue that the medical heritage has a certain centrality. More immediate, perhaps, that most syndrome names (or small sets of names that are substitutable for each other) have a history suggests that their use forges a significant link to past medical work. Unless we assume that blind repetition is itself socially or psychologically functional, we must wonder why, given the specificity that is accorded to every illness, syndromes are not simply named something like "Mr. Wang, May 27, 1979, afternoon clinic." Clearly just any name for an illness will not do. Even a name that refers systematically to characteristics of the illness revealed through analysis, if it is not already a syndrome name in the literature, is problematic; its relationship to known syndromes would (in any published place, anyway) have to be explained. Given the vast range of possibilities in the medical archive, this is hardly much of a constraint, but it does suggest that previous experience must be drawn on somehow. A "mere" technology linking eight rubrics to drug qualities, visceral systems analysis to tract affinities, and so on could presumably be ahistorical. It would as a consequence be open to rash and ill-considered applications, ignorant of past mistakes and victories.

Yinyang Reexamined

Yinyang has proven throughout this discussion to be important in understanding the significance and entailments of many statements. It has been shown to be a general form of relating the two terms of almost any dyad together into generative dynamic relations. The concept is profoundly relative and (philosophers might argue) overflexible; just about any effect can be divided into active and structive aspects, and the source of any event can be traced infinitely backward into prior conditions that either are invisible (and hence "unverifiable") or have quite different, even opposed qualities. It is not surprising, then, that "yingyang" (pronounced with too many *g*'s and a twang) should have become almost a parody of the fabled mysticism or fuzzy thinking of "the Orient." For better or for worse, however, the double concept cannot be avoided in a study of traditional Chinese medicine. Having worked through the practical logics of the clinical encounter, then, I now want to make one last attempt to rescue yin and yang from the clutches of the idealists and the mystics.

To begin with the material just covered, elements of the clinical encounter itself can be said to relate to each other in yinyang ways. For example, in a locational sense the *zhengzhi* pivot may be said to be more inside medicine and the doctor's consciousness than reported signs and assembled drugs. Thus, the former is classifiable as yin, whereas the latter is yang. In a dynamic sense, however, the *zhengzhi* pivot can be seen as a yang (active) source, whereas the formula and its material manifestation in a bundle of drugs are the yin (structed) result of this particular yang stimulus. Syndrome (*zheng₃*) and treatment method (*zhi*) could themselves be understood as yang and yin, respectively, which understanding would make the widespread idea that treatment method both expresses and opposes the syndrome more coherent. In all these examples the situation-dependence of any yinyang analysis is evident: The treatment method may be yin to the syndrome's yang, but it is yang to the yin of the written formula. Similarly, the relatively silent and tacit *zhengzhi* pivot of the clinical encounter is classificatorily yin but dynamically yang (vis-à-vis therapeutic action). Put another way, yin and yang have no ultimate content; they are abstract relational principles that can be applied to the task of clarifying the dynamics of concrete situations.

The relativity and contingency of yin and yang appear both natural and necessary when the transformative metaphysic of Chinese indigenous science is acknowledged. When the "ontological ground" of effects is a state of constant transformation, when there is no European metaphysic requiring fixity of essence or discreteness of material form as a criterion of "reality," it is patterns in and of time and space, rather than material structures and mechanical functions, that must be perceived. And for this profoundly temporal project, applied in medicine, yinyang is a clarifying model.

Two major aspects of yinyang have been explored herein: their aspect as classificatory rubrics and their aspect as dynamic relationship. (These two aspects can, of course, also be understood as having a yinyang relationship, the "structures" that can be classified having resulted from dynamic "action" as yin results from yang.) As classificatory rubrics yin and yang require that the qualitative resemblances and differences among effects be perceived. Things that are yang in quality in a given situation resonate to and support the activity of other things, possibly in other realms, that are also yang in the quality of their activity. They do this, not by simply replenishing materially, but by stimulating specific kinds of action. Thus it is that formulae and drugs that are classified as Warm can strengthen and supplement the warming functions of the body's yang qi. The relations of commonality in the eight rubrics operate effectively in this way to characterize a number of illness facets through classification, allowing drugs that can intervene in dynamic excesses and deficiencies to be selected.[18]

As a dynamic relationship of "struggle, interdependence, and mutual transformability," yinyang emphasizes not resemblances but differences among things, relying on processes of differentiation that can place a given effect into productive relations with other effects. These relations of tension and interaction are polar and work by opposition, but such oppositions hold only up to that point at which a transformation can take place and reverse, alter, or revalue the elements in play. Thus, classificatory yinyang relations (resemblances) are always being revised and renewed via the dynamic of yinyang (i.e., polar difference) that pervades all the things of the world. The placing of the things or events that have been perceived through classificatory characterization (syndromes, formulae, drugs) in networks of interactive influence and/or struggle is the essence of action in the Chinese medical world. Once position has been acted on, generation of new or altered effects will take care of itself. Classification of the specific kind described herein, the character of which cannot be understood without reference to a yinyang form of relating, is fundamental to medical intervention in the flow of events.

The place of the human agent in a transforming world that can be made both coherent and (in situations of illness) less painful through the application of yinyang classification entails neither complete separation from these processes nor complete subjection to them. Agency is a feature of all the myriad things in this universe; nothing that comes from qi is isolated from the changes. Activity is assumed, but human (medical) activity, because it is informed by past patterns and past interventions, can always play on contingency, bring the powers of drugs to bear on the manifestations of illness, and introduce desired priorities and emphases against the undesired unevenness of the yinyang relations that appear as pathology among the *wanwu,* the ten thousand things.

I doubt whether any Chinese materials present yinyang analyses that are not highly situational and involve a predominance of either the yin or yang

---

18. The term *replenishment,* like other English words with which Euro-American scholars have struggled to express Chinese medical concepts, connotes a metaphor of fluids (in implicit vessels) that can diminish and be replaced. Although I do not think such phrasings and the stubbornly massy metaphors that underlie them can be improved on for our translations, their limitations should be acknowledged. Even very rich English metaphors may mislead where cosmology differs so much. Chinese medical physiology is not completely understandable as an anatomy of fluids; such a metaphorically induced notion would make its therapies appear structurally ludicrous. Rather, we must think in terms of a physiology of functions or activities, as Manfred Porkert has insisted in *The Theoretical Foundations of Chinese Medicine* (Cambridge, Mass.: MIT Press, 1974); and as I try to make clear in much of this book.

dimension. Every episode of *kanbing* locates the yinyang character of a physical disorder, perceiving its excesses and deficiencies, and positions an intervention that is oppositely weighted in intimate yinyang struggle. This is not, of course, a one-shot miracle cure; consistent with the logic of transformativity, Chinese medical practice is a sort of recovery management, periodically reanalyzing the patient's condition and redesigning his therapy. When no excess or deficiency of yin or yang can be perceived, there is no illness, and curative intervention is no longer required. Yin flows forth evenly, and yang hides within it. But just as there can never be a state that is not either day or night or transition between them, there can never be a place or time that does not have its yin or yang ascendancy as the partly determining ground of any action.

*　*　*

The practical form and methodological capabilities of the clinical encounter in Chinese medicine have been shown here to depend neither on a fixed base of essences instantiated in material forms (the single "real world" of positivism) nor on an abstract body of scientific standards by means of which the truth or falsity, adequacy or inadequacy of statements can be evaluated. Knowledge, method, theory, even the medical archive itself, have been shown to derive their value from practical processes in which the virtuosity of the doctor and his mastery both of his own clinical experience and that recorded in medical history are highly valued. Practicality, artistry, and seasoned wisdom are not, of course, confined to the world of Chinese medicine. But Chinese medicine appears to have developed unique means of acknowledging, understanding, and refining the skills of its practitioners. Skill, specificity, and contingency are in its discourse central to the practice of knowing. In textbooks, classrooms, journal articles, theoretical writing, and clinic rounds, it is not impersonal knowledge but experience—a very historical and social development—that brings order and goodness to the whole edifice of human agency and material powers that is healing.

Conclusion

THERE ARE MANY OTHER ways I could have written this book and much more that I could have said about contemporary Chinese medicine. I merely hinted at the symbolic and ideological riches to be found in the literature and practice of traditional medicine, for example, and I purposely neglected the anthropologist's usual task of describing "culture." Furthermore, I have not even begun to explore systematic variations of practical medical work in different institutional settings, in different geographical areas, or under the influence of different leading doctors. Nor have I extended the many social implications of the practice of the clinical encounter into any pretense at a sociology of Chinese medicine.

Such studies can and undoubtedly will be done, some of them by me. But I would not like to see them done without serious consideration of the issues explored herein. Too often our sociologies of knowledge and ethnographies of medicine take on an almost behaviorist tone—the technical and philosophical concerns of knowing and healing, about which our adept subjects are often quite willing to instruct us, are held separate from the social and the symbolic, as if mental disciplines and physical skills everywhere vary independently of social relations and cultural ideologies or are a mere reflection of them. Such assumptions can lead, for example, to studies of "the doctor-patient relationship" that do not address the goals and fears that are most salient to doctors and patients while they *kanbing*. These assumptions also lead to interpretations of, for example, the language of diagnosis that seek referents in ancient philosophy or popular culture before attending to the particular complaints being addressed in any actual setting of use.

I have chosen instead to start with the concerns that Chinese medical insiders take to be central—those required to practice healing. After we have begun to see why pulse-taking must be attentive and why it should be checked against tongue image and a full illness history, how eight rubrics analysis can be refined in very nuanced ways by other analytics, how treatment methods are implemented through a quantitative technique for designing formulae, and what has been recorded and compiled about the vast materia medica, we can begin to place specific actions into a context that (dimly, to be sure) resembles the environment in which Chinese doctors act.

In privileging a certain "native point of view," that of doctors of traditional Chinese medicine working in an urban clinic, I have not departed from long-held biases of cultural anthropology. I have, perhaps, been more careful than some not to totalize the insights gained from a study of the discursive practices of Chinese doctors into "deep structures" of Chinese thought or stable attributes of "Chinese culture." But this book would be fairly trivial if it did not aim at relevance to some larger projects.

I suppose it hardly needs to be argued that the methods and findings of this book might be of interest to other scholars of the traditional Chinese sciences. This is a growing and increasingly lively field, thanks to the continuing inspiration of Joseph Needham and his many collaborators. Since medicine is the only indigenous Chinese science to continue into the twentieth century in a way that is institutionally and discursively prominent, it would not be surprising if an ethnographic study of Chinese medicine and an analysis of its contemporary discourse were to reveal certain continuities with many Chinese textual traditions that have disappeared or have been denounced as "superstition." The nature of these continuities cannot be predicted. As I argued in Chapter 1, much has changed in the world of Chinese medicine, and some of this alteration has both subtly and profoundly influenced "basic theory."

Historians may find, however, that certain observations I have made can shed light on old problems. If, for example, contemporary Chinese assumptions about the function of language, and their expression in modes of recordkeeping, are explicitly attended to, we might begin to read sources with more attention to rhetoric and less to representation. If filiality and pedagogy are taken as a social complex that informed a great deal of text production, scientific works might be more powerfully contextualized with reference to family chronicles, biographies, and general histories. And if my sinological colleagues see some value in the analytic complex I have described here—that is, a coordinated use of "logically inconsistent" methods to produce a nuanced specificity—they may begin to discern analogous complex practices in much more ancient texts.

I hope, further, that this book can function as a caution against wholesale idealization in the historical study of Chinese knowledge. I do not wish to minimize the difficulty of inferring a practical dimension from old and fragmentary texts, but I hope that the continuities of the knowing practice I have explored herein will convince us that no history of medicine should be solely a history of ideas. After all, wherever medical work has emerged as a developed genre of practice, it is often messy and smelly and most of the time very mundane. It can also be saddening, infuriating, or frightening. The most general condition of medical strategy is uncertainty of outcome, making medical intervention in the world always a form of gambling. The serene autonomy of development, contradiction, and decline that we associate with histories of ideas is remote not only from Chinese medicine but also quite possibly from other indigenous Chinese sciences. Perhaps the complex connections between a philosophical language deriving from the long history of speculative thought in China and the subtle practices and thorough embodiment of knowledge still evident in the contemporary world of Chinese medicine will offer a few paths out of idealism and mysticism in Chinese studies.

There is, however, a more immediate arena to which a book of this kind will be referred, that of professional ("Western") biomedicine. Much of my extended explanation of the clinical encounter owes its form, of course, to an implicit comparison of Chinese medicine with Western medicine. Academic writing is, after all, a form of pedagogy, and I cannot ignore the assumptions of my likely readers (most of them academic Americans) as I try to make clear to them a form of healing that differs quite drastically from that they know. My own assumptions have also played no small role as I have subtly and not so subtly shaped the object I have called Chinese medicine. Some medical readers, perhaps already put on the defensive by popular criticisms of biomedical practice, may find the very seriousness with which I address a practice quite different from theirs to betray an ill-considered and poorly supported critical stance. The situation is more complicated than this, however.

I have felt unqualified to condemn any aspect of biomedical expertise by making explicit comparisons demanding that one side be belittled if the other is to be accorded any dignity. This discussion might have been rendered a good deal more readable had I been willing to compare and contrast what I know of biomedical practice with what I know of Chinese medical practice. But the comparisons would not be just and would in most cases lead to a false complacency about our understanding. What I know about biomedicine is a result of a personal career as patient; laboratory research assistant; friend of nurses, doctors, and scientists; and reader of a smattering of sociological studies. My knowledge of Chinese medicine results from months of auditing intensive classes for doctors, more or less systematic observations in urban and rural clinics and hospitals, interviews with scholar-doctors of several generations and levels of training, and fairly wide reading and careful analysis of published and unpublished professional writings. It follows that the two "medicines" to be compared are produced by quite different methods, and although I do not always resist herein a negative that is clearly motivated by characteristics of biomedicine (e.g., "Chinese medicine is not reductive"), I have by no means made a full-scale comparison.

One reason to be wary of obvious comparisons, of course, is the danger of reification. The differences discussed are not really between two separate

unities or two autonomous "health care systems." The more one under-
stands of the activities in contemporary Chinese clinics, the more elusive
Chinese medicine as a meaningful unity becomes. Blood pressures and
X-rays are added to pulse and tongue images; classic formulae are modified
with acetyl-salicylic acid and vitamin C. Cardiac workups are recommended
for patients with chest pain, and acupuncture is used to speed recovery from
surgery. Biomedical diagnostic categories are used alongside or instead of
syndrome names, and explanations are almost as often couched in anatomical terms as in yinyang functional terms.

By focusing on the practical logics of the clinical encounter, I have not
tried to reduce this marvelous complexity to a single correct or pure form of
Chinese medicine. Rather, I have sought to render intelligible a rather stable
practical form within it: An X-ray may be ordered, but an herbal prescription
is issued at the same time; a Western medical specialist may be recommended, but the patient need not forego her visits to her Chinese medical
doctor in his small room with his humble tools. No comprehensive account
of the meaning or underlying principles of a profession that can be drawn
apart from and readily compared to Western medicine is claimed; any anthropology of the sort I have attempted here, when applied to our own
medical world, would equally destabilize any illusion that biomedicine is
one clearly delimited social institution.

Although I warn readers not to seek in Chinese medicine facile responses
to the widespread discontent stimulated by the work of biomedicine in
North America and Western Europe, there is still perhaps something to be
learned from a comparison. I would not be surprised, for example, if experienced clinicians of Western medicine are able to recognize in the adeptness
and sense of timing cultivated by senior Chinese doctors something of their
own hard-won (and perhaps less articulately acknowledged) skills. I am
tempted to believe (and much medical anthropology supports me in this
belief) that the conditions in which all healing takes place produce similar
dilemmas, however different the resources and techniques involved. The
very open-endedness of all clinical encounters, their uncertainty of outcome, and (in many cases) the relative clarity in distinguishing good outcomes from bad ones make medical action a particularly fascinating topic
for sociological study. Consequently, some dimensions of a medicine-to-
medicine comparison, however divergent the histories and social worlds of
the practices considered, should yield both satisfying resemblances and fascinating specificities.

The most general insight I can offer from this comparative project is
something on which Chinese medical philosophers and practice-oriented
anthropologists agree: Knowledge and the social are not ultimately divisible.
Both sorts of scholars have good reason to avoid simplistic reflection models
of the kind that finds a hierarchical logic (e.g., of drug formula design)

"arising from" a hierarchical social order. The complexities of history, healing, and human creativity for which social scientists try to account can only be distorted in models that match socioeconomic structures with ideological structures as if the former somehow explain the latter. And medical people in a Marxist intellectual world cannot convincingly justify their subtlety and efficacy with a simplistic base-superstructure analysis. Nevertheless, both discourses advance the demand that knowledge be seen in the final analysis as social and that social life be understood in a way that does not reduce its intellectual, aesthetic, and political richness. This is more than an academic point: American medical reformers appear to believe that the social relations of clinical work can be made more "humanistic" with no alteration in the science and technology of advanced biomedicine; and the vast apparatus that is research bioscience proceeds on the assumption that the social consequences of the ideologically pure knowledge it is generating can be worked out by experts of another kind later on.

I have no intention of taking on these massive topics, at least not here. Rather, I wish to explore one last example of the ways in which knowledge entails practices and practices produce knowledge in Chinese medicine, problematizing the sense we have of both terms while preserving a role for human agency. Thus, can the statement "An accelerated and strung pulse image indicates a yang repletion," be called knowledge? Certainly this statement can be found presented as factual in books, and it can be incorporated in a table of correspondences. It can be included in self-study curricula published in magazines and sold in popular bookstores, and it has been known in similar statement form for a very long time. No insider to Chinese medicine would contest it, and any scientist wishing to falsify it would have to destroy the natural clinical conditions in which it is true. (In other words, to determine whether the yang repletion was actually the case, one would have to first redefine the yang repletion pathology as an anatomical lesion and then perform immediate exploratory surgery, or at least fairly invasive tests, which would alter both the nature of the functional pathology and the pulse image that would be discerned if anyone bothered to recheck it.)

Unless we wish to indulge certain classic anthropological a prioris and arbitrarily refer to this correspondence of pulse to pathology as a (mere) "belief," we must admit that it has all the earmarks of a stable and relatively impersonal bit of genuine knowledge. How does such knowledge, then, relate to "practice"? In one sense, of course, it *is* a set of practices—reading, writing, publishing, and archiving all allow the maintenance of this correspondence as knowledge in a more or less stable form as well as contributing to its social and historical authority. Such knowledge is also grounded in the particular diagnostic practice of pulse-reading and propagated in the clinic through apprenticeship relations in which senior doctors expect their juniors to emulate and incorporate their particular habits of clinical work.

But (in what seems like a reversal but is not) the practices that "support" the truth that an accelerated and strung pulse indicates a pathology of the yang repletion type are also partly determined by it. Pulses are read because doctors know their specific manifestation can be linked not only with physiological sources but also with a written history of therapies. Books on pulse lore are published because their authors know that certain kinds of truths can be written down and taught to those who read about them. To call the relationship of knowledge and practice a dialectic under such circumstances is an understatement; rather, it begins to appear the height of arbitrariness to separate them as two dimensions (or "moments") at all. Put another way, we need not rise above the level of practice (base, material stuff) into some ontologically distinct realm of the ("immaterial"?) word and idea to trace the complex paths of specific forms—for example, the relationship of accelerated strung pulse to yang repletion—through historical instances of describable practices. This should be the case for any fact, as Bruno Latour, among others, has begun to show in his series of studies of laboratory science.[1]

But reading pulses and inferring pathology from them need not be separated out as a "facteme" from a much vaster array of forms in what might now be called the knowing practice of Chinese medicine (in the latter half of the twentieth century, in provincial-level colleges and hospitals of traditional medicine, as practiced by those who did not mind talking to a foreign anthropologist, and so on). Any practice can have entailments going far beyond a few allied clinical activities and a few pages of a handful of books. Practice can be placed within a sequence of interdependent effects, and its coherence with much more of the world of Chinese medicine can be made clear.

Thus, it should by now be evident that the sort of experience (*jingyan*) on which many claims for the legitimacy of Chinese medicine are based is far from being a collection of events imprinted on a passive consciousness. Rather, this experience is a cultivation of skills of the pulse-reading sort, a slow development of adeptness through the living of a clinically useful life. Although the importance of the notion of experience in the contemporary discourses of Chinese medicine undoubtedly has something to do with the prominence in scientific socialism of a borrowed term meaning "empiricism" (*jingyanzhuyi*), this knowing practice is not an empiricism of a kind we "moderns" would immediately recognize. Perhaps most central, the knower is not drawn apart from the known. Although quantification is fundamental to pulse discrimination, that an image such as acceleration is

---

1. Bruno Latour and Steve Woolgar, *Laboratory Life* (Princeton: Princeton University Press, 1986); Bruno Latour, *Science in Action:* (Milton Keynes, Oxfordshire: Open University Press, 1987); and Bruno Latour, *The Pasteurization of France* (Cambridge, Mass.: Harvard University Press, 1988).

gauged against the doctor's own breathing, rather than against an objective time standard, is telling. This sort of knowing is concrete and social.

The things doctors must know are closely related to their opportunity and capacity to cultivate themselves as they become "experienced"—it should thus be no surprise that most patients prefer older practitioners and that these seniors wield considerable power in the institutions of traditional medicine. They not only "know" medicine better than their juniors; they also embody it more fully. For the moment, it is they who translate their hard-won virtuosity into spoken and written instruction and clinical service, defining what Chinese medicine is while keeping a firm grip on their privileged standing as ever-more-powerful adepts.

One cannot be content, however, with arguing that gerontocracy somehow "goes with" forms of knowledge that must be embodied through time or for that matter that invasive diagnostic technologies must be present where knowledge is of visualized anatomical structures. These are historically specific relationships that will not escape revision. To suggest otherwise would be to commit an old anthropological sin—to naturalize the contingent, insisting that because things are clearly of a piece, they must be coherent in just that way forever. To adopt Kuriyama's metaphor, the technique of discerning the chicory bouquet of a 1935 Bordeaux is efficient and appropriate to the social life of which enjoying good wines is a part. Reading pulses, including such techniques as judging acceleration against the rhythm of one's own breathing, is a useful means of inferring physiological processes and is a practice that can mobilize a rich traditional therapeutics throughout which the doctor's refined judgment operates. But there is now an industrial chemistry of wine flavors directed at simulation and regulation and an electrical engineering of pulsography[2] directed at objective replication of diagnostic findings. We cannot be certain that future wine labels will not include chemical analyses or that future traditional Chinese doctors will not be reluctant to treat until the lab has sent back the pulse image traced on a curl of graph paper.

Many hospitals of traditional medicine now offer magnetic resonance imaging (MRI) services, and it is in keeping with the (somewhat uneven but widespread) "anatomicization" of Chinese medical language that applications of MRI equipment to problems of traditional medical diagnosis will be (or have already been) designed. As more dynamic and less invasive visualization techniques are developed and acquired by Chinese hospitals, previously unthought-of forms of medical knowledge-practice will undoubtedly develop to use them. Computer-literate graduate students are already collaborating with at least one senior clinician to systematize his decision-

---

2. Hu Qingyin and Wang Wande, "*Maizhen Qiantan,*" *Heilongjiang Zhongyiyao* 83, no. 2 (1983):15–20; 83, no. 4 (1983):10–15.

making processes in the form of marketable software. Younger doctors trained in traditional medicine are not simply faddish in their romance with the technologies of bioscience; some are willing to admit that part of the purpose of such "objective" technology is to loosen the stranglehold their elders have on medical truth. It is because knowledge and the social are intimately bound up together that "science and technology" may be as much weapons as ideals in contemporary China.

Let us return for a moment to the clinical encounter, with its microcosmic version of the problem of agency. The agency allowed, even required, by the *bianzheng lunzhi* process described here may appear humble or paltry to those of us who have lived for so long with the grand Enlightenment dreams of freedom, timeless ideals, and individual power. I have tried to make it clear how in Chinese medical healing a great many material and historical constraints narrow the space within which a doctor's judgment can operate, while I have appreciated the ways in which his refined perception and his virtuoso therapeutics are centered and valorized in discourse. In such a practice, the constraints themselves are seen more as resources than as limits: Medical history provides effective techniques and minutely described drug powers, and the many contingencies embodied by each patient are not so much obstacles to clarity as they are the materials from which a clear picture of the problem is generated.

Social forces are too complex, both overdetermining and internally contradictory, to ever produce a single solution to a problem, a single course of action; we must always chart a course with inadequate guidance among abounding uncertainties, limiting as best we can the possibilities that overflow most situations. Chinese doctors pride themselves on their realism. They are consummate strategists whose therapeutic aspirations are more modest than those of the freewheeling medical saviors—speeding through a world flattened by arguments that hold only as long as "all other things are equal"—sometimes dreamed of in North American representations of biomedicine. Chinese doctors know that time must be spent, personal skills slowly cultivated, and the teaching of predecessors respectfully accepted and continued. But they also know that adeptness depends on more than embodying tradition; it resides in remaining alert to every shift in conditions, every change in the needs of patients and in the social worlds in which both doctor and patient are active and creative. There may be little by way of a recognizable dream of freedom (read, individual autonomy) here, but there is a definite struggle for personal excellence, historical contribution, and genuine moral efficacy.

These are not simply less ambitious versions of the "universal human aspirations" articulated by the European Enlightenment and claimed by modernist discourses. (This point would hardly need to be made if it were not such an important assumption of the modernization theory that has so

powerfully constituted most social science research on China are the values of a social world that continues to be differe from our own, partly because China is a socialist state and neglected truism) because it has a long history of its own. I sons that turn difference into inadequacy do not aid us in either these values or the practical conditions to which they a

This book has studied the discourses of traditional Chinese ganized around the idea that the clinical encounter can be see practical logic. It has led me finally to posit a culture-specific and agency, a notion that seems a worthwhile, if not wholly pothesis for future work in the history and anthropology of work has also invited reflection on the idea that ways of knowi where continuous with modes of action and forms of the soc the better. But perhaps my greatest ambition for this book is join with a few others in English to introduce the great trea Chinese medical literature for serious consideration by world s many kinds. The "vast body of records" that has arisen from "th of the Chinese laboring masses in their two-thousand-year stru disease" is, when read on its own terms and with attention to th in which it signifies, a contribution to human health in the broa

Appendix A

Romanization Conversion Table: Wade-Giles to Hanyu Pinyin

	Wade-Giles[a]	Pinyin
Initials	ch (e.g., chü)	j
	ch (e.g., chu)	zh
	ch'	q
	hs	x
	j	r
	k	g
	k'	k
	p	b
	p'	p
	t	d
	t'	t
	ts	z
	ts'	c
Finals	eh	e
	ien	ian
	o	e, o, or uo
	uei	ui
	ung	ong
Syllables	chü	ju
	i	yi
	yu	you
	yü	yu

[a]This table includes only romanizations that differ between the two systems.

Appendix B: Chinese and Pharmaceutical Names of Drugs Used in Cases 1–3

Drugs Used in Case 1

Prescription 1

1. Weeping forsythia (capsule); *lianqiao;* Fructus forsythiae
2. Black-roasted jasmine seed; *heizhi;* Semen Gardeniae
3. Mild skullcap (root); *dan zi qin (huangqin);* Radix Scutellariae Baicalensis
4. Wind-weed asphodel (rhizome); *zhimu;* Rhizoma Anemarrhenae
5. Fresh rhubarb; *mianwen (dahuang);* Rhizoma Rhei
6. Mirabilite; *yuanming fen;* Natrium Sulfuricum
7. Tricosanthes fruit; *gualou;* Fructus et Semen Tricosanthis
8. Citron (roasted fruit); *zhiqiao;* Fructus Ponciri
9. Four o'clock (root); *muli gen;* Radix Jasmini Sambae
10. Fresh licorice root; *sheng gancao;* Radix Glycyrrhizae
11. Dried dendrobium (stem); *Shihu;* Herba Dendrobii

Prescription 2 (New Drugs)

1. Fresh gypsum; *shigao;* calcium sulphate
3. American ginseng; *xiyang shen;* Radix Panacis Quinquefolii
6. Fresh rehmannia (rhizome); *shengdi;* Radix Rehmannia Crudae
10. Tendril-leaved fritillary bulb; *chuanbei;* Bulbus Fritillariae Cirrhosae

Prescription 3 (New Drugs)

1. "Large seed" ginseng; *taizi shen;* Radix Pseudostellariae
9. Winter melon seeds; *donggua ren;* Semen Benincasae
11. Yunnan *fuling; yunling;* Sclerotium Poriae

Drugs Used in Case 2

Patient I

1. Cangshu; *cangshu;* Radix Atractylodis
2. Magnolia bark; *houpo;* Cortex Magnoliae Officinalis
3. Mandarin orange peel; *chenpi;* Pericarpium Citri Reticulatae
4. Licorice root (see fresh licorice root, Case 1)
5. Mirabilite (see Case 1)
6. Trifoliate orange fruit; *zhishi;* Fructus Ponciri

Patient II

Unquantified drugs:
Adenophora; *sha shen;* Radix Adenophorae
Chinese angelica; *danggui;* Radix Angelicae Sinensis
Peach kernel; *taoren;* Semen Persicae
Poncirus; *zhishi;* Fructus Ponciri (= trifoliate orange fruit)
Mirabilite (see Case 1)
Sichuan lovage; *chuanxiong;* Rhizoma Ligustici
Achyranthes root; *niuxi;* Radix Achyranthis
Plantain seed; *cheqian;* Semen Plantaginis
Cassia twigs; *guizhi;* Ramus Cinnamomi Cassiae
Cairo morning glory; *wuzhaolong;* Radix et Ramus Ipomoea Cairiceae
Dangshen; *dangshen;* Radix Codonopsis

New drugs used in Opening Bones Powder:
1. Huangqi; *huangqi;* Radix Astragali vel Huangch'i
4. Charred human hair; *xueyu tan;* Crinis Carbonisatus
5. Tortoise shell; *guiban;* Carapax Testudinis

Drugs Used in Case 3

1. Smoke-dried hedgehog skin; *ciwei pi*
2. Stink bugs; *jiu xiang chong;* Aspongonpur or Coridius
3. Buddha hands (fruit); *foshou;* Citri Sarcodactylis
4. Powdered corydalis (rhizome); *yanhusuo;* Tuber Corydalis
5. Licorice root (see fresh licorice root, Case 1)
6. Meadow rue (rhizome); *maweilian;* Caudex Thalictri Foliolosi, Delavayi, et Baicalensis
7. Herbaceous peony (root); *baishao;* Radix Paeoniae Lactiflorae
8. Sichuan pagoda tree (fruit); *jinlingzi (chuan lianzi);* Fructus Toosendan
9. Citron peel; *xiang yuanpi;* Fructus Citri Medicae
10. Calciferous ark shell; *walengzi;* Concha Arcae
11. Evodia fruit; *wuzhuyu;* Fructus Evodiae

Drugs used in modified formula

Trifoliate orange fruit (see Case 2)
Amomi fruit; *sharen;* Semen Amomi
Nutgrass flatsedge rhizomes; *xiangfu;* Rhizoma Cyperi
Areca nut shell; *dafupi;* Pericarpium Arecae

SOURCE: Shiu-ying Hu. *An Enumeration of Chinese Materia Medica.* Hong Kong: Chinese University Press, 1980.

Glossary of Chinese Terms

THE GLOSSES LISTED FOR the Chinese terms used in this book are neither true definitions nor full translations. They should assist non–Chinese-speaking readers, however, as mnemonics that can recall previous discussions and uses of terms. This glossary can also help readers distinguish among similar words, such as the various terms pronounced *zheng*. Note, however, that Chinese is like English in that one cannot know from looking at a word what part of speech it is. When one word or term functions differently in two different sentences, Chinese does not usually mark this with a derived form or an inflection. For example, *bianzheng* can be a verbal form, "to differentiate syndromes" or a nominal form, "syndrome differentiation"; it can also function as an adjective or adverb. Parts of speech in Chinese are most often determined by the syntax of the sentence in which they appear. In addition, plurals are not marked in words themselves; occasionally a plural is marked with a measure word placed before the noun, but most often the reader is left to judge from context whether the reference is to one object or more than one.

ba gang	八纲	the eight rubrics
ben	本	root, basis(-ic)
bencao	本草	materia medica and the subdiscipline concerned with drug efficacies
benzhi	本质	essence, basic substantial character
bianzheng	辨证	syndrome differentiation
bianzheng fangfa	辨证方法	methods of differentiating the syndrome
bianzheng lunzhi	辨证论治	syndrome differentiation and therapy determination
bianzheng qiu yin	辨证求因	seeking the cause when differentiating the syndrome
bianzheng shizhi	辨证施治	syndrome differentiation and therapy deployment
biao	表	body exterior, opposite of *li*
biao ben	表本	branches and roots in relation to each other
bing	病	illness, sickness, disease

bingbing	并病	simultaneous illnesses
bingli, binglixue	病理，病理学	pathology
bingshi	病势	configuration and force of illness
bingyin	病因	illness factor
bu	补	to bolster
bu renzhen	不认真	not serious, responsible, or careful; sloppy
cailiao	材料	materials (for analysis)
cao	草	grass, plant
cengci	层次	level, stratum
chen	沉	to sink inward
Chong (mai)	冲脉	the highway tract, one of the auxiliary circulation tracts
chuan (bian)	传变	transmission between warp classes (in six warps analysis)
chuanhua	传化	transmission and transformation (between sectors, in four sectors analysis)
dafa	大法	the methods used in modern clinical practice
dan	淡	Clear (drug flavor)
danhong	淡红	pink (tongue color)
Du (mai)	督脉	the superintendent tract, one of the extraordinary tracts
duili tongyi	对立统一	the unity of opposites
fa	法	methods, methodology
fang	方	formula(e) of drug prescriptions
fangfa	方法	techniques, methods
fangfalun	方法论	methodology (as a theoretical investigation)
fangji	方剂	same as *fang*
fangjixue	方剂学	formulary, the subdiscipline covering drug formula design
fanglun	方论	discourse on formulae
fanzhi	反治	reversed therapy, (i.e., using a method the reverse of one that directly opposes the heteropathy)
faze	法则	methods
fen	分	sector
fenxi	分析	to analyze
fu	腑	the yang (hollow) visceral systems of function: Stomach, Gall Bladder, Large and Small Intestines, Urinary Bladder, and Triple *Jiao*
fu	辅	the supporting role in drug formulae

fu	浮	to float to the surface
fuke	妇科	women's medicine, Chinese medical gynecology
fuzhu	辅助	same as *fu* in formulary
gaikuo	概括	summary, to summarize
gaodu gaikuo	高度概括	epitome, to epitomize
ge	隔	to cross-cut
Ge shou qi xiang.	各守其乡	Each will take care of its own domain.
gongxia	攻下	to attack downward
gongxiao	功效	efficacies of drugs
guancha	观察	examination, inspection
guanxi	关系	personal relationships, connections
guiding	规定	to determine, fix according to standard principles
guijing	归经	tract affinities of drugs
guilu	规律	principles, rules, regularities
guina	归纳	inference, to infer
han yin han yong	寒因寒用	with Cold factors, Cold techniques used
haoxue dongxue	耗血动血	diminution or disturbance of blood
hebing	合病	corresponding illnesses
hegu	合谷	an acupuncture point, IG4
heng ni	横逆	lateral backup(s) (in pathology)
hong	红	red (tongue color)
hou	侯	a period of time of unspecified length
hu	呼	inflected tone
hua	化	to transform (often used as suffix, "-ization").
huanzhe	患者	sufferer, patient
huoxue huayu	活血化瘀	to enliven Blood and transform stasis
ji	剂	dose, dosage (in Formulary)
jiang	绛	crimson (tongue color)
Jiao	焦	See Triple *Jiao*
jibing	疾病	disease, often used for the biomedical concept of disease.
jing	精	essence; semen; transitional qi, (in physiology)
jing	经	circulation tract(s); warp classes, as in *liu jing*, six warps; classic books
jingluo	经络	the circulation tract system
jingmai	经脉	circulation tract(s)

jingqi	精气	nutritive essence
jingshen shizhi	精神实质	spirit and essence
jingyan	经验	experience
jingyanzhuyi	经验主义	empiricism
juan	卷	chapter or section (used in classical texts)
jue	角	musical note
jueyin	厥阴	attenuated yin, one of the six warp classes
jun-chen	君臣	monarch-minister relations in drug formulae
kanbing	看病	to look at illness, to consult a doctor
keguan	客观	objective
kexuehua	科学化	scientization, to scientize
lao	老	old or senior, an honorific form of address
laozhongyi	老中医	senior Chinese doctor(s)
li	里	body interior, opposite of *biao*
li, fa, fang, yao	理法方药	theory, methods, formulae, and drugs (Chinese medicine's basic arsenal)
lilun jichu	理论基础	theoretical foundation(s)
linghuo	灵活	flexible, adept, sensitive, efficacious, virtuoso
liu jing	六经	the six warp classes of Cold Damage theory
liu yin	六淫	the six (external) excesses
Lower *Jiao*	下焦	See Triple *Jiao*.
lun		discourse, discussion
lunzhi	论治	treatment determination, discourse on therapies
mai	脉	circulation vessel(s)
maixiang	脉象	pulse image(s)
Middle *Jiao*	中焦	See Triple *Jiao*.
ming laozhongyi	名老中医	renowned senior Chinese doctor(s)
Nali you bing?	那里有病？	Where (why) is (your) illness?
neihangren	内行人	insiders (to a field or specialty)
neike	内科	internal medicine
neirong	内容	content(s), characteristics
ping	平	even, level; Neutral drug character (in pharmacy)
pingren	平人	healthy people, in the *Treatise on Cold Damage*
qi	器	thing, object, device

qi	气	configurational energy, energetic configuration (Porkert); air, breath; vitalities, energies (Sivin)
qi fen	气分	active qi sector
qi qing	七情	the seven emotional states: joy, anger, sorrow, worry, grief, apprehension, fear
qihua	气化	qi transformation
qing	清	to clear
qingxie	清泻	to clear and drain (Heat)
Ren (mai)	任脉	the conception tract, one of the auxiliary circulation tracts
renshi	认识	to recognize, know, to discern
renshilun	认识论	epistemology
sanjiaoshu	三焦俞	an acupuncture point, VU22
shaoyang	少阳	immature yang, one of the six warp classes
shaoyin	少阴	immature yin, one of the six warp classes
shen	身	body, whole person, self
shen	神	vitality, spirit(s)
shenghua	生化	generation (of physiological substances)
shengli, shenglixue	生理, 生理学	physiology, physiological
shengli huodong	生理活动	physiological activity
shenshu	肾俞	an acupuncture point, VU23
shi	使	emissary or sending role in drug formulae
shier jing	十二经	the twelve cardinal circulation tracts used in acupuncture
shijian	实践	practice
shiwu	事物	effects, things
shu	暑	Summer-Heat
shuidao	水道	the watercourse, fluid metabolism managed by the Triple *Jiao*
shuxie	疏泻	dredging and draining, a function of the Liver system
shuxing	属性	characteristic features, classification, category membership
sizhen	四诊	the four methods of examination
Sizhen hecan.	四诊合参	The four examinations work jointly.
taiyang	太阳	mature yang, one of the six warp classes
taiyin	太阴	mature yin, one of the six warp classes

tanyin	痰饮	physiological and pathological Mucus and Phlegm
tiaoji	调剂	to regulate volumes of drug
tong	统	to encompass, to gather, to unify
tongxue	同学	fellow student(s)
Triple *Jiao*	三焦	a yang visceral system that rules fluid metabolism in the three bodily regions of upper, middle, and lower
Upper *Jiao*	上焦	see Triple *Jiao*.
wanwu	万物	the myriad phenomena, the "10,000 things"
wei	味	flavor(s) of drugs
wei qi	卫气	defensive qi
wei qi fen	卫气分	defensive qi sector
wei qi ying xue	卫气营血	four sectors analyzed in Warm Illnesses diagnostics
wen	闻	listening/smelling, one of the four examinations
wenxie	温邪	Warm heteropathy
wuyun	五运	the five cyclic components
wuzhi	物质	substance, substantial
xiandaihua	现代化	modernization
xiang	象	image, external appearance, visible form
Xiang yu xuan she.	相有宣摄	The one gives off and the other takes in.
xie	泄	to drain
xie qi	邪气	heteropathic qi
xinde	心得	heart-mind attainment, knowledge, understanding
xing	性	drug character; character or quality in general
xingti	形体	material form, body
xingwei	性味	character and flavor of drugs
xingzhi	性质	quality(-ies), character
xinliang jie biao	辛凉解表	using Pungent and cooling drugs to flush Heat from the exterior
xitonglun	系统论	systems theory
xiu shen	修身	refinement or cultivation of the self
xiyi	西医	Western medicine, biomedicine
xu han	虚寒	depletion Cold
xuan	玄	dark generative potential
xue fen	血分	Blood sector
yang	阳	active aspect of dynamic phenomena

yangming	阳明	yang brightness, one of the six warps
yang sheng	养生	cultivation of life
yi caolei wei zhibing de jiben	以草类为治病的基本	taking herbals to be the root and basis of treating illnesses
yin	阴	structive aspect of dynamic phenomena
yin	因	cause, reason
yin ping yang mi	阴平阳秘	yin even, yang hidden
yincang	隐藏	concealed inside
ying fen	营分	constructive qi sector
yingyong	应用	usage of drugs (in pharmacy)
yinyang	阴阳	the dynamic relation of active (yang) and structive (yin) aspects of phenomena
You shemma bing?	有什么病？	What is (your) illness?
You shemma bushufu?	有什么不舒服？	What are (your) discomforts?
yuan	元	origin, source, original
yuan wen	原文	original text
yuanqi	元气	primordial qi
yufang	预防	prevention (of disease)
yufangxing	预防性	preventive character, preventive emphasis
yunhua	运化	transmission and assimilation, a Spleen system function
zang	脏	the yin (solid) visceral systems of functions: Heart, Lungs, Liver, Spleen, and Kidney.
zangfu	脏腑	visceral system(s) of functions
zangxiang	脏象	visceral systems imagery
zhenduan	诊断	diagnosis
$zheng_1$	征	sign(s) of illness
$zheng_2$	症	symptom(s) of illness
$zheng_3$	证	illness syndrome(s)
$zheng_4$ (qi)	正气	orthopathic qi
zhenghou	证候	illness syndrome(s)
zhengtiguan	整体观	holism, view of the whole
zhengzhi	正治	straight therapy (i.e., using direct methods against heteropathy)
zhengzhi	证治	short for *bianzheng lunzhi*
zhengzhuang	症状	symptoms
zhenqi	真气	true qi
zhenyuan (qi)	真元气	steady original (qi, in cosmogony)
zhi	治	to treat or manage an illness or a disorder
zhibing	治病	to treat illness

Zhibing qiu ben.	治病求本	When treating illness, trace the root.
zhifa	治法	treatment method(s)
zhize	治则	therapeutic principles
zhong	中	intermediate, middle
zhongchengyao	中成药	Chinese patent medicines
zhongyi	中极	an acupuncture point, JM3 or Ren-3
zhongyaoxue	中药学	pharmacognosy, Chinese materia medica
zhongyi	中医	Chinese medicine
zhu	主	to rule or govern: ruling role in drug formulae; to be chief among, to unfold or ramify outward (in visceral systems imagery); to be in charge of; main or central
zhuguan	主观	subjective
zhuzhi	主治	main illness treated (in pharmacy)
ziran	自然	"self-so," the unceasing, spontaneous generativity of the cosmos
ziran bianzhengfa	自然辩证法	the dialectics of nature
ziwuliuzhu	子午流注	a tract-based diagnostic method emphasizing temporal patterns of effects
zong qi	宗气	genetic qi
zonghe	综合	to synthesize
zongze	总则	general principles
zuo	佐	assistant role in drug formulae
zusanli	足三里	an acupuncture point, V36

Bibliography

Adorno, Theodor. *Negative Dialectics.* New York: Seabury Press, 1973.

Ågren, Hans. "Patterns of Tradition and Modernization in Contemporary Chinese Medicine." In *Medicine in Chinese Cultures: Comparative Studies in Health Care in Chinese and Other Societies,* edited by Arthur Kleinman et al., 37–59. Washington, D.C.: John E. Fogarty International Center, 1975.

Ahern, Emily M. "Chinese-Style and Western-Style Doctors in Northern Taiwan." In *Culture and Healing in Asian Societies,* edited by Arthur Kleinman, 101–110. Cambridge, Mass.: Schenkman, 1978.

Ames, Roger T. *The Art of Rulership.* Honolulu: University of Hawaii Press, 1983.

Anderson, Eugene N., Jr., and Marja L. Anderson. "Modern China, South." In *Food in Chinese Cultures,* edited by Kwang-chih Chang, 317–382. New Haven: Yale University Press, 1977.

Ban Gu. *Han Shu Yiwen Zhi* (Bibliographical Record in the History of the Former Han). 1st century A.D. Shanghai: Commercial Press, 1955.

Barnes, Barry. *Interests and the Growth of Knowledge.* London: Routledge and Kegan Paul, 1977.

————. *T. S. Kuhn and Social Science.* New York: Columbia University Press, 1982.

Beijing College of Traditional Chinese Medicine, ed. *Zhongyixue Jichu* (Foundations of Chinese Medicine). Shanghai: Shanghai Science and Technology Press, 1978.

Beijing College of Traditional Chinese Medicine et al., eds. *Essentials of Chinese Acupuncture.* Beijing: Foreign Languages Press, 1980.

————. *Shiyong Zhongyixue* (Practical Chinese Medicine). 2 vols. Beijing: Beijing Press, 1975.

Bennett, Stephen J. "Patterns of the Sky and Earth." *Chinese Science* 3 (1978):1–26.

Bourdieu, Pierre. *The Logic of Practice.* Translated by Richard Nice. Stanford: Stanford University Press, 1990.

————. *Outline of a Theory of Practice.* Translated by Richard Nice. Cambridge: Cambridge University Press, 1977.

Chen Guying, ed. *Laozi Zhuyi ji Pingjie* (Laozi with Annotations and Commentary). Beijing: Chinese Book Company, 1984.

Cheng Shide et al., eds. *Suwen Zhushi Huicui* (The Compiled and Annotated Basic Questions). Beijing: People's Health Press, 1982.

Chengdu College of Traditional Chinese Medicine et al., eds. *Zhongyaoxue* (Chinese Pharmacognosy). Shanghai: Shanghai Science and Technology Press, 1978.

Cihai Editing and Compiling Committee, ed. *Cihai* (Reservoir of Words). Compressed character edition. Shanghai: Shanghai Dictionaries Press, 1980.

Clifford, James, and George E. Marcus. *Writing Culture: The Poetics and Politics of Ethnography*. Berkeley and Los Angeles: University of California Press, 1986.

Collingwood, Robin G. *An Essay on Metaphysics*. Lanham, Md.: University Press of America, 1972.

Comaroff, Jean. *Body of Power, Spirit of Resistance: The Culture and History of a South African People*. Chicago: University of Chicago Press, 1985.

Croizier, Ralph. *Traditional Medicine in Modern China*. Cambridge, Mass.: Harvard University Press, 1964.

Deng Tietao. *Shiyong Zhongyi Zhenduanxue* (Practical Diagnosis in Chinese Medicine). Shanghai: Shanghai Science and Technology Press, 1988.

———. "*Wanli Yuntian Wanli Lu*" (A Long and Clouded Road). In *Ming Laozhongyi zhi Lu*, edited by Zhou Fengwu et al., vol. 2:1–8. Jinan: Shandong Science and Technology Press, 1984.

———. *Xueshuo Tantao yu Linzheng* (Theoretical Inquiries and Clinical Encounters). Ghangdong: Guangdong Science and Technology Press, 1981.

Deng Tietao, ed. *Zhongyi Jichu Lilun* (Fundamental Theory of Chinese Medicine). Guangzhou: Guangdong Science and Technology Press, 1982.

Derrida, Jacques. *Of Grammatology*. Translated by Gayatri C. Spivak. Baltimore: Johns Hopkins University Press, 1976.

Du Huaidang, ed. "*Tantan Zhiliao Weiwan Tongde Jingyan*" (Remarks on Experience of Treating Stomach Cavity Pain). *Xin Yiyao Zazhi* 10 (1977):15.

Editing Committee of the Dictionary of Chinese Medicine. *Jianming Zhongyi Cidian* (Abridged Dictionary of Chinese Medicine). Beijing: People's Health Press, 1979.

Editing Committee of the Unabridged Dictionary of Chinese Medicine. *Zhongyi Dacidian, Fangjixue Fence* (Unabridged Dictionary of Chinese Medicine, Formulary Volume). Beijing: People's Health Press, 1983.

———. *Zhongyi Dacidian, Jichu Lilun Fence* (Unabridged Dictionary of Chinese Medicine, Theoretical Foundations Volume). Beijing: People's Health Press, 1982.

———. *Zhongyi Dacidian, Zhongyao Fence* (Unabridged dictionary of Chinese Medicine, Materia Medica Volume). Beijing: People's Health Press, 1982.

Editors, Shandong Zhongyixueyuan Xuebao. Cover essay. *Shandong Zhongyixueyan Xuebao*, no. 2 (1980).

Evans-Pritchard, E. E. *Witchcraft, Oracles and Magic Among the Azande*. Oxford: Clarendon Press, 1937.

Farquhar, Judith. "Body Contingency and Healing Power in Traditional Chinese Medicine." *Discours Social/Social Discourse* 3, nos. 3–4 (1990–1991):53–70

———. "Objects, Processes, and Female Infertility in Chinese Medicine." *Medical Anthropology Quarterly* (NS) 5, no. 4 (December 1991):370–399.

———. "Problems of Knowledge in Contemporary Chinese Medical Discourse." *Social Science and Medicine* 24, no. 12 (1987):1013–1021.

———. "Speech, Text, and Silence: Text Production and the Unsaid in the Contemporary Practice of Chinese Medicine." Paper presented at the Fifth International Conference on the History of Science in China, San Diego, California, August 5–10, 1988.

———. "Time and Text: Approaching Contemporary Chinese Medical Practice Through Analysis of a Published Case." In *Paths to Asian Medical Knowledge*, edited by Charles Leslie and Allan Young. Berkeley and Los Angeles: University of California Press, 1992.

———. "Rewriting Traditional Medicine in Post-Maoist China." Paper presented at the Conference on Epistemology and the Scholarly Medical Traditions, McGill University, Toronto, Canada, May 1992.

Feyerabend, Paul. *Against Method*. London: New Left Books, 1975.

———. *Realism, Rationalism and Scientific Method: Philosophical Papers*, vol. 1. Cambridge: Cambridge University Press, 1981.

Foucault, Michel. *The Archaeology of Knowledge*. Translated by A. M. Sheridan Smith. New York: Harper and Row, 1972.

———. "Nietzsche, Genealogy, History." In *Language, Counter-memory, Practice: Selected Essays and Interviews*. Edited by Donald F. Bouchard, 139–164. Ithaca, N.Y.: Cornell University Press, 1977.

———. *The Order of Things: An Archaeology of the Human Sciences*. New York: Vintage, 1973.

Fu Weikang *Zhongyixue Shi* (History of Chinese Medicine). Shanghai: Shanghai Science and Technology Press, 1990.

Gould-Martin, Katherine. "Hot Cold Clean Poison and Dirt: Chinese Folk Medical Categories." *Social Science and Medicine* 12B (1978):39–46.

———. "Ong-ia-kong: The Plague God as Modern Physician." In *Culture and Healing in Asian Societies*, edited by Arthur Kleinman, 41–68. Cambridge, Mass.: Schenkman, 1978.

Gove, P. B., ed. *Webster's Third New International Dictionary of the English Language, Unabridged*. Springfield, Mass.: G. and C. Merriam, 1969.

Granet, Marcel. *The Religion of the Chinese People*. New York: Harper and Row, 1975.

Guangdong College of Traditional Chinese Medicine, ed. *Zhongyi Zhenduanxue* (Chinese Medical Diagnosis). 1964. Reprint. Shanghai: Shanghai Science and Technology Press, 1982.

Guangzhou College of Traditional Chinese Medicine, ed. *Fangjixue* (Formulary). Shanghai: Shanghai Science and Technology Press, 1979.

Hall, David L., and Roger T. Ames. *Thinking Through Confucius*. Albany: State University of New York Press, 1987.

Haraway, Donna. "The Biopolitics of Postmodern Bodies: Constitutions of Self in Immune System Discourse." In *Simians, Cyborgs, and Women: The Reinvention of Nature*, 203–230. New York: Routledge, 1991.

Hay, John. "The Human Body as a Microcosmic Source of Macrocosmic Values in Calligraphy." In *Theories of the Arts in China*, edited by Susan Bush and Christian Murck, 74–102. Princeton: Princeton University Press, 1983.

Hevia, James. "Guest Ritual and Interdomainal Relations in the Late Qing." Ph.D. diss., University of Chicago, 1986.

Hirst, Paul, and Penny Woolley. *Social Relations and Human Attributes*. London: Tavistock, 1982.

Hong Menghu. *"Ping 'Qi' ji Biao Wuzhi you Biao Jinengde Liangyishuo"* (Comments on the Hypothesis of "Vital Energy" (Qi) Denoting Both Material and Function). *Zhongyi Zazhi* 24, no. 3 (March 1983):4–7.

Hou Can. *"Cong Kexue Fangfalun Kan Woguo Yixue Keyande Xuanti"* (Consideration of Selected Problems of Scientific Research on Chinese Medicine from the Point of View of Scientific Methodology). *Yixue yu Zhexue* 83, no. 3 (1983):4–6.

Hu Qingyin, and Wang Wande. *"Maizhen Qiantan"* (Comments on Pulse Diagnosis). *Heilongjiang Zhongyiyao* 83, no. 2 (1983):15–20; 83, no. 4 (1983):10–15.

Hu, Shiu-ying. *An Enumeration of Chinese Materia Medica.* Hong Kong: The Chinese University Press, 1980.

Hua Shou. *Nan Jing Benyi.* Vol. 18 of *Gujin Yitong Zhengmai Quanshu* (Collected Medical Sources, Old and New). Taibei: Yiwen Yinshuguan, 1967), p. 513.

Huang Jitang. *"Zhongyixue Shi"* (History of Chinese Medicine). In *Ziliao Huibian* (Selected Materials), edited by the Dialectics of Nature Research and Teaching Section, Guangzhou College of Traditional Chinese Medicine, vol. 2:1–19. Guangzhou: Guangzhou College of Traditional Chinese Medicine, 1982.

Huang Jitang et al., eds. *Zhongyixue Daolun* (Introduction to Chinese Medicine). Guangzhou: Guangdong Higher Education Press, 1988.

Huang Meilin. *"Tongyi Waigan Rebing Bianzheng Ganglingde Yanjiu Gaikuang"* (Survey of Research on Unifying the Diagnostic Categories of Exogenous Heat Illnesses). *Guangxi Zhongyiyao* 83, no. 5 (1983):44–48.

Hubei College of Traditional Chinese Medicine, ed. *Shang Han Lun Xuandu* (Selected Readings from the Treatise on Cold Damage). Shanghai: Shanghai Science and Technology Press, 1979.

Inden, Ronald. *Imagining India.* Oxford: Basil Blackwell, 1990.

Jiang Keming, and Bao Minghui, eds. *Jianming Fangji Cidian* (Simplified Dictionary of Formulary). Shanghai: Shanghai Science and Technology Press, 1989.

Jiangsu New Medical College, ed. *Zhongyao Dacidian* (Unabridged Dictionary of Chinese Materia Medica). 3 vols. Shanghai: Shanghai People's Press, 1977.

Jiangsu Province Department of Health, ed. *Zhongyi Jichu* (Foundations of Chinese Medicine). Suzhou: Jiangsu Science and Technology Press, 1977.

Judovitz, Dalia. *Subjectivity and Representation in Descartes: The Origins of Modernity.* Cambridge: Cambridge University Press, 1988.

Kaptchuk, Ted J. *The Web That Has No Weaver: Understanding Chinese Medicine.* New York: Congdon and Weed, 1983.

Kleinman, Arthur. *Patients and Healers in the Context of Culture.* Berkeley and Los Angeles: University of California Press, 1980.

Kuhn, Thomas S. *The Structure of Scientific Revolutions.* 2d ed. Chicago: University of Chicago Press, 1970.

Kuriyama, Shigehisa. "Pulse Diagnosis in the Greek and Chinese Traditions." In *History of Diagnostics,* edited by Yosio Kawakita, 43–67. Osaka: Taniguchi Foundation, 1987.

Kwok, D.W.Y. *Scientism in Chinese Thought, 1900–1950.* New Haven: Yale University Press, 1965.

Lampton, David M. *The Politics of Medicine in China.* Boulder: Westview Press, 1977.

Latour, Bruno. *The Pasteurization of France.* Cambridge, Mass.: Harvard University Press, 1988.

——. *Science in Action: How to Follow Scientists and Engineers Through Society.* Milton Keynes, Oxfordshire: Open University Press, 1987.

Latour, Bruno, and Steve Woolgar. *Laboratory Life: The Construction of Scientific Facts.* Princeton: Princeton University Press, 1986.

LeBlanc, Charles. *Huai Nan Tzu: Philosophical Synthesis in Early Han Thought.* Hong Kong: Hong Kong University Press, 1985.

Lewontin, R. C., Steven Rose, and Leon J. Kamin. *Not in Our Genes.* New York: Pantheon, 1984.

Li Jinyong et al., eds. *Zhongyixue Bianzhengfa Jianlun* (The Dialectics of Chinese Medicine Simply Explained). Taiyuan: Shanxi People's Press, 1983.

Liu Changlin. *Neijingde Zhexue he Zhongyixuede Fangfa* (The Philosophy of the *Inner Canon* and the Methods of Chinese Medicine). Beijing: Science Press, 1982.

Liu Daoqing et al., eds. *Zhongguo Minjian Liaofa* (Chinese Folk Therapeutics). Hebei: Farmers' Press of the Central Plains, 1987.

Liu Hsieh. *The Literary Mind and the Carving of Dragons.* Translated by Vincent Yu-chung Shih. New York: Columbia University Press, 1959.

Liu Ruchen et al., eds. *Zhongyixue Bianzhengfa Gailun* (Outline of Chinese Medical Dialectics). Guangzhou: Guangdong Science and Technology Press, 1983.

Liu Yanchi. *The Essential Book of Traditional Chinese Medicine.* Translated by Fang Tingyu and Chen Laidi. 2 vols. New York: Columbia University Press, 1988.

Liu Yanchi, Song Tianbin, Zhang Ruifu, and Dong Liantong, eds. *Zhongyi Jichu Lilun Wenda* (Questions and Answers on the Fundamental Theory of Chinese Medicine). Shanghai: Shanghai Science and Technology Press, 1982.

Lu, Gwei-djen, and Joseph Needham. *Celestial Lancets: A History and Rationale of Acupuncture and Moxa.* Cambridge: Cambridge University Press, 1980.

Lyotard, Jean-Francois. *The Post-Modern Condition: A Report on Knowledge.* Translated by Geoff Bennington and Brian Massumi. Minneapolis: University of Minnesota Press, 1984.

Lyotard, Jean-Francois, and Jean-Loup Thebaud. *Just Gaming.* Minneapolis: University of Minnesota Press, 1985.

MacIntyre, Alasdair. "Essence." In *Encyclopedia of Philosophy,* 59–61. New York: Macmillan and Free Press, 1967.

Mao Zedong. "On Practice." In *Selected Readings from the Works of Mao Tsetung,* 65–84. Beijing: Foreign Languages Press, 1971.

Mao Zedong. "On Contradiction." In *Selected Readings from the Works of Mao Tsetung,* 85–133. Beijing: Foreign Languages Press, 1971.

Marin, Louis. *Portrait of the King.* Minneapolis: University of Minnesota Press, 1988.

McCloskey, Donald. *The Rhetoric of Economics.* Madison: University of Wisconsin Press, 1985.

Mitchell, Timothy. *Colonising Egypt.* Cambridge: Cambridge University Press, 1988.

Nanjing College of Traditional Chinese Medicine, ed. *Wenbingxue* (Warm Illnesses). Shanghai: Shanghai Science and Technology Press, 1979.

Needham, Joseph. "Human Law and the Laws of Nature." In *The Grand Titration*, 299–331. London: Cambridge University Press, 1969.

————. *Science and Civilization in China*. 7 vols. (projected). Cambridge: Cambridge University Press, 1954–.

Office of the 1977 Physicians of Western Medicine Class in Chinese Medicine, Guangdong College of Traditional Chinese Medicine, ed. *Zhongyi Jichuxue* (Foundations of Chinese Medicine). Guangzhou: Guangdong College of Traditional Chinese Medicine, 1977.

Ou Ming et al., eds. *Han Ying Zhongyi Cidian* (Chinese-English Dictionary of Traditional Chinese Medicine). Guangzhou: Guangdong Science and Technology Press, 1986.

Pokert, Manfred. *The Essentials of Chinese Diagnostics*. Zurich: Chinese Medicine Publications, 1983.

————. *The Theoretical Foundations of Chinese Medicine: Systems of Correspondence*. Cambridge, Mass.: MIT Press, 1974.

Potter, Jack M. "Cantonese Shamanism." In *Religion and Ritual in Chinese Society*, edited by Arthur P. Wolf, 207–232. Stanford: Stanford University Press, 1974.

Reiss, Timothy. *The Discourse of Modernism*. Ithaca, N.Y.: Cornell University Press, 1982.

Rorty, Richard. *Contingency, Irony, Solidarity*. Cambridge: Cambridge University Press, 1989.

————. *Philosophy and the Mirror of Nature*. Oxford: Basil Blackwell, 1980.

Shan Shujian. "*Shilun Wu Zhitong dui Zhongjingde Jicheng he Fazhan*" (Discussion of Wu Zhitong's Continuation and Development of Zhang Zhongjing's Teachings). *Jilin Zhongyiyao* 83, no. 2 (1983):4–7.

Shandong College of Traditional Chinese Medicine. *Shandong Zhongyixueyan Xuebao*, nos. 3, 4 (1980).

Shandong College of Traditional Chinese Medicine and Hebei College of Medicine, eds. *Huangdi Neijing Suwen Jiaoshi* (Basic Questions, Annotated). Beijing: People's Health Press, 1982.

Shanghai College of Traditional Chinese Medicine, ed., *Zhongyi Fangji Linchuang Shouce* (Clinical Handbook of Chinese Medical Formulary). Shanghai: Shanghai People's Press, 1973.

————. *Zhongyi Neikexue* (Chinese Internal Medicine). 1964. Reprint. Shanghai: Shanghai Science and Technology Press, 1982.

Sivin, Nathan. "Man as a Medicine: Pharmacological and Ritual Aspects of Traditional Therapy Using Drugs Derived from the Human Body." In *Chinese Science: Explorations of an Ancient Tradition*, edited by Shigeru Nakayama and Nathan Sivin, 203–272. Cambridge, Mass.: MIT Press, 1973.

————. *Traditional Medicine in Contemporary China*. Ann Arbor: Center for Chinese Studies, University of Michigan, 1987.

Skillen, Tony. *Ruling Illusions: Philosophy and the Social Order*. Sussex: Harvester, 1977.

Smith, Barbara Herrnstein. *Contingencies of Value*. Cambridge, Mass.: Harvard University Press, 1988.

Smith, Paul. *Discerning the Subject*. Minneapolis: University of Minnesota Press, 1988.

Som, Tjan Tjoe, trans. *Po Hu T'ung: The Comprehensive Discussions in the White Tiger Hall.* 2 vols. Leiden: Brill, 1949, 1952.

Topley, Marjorie. "Chinese Traditional Etiology and Methods of Cure in Hong Kong." In *Asian Medical Systems,* edited by Charles Leslie, 243–265. Berkeley and Los Angeles: University of California Press, 1976.

Paul Unschuld, *Medical Ethics in Imperial China.* Berkeley and Los Angeles: University of California Press, 1979.

———. *Medicine in China: A History of Ideas.* Berkeley and Los Angeles: University of California Press, 1985.

———. *Medicine in China: A History of Pharmaceutics.* Berkeley and Los Angeles: University of California Press, 1986.

———. *Nan Ching: The Classic of Difficult Issues.* Berkeley and Los Angeles: University of California Press, 1986.

Veith, Ilza. *Huang Ti Nei Ching Su Wen: The Yellow Emperor's Classic of Internal Medicine.* Berkeley and Los Angeles: University of California Press, 1966.

Walsh, W. H. "Metaphysics, Nature of." In *Encyclopedia of Philosophy,* 300–307. New York: Macmillan and Free Press, 1967.

Wan Yousheng. *Han Wen Tongyi Lun* (On the Unification of Cold Damage and Warm Illnesses Doctrines). Shanghai: Shanghai Science and Technology Press, 1988.

Wang Qingqi, and Qian Chenghui, eds. *Zhongyi Zangxiangxue* (Visceral Systems Imagery in Chinese Medicine). Shanghai: Shanghai College of Traditional Chinese Medicine, 1987.

Wang Xudong. *Zhongyi Meishuxue* (Aesthetics of Chinese Medicine). Nanjing: Dongnan University Press, 1989.

Wang Zhong. "*Zhongyixue Bianzhengfa Yanjiu*" (Research on Chinese Medical Dialectics). In *Ziliao Huibian.* (Selected Materials), edited by the Dialectics of Nature Research and Teaching Section, Guangzhou College of Traditional Chinese Medicine, vol. 3: 48–114. Guangzhou: Guangzhou College of Traditional Chinese Medicine, 1983.

Wilson, Bryan R., ed. *Rationality.* Oxford: Basil Blackwell, 1977.

Woolgar, Steve. *Science: The Very Idea.* New York: Tavistock and Ellis Horwood, 1988.

Wu Dingbang. "*Shanghan Wenbing Shaoyang Zheng Yitong Chuxi*" (Preliminary Analysis of the Similarities and Differences of Minor Yang Syndromes in Cold Damage and Warm Illnesses Schools). *Hubei Zhongyi Zazhi* 83, no. 1 (1983):51–52.

Xiao Shafu, and Li Mianquan, eds. *Zhongguo Zhexueshi* (History of Chinese Philosophy), vol. 1. Beijing: People's Press, 1983.

Xu Chengzu. "*Cong Renshilun Tan Zhongyi Fenxing Lunzhi*" (An Epistemological Consideration of Chinese Medicine's Classificatory Treatment Determination). *Yixue yu Zhexue* 83, no. 2 (1983): 9–11.

Xu Fulin. *Gujin Jiu Wu* (Correcting Therapeutic Errors, Old and New). Changsha: Hubei Science and Technology Press, 1985.

Yoshida, Tadashi. "Some Problems in the Analysis of Manifestations of Sickness." In *History of Diagnostics,* edited by Yosio Kawakita, 210–214. Osaka: Taniguchi Foundation, 1987.

Young, Allan A. "Mode of Production of Medical Knowledge." *Medical Anthropology* 2, no. 2 (1978):97–122.

Yu Yingao, and Gao Yimin, eds. *Xiandai Ming Laozhongyi Leian Xuan* (Cases of Renowned Contemporary Senior Chinese Doctors, Selected and Classified). Beijing: People's Health Press, 1983.

Yuan Baoting. "*Shilun Zhang Zhongjing Zhi Wen Xueshu Chengjiu*" (Consideration of Zhang Zhongjing's Scholarly Achievements in the Treatment of Warm Illnesses). *Henan Zhongyi* 83, no. 5 (1983): 10–12.

Zhang Sun Wuji et al., *Sui Shu Jingji Zhi* (Bibliography of the Sui Dynasty with Supplement). 7th century A.D. Shanghai: Commercial Press, 1957.

Zhao Fen, ed. *Zhongyi Jichu Lilun Xiangjie* (Detailed Explanation of the Fundamental Theory of Chinese Medicine). Fuzhou: Fujian Science and Technology Press, 1981.

Zhao Hongjun. *Jindai Zhongxiyi Lunzhengshi* (History of Chinese and Western Medicine Controversies). Anhui: Anhui Science and Technology Press, 1989.

Zhong Weichen. "*Ziwu Liuzhu Paoyaofa Chutan*" (Preliminary Investigation of Drug Preparation Methods According to *Ziwu Liuzhu*). *Shandong Zhongyi Zazhi* 83, no. 5 (1983): 6–7.

Zhou Fengwu et al., eds. *Ming Laozhongyi zhi Lu* (Paths of Renowned Senior Chinese Doctors). 3 vols. Jinan: Shandong Science and Technology Press, 1981–1985.

Zito, Angela. "Grand Sacrifice as Text/Performance: Writing and Ritual in 18th Century China." Ph.D. diss., University of Chicago, 1989.

About the Book and Author

This book examines the theory and practice of traditional medicine in modern China. Farquhar describes the logic of diagnosis and treatment from the inside perspective of doctors and scholars. She demonstrates how theoretical and textual materials interweave with the practical requirements of the clinic. By showing how Chinese medical choices are made, she considers problems of agency in relation to different forms of knowledge. *Knowing Practice* will be of value not only to anthropologists interested in medical practice but also to historians and sociologists interested in the social life of technical expertise and traditional teachings.

Judith Farquhar is associate professor of anthropology at the University of North Carolina–Chapel Hill.

Index

Academy of Traditional Chinese Medicine, Beijing, 5
Acupuncture, 36, 43, 46, 51–53, 74, 212, 224
Adeptness. *See Linghuo*
Aesthetics, 190, 216
Agency, theoretical problem of, 4, 126, 148, 150–151, 160, 167–174, 179, 202, 206, 219, 220, 222, 224–225, 228–229
Anatomy, 24–25, 38, 73, 92–93, 99–100, 110(n63), 148–149
Archive, Chinese medical, 38, 69, 155, 157, 160, 168–173, 176, 177(n3), 179, 181, 201, 206, 208, 217, 220

Barrier Cooling Powder, 48–49, 128, 183–184, 187–188
Basic Questions (Suwen), 29, 157, 162, 164, 166(n27), 206
Beijing, 4, 10
Beijing College of Traditional Chinese Medicine, 7, 10, 66
Bencao Gangmu. *See Systematic Materia Medica*
Bianzheng lunzhi. *See* Syndrome differentiation and therapy determination
Biographies, 16–17
Biomedicine, 10(n3), 12(n6), 13, 20, 69, 148(n3), 154, 191, 223–225, 227–228. *See also* Western medicine
Blood
  as body substance, 34, 99, 101, 104, 106, 109–110, 112–113, 115, 118, 121, 132(n90), 152, 178, 189, 194
  in relation to qi, 102, 106, 112, 165, 169, 197

Bolster Spleen Increase Qi Decoction, 178
Book of Chinese (Yi Jing), 208
Bulletin of the Shandong College of Traditional Chinese Medicine (*Shandong Zhongyixueyuan Xuebao*), 16–17

Calligraphy, 96(n)
Calming Stomach Powder, 50–52
Case histories, published, 5, 47, 151, 155(n), 168, 172, 176, 205(n8), 215
Case records, 41–44, 69, 130, 151–152, 204, 206
  Case 1, 46–50, 64–65, 72, 75, 83–85, 89, 91, 116–117, 120, 129–131, 134, 152, 157, 161, 172, 175, 183, 195, 197, 208, 211
  Case 2, 46, 50–53, 75, 83–85, 88, 97(n), 134, 152, 162, 172, 175–176
  Case 3, 46, 53–55, 64–65, 75, 83–85, 92, 105, 107, 127, 134, 152, 168, 172, 175, 195
Cassia Aconite Eight Flavor Pills, 178
Cheng Guopeng, 179
Chinese Communist Party, 12(n6), 13(n8), 15, 19(n20)
Chinese Medicine Bureau, 12
Chronic illness, 19, 44, 99, 164
Circulation tracts, 74–75, 112, 115, 117–118, 120–125, 129, 131–133, 157, 195–196, 199
Classification, clinical practice of, 32, 37–39, 55, 59, 61, 62–63, 70–73, 75–81, 83–84, 88, 91, 108, 113, 115–117, 119, 123–126, 129, 131–132, 134–135, 153, 155–157, 159, 173, 178–180, 198–199, 201, 203, 208, 210–211, 214, 216, 219

Treatment method or principle (*zhifa*), 43,
   46, 55, 57, 85, 151–152, 160–169,
   172–173, 175–181, 184, 187–189,
   192, 196, 199, 204–205, 213–214,
   216, 218, 221
"Treat the root," 20, 32, 36, 86, 90, 102,
   107, 157, 159–160, 162–163, 191
Triple *Jiao* visceral system, 92, 96–97, 101,
   116, 123, 133, 187–188, 194–196
Two Mothers Powder, 192

Unschuld, Paul, 15
Urinary Bladder visceral system, 96, 122,
   131

Virtuosity. *See Linghuo*
Visceral systems of function (*zangfu*), 6,
   31, 74–75, 91–96, 99, 101–102, 104,
   107, 112–113, 115, 118, 121, 123–
   125, 128–129, 132(n90), 152, 157,
   169, 178, 196–197, 214, 216
   Visceral systems diagnostic, 70, 72–76,
      89, 91, 96, 98, 104, 107–108, 122,
      131, 133–134, 147, 169, 201, 215,
      217
   See also Yin visceral systems; Yang visceral
      systems

Wang Bing, 94
Wang Qingren, 53
Wang Yangming, 171
Warm Illnesses school, 71, 73, 108–110,
   112, 115–116, 118–120, 126–127,
   129–130, 132(n92), 134, 187. *See
   also* Four sectors diagnostic
Western medicine (*Xiyi*), 2, 10, 12,
   13(n10), 45
   contrasted with Chinese medicine,
      10(n3), 11, 18, 46, 68–70, 75(n), 90,
      94, 111(n), 148–150, 158(n16)
   See also Biomedicine

White Tiger Decoction, 121, 125, 128,
   214

Yang (qi), 23, 32–33, 36, 165
Yang visceral systems (*fu*), 91–93, 96–98,
   105–106
Ye Guitiao (Ye Tianshi), 107–108
Ye Xichun, 49, 116, 118, 127–130, 187–
   188
Yellow Emperor's Inner Canon (*Huangdi
   Neijing*), 28–29, 37(n26), 93, 121,
   126, 148, 157–158, 166
Yi Jing. See Book of Changes
Yin (qi), 23, 32–33, 36, 165
Yin visceral systems (*zang*), 91–93, 96–98,
   105–107
Yinyang
   as dynamic process, 23, 31, 32–33, 35–
      36, 71, 78, 80, 131, 157, 165–167,
      189
   as explanatory method, 24, 32, 101,
      131, 159, 169, 179, 217–220, 224
   as relationship, 23, 30–32, 35, 76, 101,
      124, 164, 166, 206–207, 218–219
   as rubrics in eight rubrics diagnostic,
      71–72, 77, 79–80, 85, 91
   as term, 24, 35, 110(n63)
   as types of force, 91
   See also Yin; Yang
Yun Tieqiao, 14

Zhang Ji (Zhang Zhongjing), 119–122,
   128–129, 131, 156
Zhang Jiebin, 94
Zhao Fen, 7, 23–24
Zhong Jianhua, 54, 105–107, 134, 169,
   196–197
Zhu Peiwen, 14
Ziwu Liuzhu diagnostic, 72(n14)